THE PARENT AS CITIZEN

The Parent as Citizen

. . . .

A Democratic Dilemma

Brian Duff

University of Minnesota Press
Minneapolis
London

Portions of chapters 1 and 3 were previously published in the journal *Ethics and Politics* and in *Rousseau and Desire,* ed. Mark Blackell, John Duncan, and Simon Kow (Toronto: University of Toronto Press, 2009).

Published by the University of Minnesota Press
111 Third Avenue South, Suite 290
Minneapolis, MN 55401-2520
http://www.upress.umn.edu

Library of Congress Cataloging-in-Publication Data

Duff, Brian.
The parent as citizen : a democratic dilemma / Brian Duff.
p.   cm.
Includes bibliographical references and index.
ISBN 978-0-8166-7272-1 (hc : alk. paper)
ISBN 978-0-8166-7273-8 (pb : alk. paper)
1. Parenthood. 2. Parents. 3. Citizenship. I. Title.
HQ755.8.D83 2011   306.87401—dc22
2010036536

For my mother and father

Contents

Acknowledgments

WHEN PEOPLE HEAR that I have written a book on the problems with parenthood as a political identity, they often ask if I am a parent myself. I am not. There are a number of people who deserve some credit for that, I suppose, though mostly it's on me. But here I would like to acknowledge and thank those people whose help has been invaluable along the way to the birth of this book.

My interest in political theory was spurred by several inspiring mentors at the University of North Carolina, especially Stephen Leonard and the late Jeffrey Obler. That early fortune was multiplied when I arrived at the University of California, Berkeley, where I was lucky to find a group of colleagues full of humor and encouragement (and allergic to grad-school malarkey), especially Robin Brooks, Laura Henry, Jill Hargis, Sara Rushing, Cara Wong, Jake Bowers, Shalini Satkunanandan, and Michael Swaine. My Berkeley-born friendship with Maria Rosales has profoundly affected my ideas about politics and family. I am indebted to many scholars at Berkeley for their guidance during the early stages of this project: Laura Stoker likes to insist that she is "not a theorist," but her insight and advice were as invaluable as her humor and encouragement were welcome. The late Mike Rogin was a challenging, kind, and thoughtful advisor who taught me that we can enrich our care for the world if we engage what is disturbing in it. Wendy Brown is the sort of mentor that every scholar hopes for and too few encounter; one would think it impossible to feel supported and encouraged by someone who gives you comments so uncompromisingly tough-minded, but Wendy pulls it off with grace. Hanna Pitkin, Jack Citrin, Fred Dolan, and Shannon Stimson all offered valuable advice and guidance.

Along the way this project benefited from the generous support of the Center for Working Families and the Department of Political Science at UC Berkeley; the Center for Political Studies at the University of Michigan; and the University of New England. At Michigan, I appreciated the

advice of Nancy Burns and Don Kinder; enjoyed the camaraderie of Mike
Hanmer, Ismail White, and Won-ho Park; and was grateful for many din-
ners and conversations with the Bowers-Wongs. My colleagues at the
University of New England, especially Ali Ahmida and Ariel Yablon, provided friendship and constant encouragement during the later stages of
this project. My students have inspired me with their hard work and desire
to learn. The Maine political theory group (in particular, stalwarts Ron
Schmidt, Jason Read, and Jill Gordon) has been a consistently enlighten-
ing group of interlocutors. Laura Henry and the Douhovnikoff men (Vlad,
Leo, and Alexei) are like a surrogate family here in Maine, offering many
insights into both politics and parenting.

I am indebted to colleagues who read all or part of the manuscript and
provided thoughtful and challenging comments: Jamie Martel, Laura Janara,
Elizabeth Cohen, Kennan Ferguson, Ali Ahmida, Liz Wingrove, Maria
Rosales, Laura Henry, and several anonymous reviewers. I appreciate the
excellent advice of Pieter Martin, my editor at the University of Minnesota
Press, as well as the expert copyediting of Carol Lallier. Marc Taurisano's
careful reading produced countless useful suggestions. Michael Swaine
never got around to it. Rebecca Goldfine found ways to improve every
page and managed to couch every suggestion sweetly.

Finally, I owe my deepest gratitude to my family. I appreciate the support and encouragement of my sisters Jennifer, Elizabeth, and Regina.
Regina took the extra step of moving nearby during a critical stage in this
project and provided her support in person: no one has ever been a better friend to me, and our monthly dinner out will always be among my
favorite traditions. There might be a certain irony in the fact that I could
only have completed this project about the limitations of parenthood as a
political identity thanks to the love, encouragement, and unflagging support of my parents, Bill and Jean Duff. There is no limit to their virtues as
parents, and I dedicate this book to them.

The Parent and the Citizen

IT WAS AN ARGUMENT over the political significance of parenthood
that gave birth to liberal-democratic political theory. When Sir Robert
Filmer offered Western political thought's last great defense of kingly sovereignty, he based his claims entirely on the monarch's rights as father.[1]
John Locke perceived great dangers in Filmer's poor thinking about parenthood, warning readers against Filmer's "Omnipotent *Fatherhood,* which
can serve for nothing but to unsettle and destroy all the Lawful Governments in the World, and to Establish in their room Disorder, Tyranny, and
Usurpation." Responding to Filmer in *Two Treatises on Government,* Locke
shattered sovereign power into as many pieces as there were citizens. But
even so divided, the relationship between parental authority and political
sovereignty—between parenthood and citizenship—was preserved in a
new form. Locke argued that paternal authority should not be arbitrary
or automatic but rather based on the parent's ability "to inform the mind"
until the child "comes to the Estate that made his *Father a Freeman.*"[2] It
was a formulation that defined a new problem: What makes a person ready
for citizenship? What makes a citizen worthy of his part of sovereignty?[3]
Further, this formulation suggested a crucial realm in which this problem
would be negotiated: in the parent's relationship with a child.

Democratic politics has never quite severed itself from these origins.
Defining the qualities that make a person a good "freeman" and a worthy
citizen has preoccupied political theorists and political entrepreneurs in
the centuries that have followed Locke. Over these centuries, theorists,
politicians, and citizens have repeatedly returned to parenthood as the
central experience informing citizenship. In modern times, people have
come to know themselves as citizens—to *become* themselves as citizens—
through thinking about a parent's relationship to children.[4]

Thus it was a representative moment in American politics when
George W. Bush—ending his second term as the economy staggered and
two wars stagnated; preparing, as the scion of one of the nation's most

powerful families, to pass his office to the first black president and the son
of an impoverished single mother—summarized his impression of Barack
Obama for the American people:

> Clearly, this guy is going to bring a sense of family to the White
> House, and I hope Laura and I did the same thing. But I believe
> he will, and I know his girls are on his mind and he wants to make
> sure that first and foremost, he is a good dad. And I think that's
> going to be an important part of his presidency.[5]

Privileging the role of parent as the "first and foremost" in democratic politics is not a mere feel-good rhetorical device one can turn to at a difficult
or awkward political moment. Such words are meant to reassure in times
of uncertainty, and they succeed in reassuring because of the depth of their
resonance. They reflect a way of thinking about modern citizenship that is
rooted in the way both citizens and theorists have wrestled with central
questions inherent to democratic sovereignty. This book examines how
the creation of a sovereign self became enmeshed with the creation of another person through parenthood and how becoming a worthy citizen became intertwined with the creation of new citizens. It shows that modern
political theory and democratic politics have been ill served by this way of
thinking. As Locke warned about Filmer, our own ideas about parenthood
and citizenship introduce insecurities into democratic politics and offer
inroads to tyranny.

This book reveals how two of the most compelling and influential
theorists of modern politics, and two of their most popular contemporary counterparts, have deliberately sought to generate and employ the
passions and emotions surrounding parenthood in the crafting of their
political projects. These readings of Jean-Jacques Rousseau, Friedrich
Nietzsche, Richard Rorty, and Cornel West expose ideas about the power
of parenthood to provide direction to human lives and anxieties about
the truths that a child's imitation of its parents threaten to uncover. These
readings show that these ideas and anxieties are embedded in the foundational texts of liberal democratic society, the most incisive critiques of
that society and its institutions, and popular contemporary efforts to articulate a vision of liberal-democratic citizenship that incorporates those
critiques. These investigations help us understand just where the desire
to make use of parenthood in theorizing citizenship comes from, why

it continues to be so tempting, and why it so often goes wrong. When parenthood is imagined to summon a confidence in our political virtues, it often reveals profound insecurities. When parenthood is thought to instill the openness to contingency and change appropriate to democratic political contest, it often produces unexpected fundamentalisms and stagnation. While these problems—elusive virtue or unbearable conflict—are perhaps unavoidable in the context of family life, the search for political solutions to these problems when they emerge in the context of citizenship can be disastrous.

Parenthood and Values in American Politics

While Locke sought to recast the work of parenthood into the rational-sounding business of "informing the mind" of the child so the child can achieve the "estate" (the mental state) of the father, Rousseau, Nietzsche, Rorty, and West all conceive of the parent–child relationship in terms that delve deeper into the soul. In this they are mirrored by American political rhetoric, which repeatedly reinscribes the idea that the most important, fulfilling, and politically significant experience a person can have is becoming a parent. In contemporary American political discourse, the notion of virtue tends to be recast into the language of "values"—values continually couched in terms of what adults pass on to the next generation. Contest, in turn, is often imagined in terms of a debate over just which values we should strive to pass on to children, or the best way to do so—Does it take a family or a village? as the shorthand goes.

The speeches of George W. Bush provide a good example of the contemporary political use of the idea that children are the best source of meaning for a human life. As he put it in the 2005 State of the Union Address that began his second term in office, "So many of my generation, after a long journey, have come home to family and faith, and are determined to bring up responsible, moral children." Along with this parental determination comes a political responsibility, Bush explained, the "great responsibility to our children and grandchildren [to] honor and to pass along the values that sustain a free society."[6] Responding to the prominence of such rhetoric, Lauren Berlant describes a political culture in which "a nation made for adult citizens has been replaced by one imagined for fetuses and children."[7] Lee Edelman has suggested the label "reproductive futurism" for this "oppressive" political culture in which there is a "social consensus" that "public appeals on behalf of America's children . . . [are] impossible to refuse."[8] Both Berlant and Edelman point out that in its singular focus on the transmission of a particular set of values, this political rhetoric usually has little to do with the actual health and well-being of children.

Instead, this values rhetoric focuses on the importance of one generation passing on to the next their deepest convictions regarding what is most important and the right way to live. The forces that threaten to instill a different and perhaps harmful set of values in children pose the deepest political problems from this perspective. Though often associated with conservatives, these concerns preoccupy both sides of the political spectrum.[9] Writing about values in his second book, *The Audacity of Hope*, Obama reports, "Every parent I know, liberal or conservative, complains about the coarsening of the culture, the promotion of easy materialism and instant gratification, the severing of sexuality from intimacy. . . . [T]hey want those concerns recognized, their experiences validated." He notes that Americans see "raising kids with the right values" as the "most important moral challenge facing the nation."[10] After listing the challenges to American values exclusively in terms of the ways we might let down "the next generation," "children," and "our families," Obama urges that "we hang on to our values. . . . Those values are our inheritance, what makes us who we are as a people. . . . To do otherwise would be to relinquish our best selves" (84).[11]

For Obama, as for Bush, to "hang on" to our best selves means more than anything else to pass on our best selves to our children. Our ability to do so is the measure of who we are. In his first month in office, Obama published an open letter to American fathers in which he described the transformative moment of his first daughter's birth and his determination "that if I could be anything in life, I would be a good father. I knew that day that my own life wouldn't count for much unless she had every opportunity in hers. And I knew I had an obligation, as we all do, to help create those opportunities and leave a better world for her and all our children."[12] Obama admires other politicians touched by a similar transformational experience. In introducing his running mate, Obama told his audience that Joe Biden "did more than become a Senator—he raised a family. That is the measure of the man standing next to me. That is the character of Joe Biden."[13] Biden's tearful recounting of his anguish at his daughter's death from a car accident became the most resonant moment in his campaign. It was a simple transition, apparently automatic and sincere, for Biden to recast the death of his child in terms that resonate with the style of values thinking in which a child with the wrong values is tragically lost. Conveying his sympathy for parents struggling to raise their children, Biden told them, "I understand what it's like as a parent to wonder [if] your kid's going to make it."[14]

In this American way of politics, contest (conceived of in terms of openness to change and self-transformation), is cast as an openness to be changed by the experience of parenting—taking on the responsibility of living by the values you hope to pass on. This is apparent in Bush's formulation of his generation "coming home to family and faith" after a period of wandering. It is clear in Obama's framing of Biden's life story in terms of his assumption of the responsibilities of single fatherhood. It was clear in religious conservatives' unperturbed reaction, in the same election campaign, to the news that the teenage daughter of the Republican vice-presidential candidate was pregnant out of wedlock. Governor Sarah Palin noted that becoming a parent "would make her grow up faster than we had ever planned. . . . As Bristol faces the responsibilities of adulthood, she knows she has our unconditional love and support."[15] Any unwholesomeness associated with teen sexuality is scrubbed clean by its culmination in procreation. "It changes your life and gives you a different perspective on the world," the conservative activist Phyllis Schlafly told the *New York Times*.[16] As Kristin Lukor found in her study of ideas about procreation among American political activists, "Sex is sacred because in [the conservative] worldview it has the capacity to be something transcendent—to bring into existence another human life."[17]

In American political culture, reproduction can also introduce the sacred, meaningful, and life-changing to relationships in which sexuality is not procreative, creating a new identity with profound political consequences. As Dan Savage wrote in the *New York Times*,

> There is a political element to gay and lesbian parenting that unfortunately is unavoidable: you can't have a baby and sit out the fight for equality. . . . Gay parents are not only making a commitment to our political future but to the future, period. . . . And many of us have decided we want to fill our time with something more meaningful than sit-ups, circuit parties and designer drugs. For me and my boyfriend, bringing up a child is a commitment to having a future.[18]

Confirming this worldview, another *Times* columnist, David Brooks, imagines a dystopia in which no citizens were parents. Without children to raise, Brooks suggests, "There are no grand designs. There are no high ambitions. Politics becomes insignificant. Even words like justice lose meaning."[19]

Edelman recoils at "this fascism of the baby's face, . . . as if the future secured by the Child, the one true access to social security, could only be claimed for the other's sake, and never for one's own—then that future can only belong to those who purport to *feel* for the other."[20] But Edelman's reaction misses the extent to which the American obsession with passing on values to children is less about getting caught up in another than it is about an examination of the self and what parenting reveals about the self. As the chapters that follow demonstrate, the modern conception of the parent as citizen, burdened with the task of passing on values, has less to do with care than it has to do with *imitation*.[21]

Parenthood and the Politics of Imitation

Locke's vision of parenthood involved the creation of a sort of imitation of oneself in one's child—raising the child to the state that made the parent worthy to be a citizen. He reminded fathers, "Children (nay, and men too) do most by example. We are all sort of chameleons that still take a tincture from things near us; nor is it to be wondered at in children, who better understand what they see than what they hear." Thus, Locke warned, "You must do nothing before [your child] that you would not have him imitate."[22] In its obsession with the "values" that we struggle to pass on to children, American political rhetoric strikes a concordant tone. In his letter to American fathers, Obama urged them "to show [your] children, by example, the kind of people [you] want them to become."[23]

This is a way of thinking about the political significance of parenthood that, as the following chapters demonstrate, resonates with Rousseau's and Nietzsche's take on the role of parenthood in the politics of virtue and contest and the reworking of their ideas in West and Rorty. Each of these theorists emphasizes the importance of imitation to the relationship between parents and children, and each puts it to use in his theory of citizenship. It is the intensity of the child's scrutiny of the parent that allows these theorists to see in the relationship the potential for a unique understanding of who we really are and how worthy we are as citizens and sovereign beings. But it is the frightening possibility that this scrutiny might uncover truths we would rather not face that makes these theorists flinch at the responsibilities and risks of democratic citizenship.

Adorno suggested in *Minima Moralia* that a child's effort to imitate his or her parents is the foundation of our best political capacities. It was an aspect of human existence that Adorno thought political theorists should be more willing to embrace. "The human is indissolubly linked with imitation: a human being only becomes human at all by imitating other human beings. In such behavior, the primal form of love, the priests of authenticity scent traces of the utopia which could shake the structure of domination."[24] Adorno thought it would encourage human flourishing if theorists would abandon the temptation to focus one's attention inward in search of a kernel of genuineness and uniqueness in each human being and rather embrace the multiplicity of social connections and social influences, the many imitations, that determine the makeup of any individual. More recently, Judith Butler has suggested that by understanding our expressions of gender as imitative, we might loosen our attachment to notions of "natural" sexuality that are both personally alienating and legitimating of current hierarchies. Gender, Butler suggests, is an imitation that produces the original it assumes.[25]

But imitation is a form of social influence that political theorists have found intriguing, less often because our experience as infantile imitators forms the basis for our adult political capacities,[26] but more frequently as a noble alternative to baser political activities of arguing, reasoning, cajoling, or using force. This is the politics of *being imitated,* not of imitating, of being the original rather the copy, and it is a tempting politics indeed. To be imitated is to be adult rather than infantile. The ability to inspire imitation means a person is able to preserve the satisfaction of genuineness and being true to oneself but also gets to lead others in the direction he or she has chosen.

So it is necessary to explore the flip side of Adorno's formulation: the importance that modern political theorists have placed on the experience of being imitated. Political theory offers many examples in which those who inspire imitation are figured as the ultimate political actors. John Stuart Mill's *On Liberty,* for example, urges readers to respect individual uniqueness and allow a diversity of approaches to life. But he cannot resist the figure of the genius, a person who takes advantage of society's freedoms to craft a way of life that is truly worth imitating.

There are but few persons, in comparison with the whole of mankind, whose experiments, if adopted by others, would be likely to be any improvement on established practice. But these few are the salt of the earth; without them, human life would become a stagnant pool. . . . I insist thus emphatically on the importance of genius. . . . The honour and glory of the average man is that he is capable of following that initiative; that he can respond internally to wise and noble things, and be led to them with his eyes open.[27]

Across the Atlantic, Ralph Waldo Emerson endorsed a similar view: "There are men, who, by their sympathetic attractions, carry nations with them, and lead the activity of the human race."[28]

Max Weber's *Politics as a Vocation* climaxes in the moment when the political actor forgoes the compromises of modern "machine" politics—material and rhetorical—and makes a stand that others may imitate if they will. This politician "somewhere reaches the point where he says: 'Here I stand; I can do no other.' That is something genuinely human and moving."[29] Bonnie Honig depicts this figure as one example of a "recasting [of] the relation between virtue and [contest]," because the figure blends Weber's ethic of responsibility (which Honig associates with contest) and the ethic of ultimate ends (which she aligns with virtue). Honig feels the pull of imitation herself and suggests "we might follow Weber's example." She compares Weber's compelling politician to Nietzsche's Zarathustra and his self-declaration: "I am who I must be; I call myself Zarathustra." Faintly invoking the politics of parenthood, Honig notes that she "prefer[s] Nietzsche's formulation to Weber's, however, because Nietzsche begins with an acknowledgement of the constating structures and identities into which human beings are born."[30]

Switching perspectives from those who are born to those who create them, the chapters that follow examine the politics of imitation wrapped up in the politics of parenthood—politics from the perspective of those, to borrow Honig's terms, who constate the structures and identities into which others are born. In democratic times, the politics of imitation need not be reserved for the rare and the elite. For every child who is initiated into politics, as Adorno supposed, through imitating, there are parents (sovereign and citizen) who are the object of scrutiny and potential emulation. But if parenthood provides access to a particularly democratic politics of imitation, it brings the challenges and pressures of citizenship along with it.[31]

Scholars who have studied the development of the modern family have found dark and desperate forces focused on the question of imitation. In particular, the spiritual self-reliance associated with Protestant beliefs changed the relationship between parents and children profoundly. The father's role as the religious leader of the household deeply intensified his scrutiny of his children and his efforts to inculcate the spirit and cant of his faith. This intensified attention to one's child worked like a mirror to provide a new form of self-scrutiny. Self-doubt regarding one's status among the "select" who were predestined for heaven—the same self-doubt that Weber placed at the heart of the spirit of capitalism—caused parents to react venomously to misbehavior on the part of their children. A bad child could indicate a bad inheritance from an unworthy (and unchosen) parent. One result was that children were beaten with much greater frequency and intensity in Protestant Europe than in Catholic communities.[32]

This way of thinking was reflected in political theory, for example, in Locke's account of parental authority as dependent on the inner qualities of the father. Rousseau would make it a central concern of his political thought in which the best quality found in both parents and citizens is that "one cannot know them without wanting to imitate them."[33] Nietzsche, Rorty, and West would in turn consider the uses of parenthood in their own political projects. In each case, the pressures created by the burden of making oneself the sort of parent and citizen worthy of imitation had dire and unintended consequences. Among these pressures is the persistent anxiety that in seeking to make oneself worthy of imitation, a citizen becomes a mere imitator in his or her own right—struggling to pass on values that we did not author and have never truly made our own. Due in part to these sorts of anxieties, Rousseau, Nietzsche, Rorty, and West each, in one way or another, recoil from the prospect of relying on the experience of parenthood to offer their account of proper citizenship. Yet none of them could resist it. Examining these theorists helps us understand the profound pull of parental thinking along with its profound flaws.

Parenthood in the Development of the Modern Citizen

The idea that children will imitate their parents has become wrapped together with other aspects of the experience of parenthood—as it has been imagined and as it is actually experienced—to make it alluring to those who would confront the responsibilities of democratic citizenship, whether figured in terms of virtue, contest, or both.[34] It has been so since modern democracy's beginnings. Jürgen Habermas and Charles Taylor suggest that it was in thinking about and discussing their roles in the family that the eighteenth- and nineteenth-century bourgeoisie most intensively developed the capacities and concerns that they would bring to the emerging democratic public sphere. As new freedoms developed, parenthood played a crucial role in the sense of self that people brought to their emergent understanding of the modern citizen—an individual who is responsible not only for the substance and direction of his or her own life but also for that of the political community as a whole. Taylor writes that in the face of new political circumstances, "what changes is not that people begin loving their children ... but that these dispositions come to be seen as a crucial part of what makes life worthy and significant."[35] These notions of what is most significant did not merely inform the politics of developing democracy but to a large extent became the substance of public discussion. As Taylor puts it,

> The intimate domain had to be defined through public interchange.... A new definition of human identity, however private, can become generally accepted only through being defined and affirmed in public space. And this critical exchange itself came to constitute a public sphere, along with, even slightly ahead of, the principle axis of exchange around matters of public policy. People who never met came to a mutually recognized common mind about the moving power of Rousseau's *Julie*.[36]

As chapter 1, "Monsters in the Garden: Rousseau on Politics and Parental Virtue," explores, the moving power of Rousseau's novel *Julie* was rooted in its depiction of a family drama centered on questions of parenthood. Habermas offers a similar account of a family-preoccupied public sphere. It was "the patriarchal conjugal family" that offered "the experiences about which a public passionately concerned with itself sought agreement and enlightenment through the rational-critical public debate."[37] As the substance of politics came to center on debates regarding the role of family in living the right sort of life, this brought new pressures to bear on people's understanding of, and their passionate concerns about, their personal experience of parenthood. Children were restricted in new ways, and parents scrutinized their relationship with their offspring for signs of success in this newly crucial aspect of life. Fears of failure haunted the new parent-centered citizen that became central to the emerging politics of democracy. The difficulty of making the actual practice of parenting match new ideals caused the normal setbacks of home life to take on new and more devastating meanings. A child's "disobedience threatens to break a parent's heart," according to Taylor, and can diminish the parent's confidence as a participant in the public sphere.[38] With modern identity focused on citizens' role as parent, insecurities became rooted in a realm where they are particularly difficult to bear and where citizens feel the deepest responsibility for failure. The consequences for a politics that privileges that identity are profound.

These public discussions, these interpretations of Rousseau, and these reflections by citizens on their own lives generated and revealed aspects of parenthood that are familiar in our own political culture. On a discursive level, citizens were conjured in modern political theory and popular rhetoric as parents. At the same time, political theorists and citizens in the public sphere helped to generate and designate the feelings, emotions, and responsibilities that would be associated with parenthood. Books regarding both the meaning and techniques of parenthood were among the most widely and intensively read among the new literate class.[39] Many of these were written by political thinkers, including Locke and Rousseau. Thus, in confronting the role of ideas about parenthood in modern political theory, it is necessary to keep in mind not only the parent as citizen but also the modern citizen who is *imagined* in terms of parenthood. In theorizing democratic citizenship as rooted in the experience of parenthood, modern political theorists have created burdens and expectations that prove problematic for both parents and nonparents, if not in precisely the same ways.[40] As the following chapters reveal, even when parenthood is appealed to as a metaphor, it is a metaphor that suffers from an inability to leave its referent behind.

What modern theorists and citizens "discovered" about parenthood (or generated as important ways of thinking about the experience of parenthood) is that it can offer us access to a sense of the magical, the miraculous, and the life-affirming in a secularized world. Parenthood can put us in touch with what William Connolly calls an "enchantment with being and becoming" in disenchanted times.[41] It can summon our sense of responsibility and authority amid the confusion of modern social forces. Parenthood can promise a meaningful and lasting relationship in a world where bonds of fellow-feeling, friendship, and love are often fleeting. It can offer an impetus to pause amid the blur of life and reorganize our lives around what is most important to us. It can deepen our sense of connection to both past and future as we reconsider our cultural and political inheritance in thinking about what we would like to pass on to the next generation.[42] In all these ways, parenthood has come to be imagined, and often lived, as a deeply felt and intimate experience that generates many of the capacities and responsibilities we hope to bring to politics. Paul Kahn suggests, "What is striking is not the occasional conflict, but the deep compatibility between the domains of politics and family." Kahn believes that this compatibility helps explain why the modern democratic citizen's relationship to the political is much deeper than liberalism has often imagined. Turning to the political resonance of the experience of parenting and deep imitation, Kahn explains, "My children are mine because they embody an idea of the self: not a narrow idea of the self as a natural body, but an idea as rich as the subject I take myself to be. They, just as much as the political world of actions and words, connect me to a world that will be. Indeed, they connect me to that same political world."[43]

These aspects of parenthood have made it attractive to citizens responsible for crafting, articulating, and judging themselves and others according to a notion of the right way to live in an era of democratic freedoms and responsibilities—a notion that informs how we act politically and what we expect from our politics. In fact, as Taylor and Habermas suggest, these sentiments and ideas initially became central to parenthood *through* emerging practices of citizenship and participation in the developing public sphere. These notions about parenthood have made it irresistible to modern political theorists as well.

But the explorations of modern political theory that follow suggest that it is counterproductive to stake so much of our capacity for democratic citizenship on the sentiments and capacities that result from the parent's relationship with the child—a relationship in which power is distributed unequally, clearly, but also one in which responsibility is felt so intimately and profoundly that conflict and failure can be devastating. Parenthood often means we must impose upon our children rules of behavior and conceptions of right and wrong that we know in our bones to be dubious. Parents' own actions, as children often observe (and imitate), too frequently betray the standards they set. The difficulties of this task can breed desperation, and sadly it is in inculcating our notions of right behavior that we most often violate them. When you witness an adult hissing at someone, manipulating someone, promising retribution, or cruelly expressing disappointment, that adult is usually communicating with his or her child. Despite the allure of parenthood, it is often the source of our deepest insecurities and uncovers (or creates) some of our most surprising fundamentalisms. When parenthood becomes central to our conceptions of citizenship, our notions of political virtue struggle to live up to these standards. Political contest can become unbearable under such conditions.

Parenthood and Two Theories of Citizenship

This book explores these dangers through investigations of the role of ideas about parenthood in the political thought of Rousseau as an exemplary theorist of virtue politics and Nietzsche as an exemplary theorist of the politics of contest. Through these theorists, I examine how two central ways of thinking about modern citizenship are undermined by their reliance on ideas about the experience of having and raising children. One approach is the theory of the virtuous citizen in which proper citizenship is marked with a particular set of admirable qualities and sentiments. Theorists of virtuous citizenship value a measure of uniformity in which members of a political community have been informed by similar experiences—like parenthood—to bring to politics a particular set of worthy values. The other approach is the contest theory of citizenship in which the values of citizens should be open to challenge and reconsideration. Advocates of this theory prize the contingency of political claims, a multiplicity of perspectives, competition between political ideals, and an openness to change.[44] Thus virtue and contest theories seek to tackle two fundamental questions of modern citizenship: First, how do we develop deeply felt notions of the good and the right way to live now that we, rather than kings or priests, are responsible for such decisions? Second, how do we communicate our convictions to other citizens and meanwhile cultivate openness to the possibility of transforming our deeply felt notions of the good in the context of democratic engagement with others? In answering these questions, theorists of both virtue and contest have relied on the way the experience of parenthood can be felt to reach into our souls. Though each of these accounts of modern citizenship has exemplary figures, like Rousseau among virtue theorists and Nietzsche among contest theorists, they are also persistently in conversation with each other.

Ideas about parenthood have become a point of connection where contemporary American political theorists like Rorty and West seek to intertwine these two theories of citizenship in an effort to find a reliable lodestar of virtue that allows us to navigate the challenging waters of contest. My readings of these theorists suggest, however, that this strategy exacerbates rather than mitigates the problems that accompany the political uses of parenthood. In theorizing citizenship, both Rorty and West have good reasons for appealing to the experience of parenthood in confronting the challenges of modern politics. But in each case, the turn to parenthood introduces unwanted complications that are difficult to overcome. In coming to rely on parenthood for political goals, these theorists figure citizens who are insecure in their virtue in ways they fear to acknowledge and who resign from the challenges of political contest at the moments when contest is most valuable.

In assessing these theorists, I hold them accountable to their own criteria regarding citizenship. One of the theorists I examine, Cornel West, admires thinkers who engage the work of others through the Hegelian method of "immanent critique," by which West means that a criticism of a thinker should appeal to that thinker's "own standards [and] principles" and "[tease] out internal inconsistencies, blindnesses and contradictions."[45] In that spirit, the chapters that follow identify the ways in which each theorist's ideas about the role of parenthood in democratic citizenship help undermine their own central political commitments. To the extent that the goals of these political theorists overlap with our own goals for our political community—the extent to which we still sympathize with Rousseau's desire to foster an earnestly engaged democratic citizenship, Nietzsche's efforts to chip away at unexamined self-righteousness and debilitating guilt, Rorty's efforts to articulate a vision of liberal citizenship that maximizes opportunities for self-creation and minimizes cruelty, and West's efforts to salvage a self-directed democracy from the nihilistic pull of market forces—it is particularly useful in our family-obsessed political culture to see what complications and contradictions emerge when ideas and feelings tied to parenthood are put in the service of these goals.[46]

The goals of these theorists also overlap with an important strain in contemporary democratic theory. Stephen K. White recently identified a trend in which many theorists acknowledge that "all fundamental conceptualizations of the self, other and world are contestable" but also hold that "such conceptualizations are nevertheless necessary or unavoidable for an adequately reflective ethical and political life."[47] William Connolly urges us to develop "an appreciation of the profound contestability of the fundamentals [we] honor."[48] In other words, contemporary theorists of democratic citizenship often seek to answer the question of how we might balance virtue and contest—how we make genuinely felt assertions about better and best ways to live as democratic citizens and how we open those assertions to challenge and reconsideration. The idea of virtue and contest as competing modes of theorizing politics has been most explicitly explored by Bonnie Honig in her *Political Theory and the Displacement of Politics*. Honig argues as a partisan of the politics as contest—for the ideas of theorists like Nietzsche and Arendt over theorists like Kant and Rawls. But after her incisive critiques of the politics of virtue from the perspective of contest, Honig concludes that the best approach to democratic politics will include both. She suggests we consider that

> virtue and *virtù* represent not two distinct and self-sufficient options but two aspects of political life. What if they signal two coexisting and conflicting impulses, the desire to decide crucial undecidabilities for the sake of human goods that thrive most vigorously in stable, predictable settings, and the will to contest established patterns, institutions, and identities?[49]

In this spirit, the chapters that follow do not argue as a partisan of the politics of virtue or the politics of contest. Rather, while noting what is compelling in each, these chapters attend to ideas about parenthood as a common and persistent source of trouble for these ways of thinking about politics. When refracted through parenthood, the citizen's desire for "stable, predictable" settings can become overwhelming even for an exemplary theorist of contest like Nietzsche.[50]

The first two chapters examine Rousseau and Nietzsche as foundational theorists of the modern politics of virtue and contest and uncover the problematic role of parenthood in each thinker's ideas. In chapter 1 on Rousseau, I argue that in relying on the experience of parenthood to plant the seed of virtue, and using the relationship with one's children as the measure of virtue, he introduced a source of profound insecurity into modern conceptions of citizenship. Rousseau was persistent and creative in exploring ways that the experience of parenthood might help produce the right sort of virtuous citizenship. The results were deeply compelling—so much so that the popularity of Rousseau's work quite literally introduced these ideas into popular conceptions of modern citizenship.[51]

Rousseau has frequently been interpreted as a theorist of the role of love, of passion, and of brotherhood in citizenship, and he was certainly all of these.[52] Many interpretations of Rousseau conceptualize these preoccupations as an effort to base democratic politics on forces that transcend the older and colder authority of patriarchy.[53] But Rousseau worked insistently to tie love and passion to the goal of virtuous parenthood in order that they might truly support virtuous citizenship. Even in the most unusual of circumstances—in pursuing forbidden love in the paternal home, for example, or in dalliances with prostitutes—Rousseau's lovers strive to become parents, and parents of the right sort. Rousseau replaces the old patriarchy with a new paternity.

But Rousseau's virtuous parenthood proves profoundly difficult to achieve, and it produces its own exacting measure regarding its proper achievement. It is the child a parent produces who provides the measure of success, the child who best perceives our true qualities and who eventually decides if he or she will aspire to imitate them. The self-scrutiny that results from the responsibility to instill in one's children a sense of the right way to live can yield profound doubts and fear of failure. This insecurity drives Rousseau to seek political solutions for the elusiveness of parental virtue and contributes to Rousseau's political despair and authoritarian impulses.

Or worse. Taylor notes that Rousseau's articulation of a "heroic and fullbodied" sense of citizenship in "a new kind of republic of virtue" marked the beginning of one path that "produced totalitarian challenges to liberal democracy in the twentieth century." He suggests that "the other path followed Nietzsche" and produced totalitarian challenges all its own.[54] But Nietzsche, like Rousseau, has become a thinker to whom theorists of democracy frequently turn to enrich our sense of citizenship. In particular, contemporary theorists have found in Nietzsche useful ways of thinking about how and why we should cultivate an openness to challenging and reconsidering our deeply held values and ideas about the right way to live.[55]

Chapter 2, "The Tragedy of Birth: Nietzsche on Parenthood and Political Contest," explores how Nietzsche, a central contest theorist, relied on the possibility of passing on a way of life through parenthood to provide the impetus for citizens to do the difficult work of self-transformation and of recrafting our fundamental values. The experience of parenthood, because

of the intensity of the relationship and the scrutiny of the parent by the developing child, struck Nietzsche as the best, perhaps only, way to communicate the results of a self-transformation that reaches deeper than mere
words or ideas—down to the level of instinct. Attention to this aspect of
Nietzsche's thought reveals that many of the ideas that contest theorists of
democracy have found most alluring in Nietzsche are deeply enmeshed
with those aspects of his thought that democrats most often try to excise
or elide—especially his attraction to aristocracy over democracy, his notions regarding gender, and his enthusiasm for grand political projects of
breeding.

While it might be satisfying to allow Nietzsche to help us claim parenthood for the politics of contest, it is not so easily done. Nietzsche's ideas
regarding parenthood as a political identity threatened to undermine his
commitment to the very notions regarding politics as contest that make
him so attractive to many contemporary theorists of democracy. In appropriating Nietzsche's ideas for a democratic politics of contest, Honig suggests that "Nietzsche's alternative ethic values not the construction and
maintenance of any single form of subjectivity but a commitment of a perpetual process of self-overcoming. . . . In matters of identity, Nietzsche insists, it is not possible to get it right."[56] But chapter 2 reveals that Nietzsche's
ideas suggest that those who seek to embody a version of himself or herself
in a child can become deeply attached to one perspective on life. Political
projects relying on parenthood can prove too dear to abandon—leading
to fundamentalism, stagnation, and love of the same. Thus my reading of
Nietzsche reveals that when conceived of as an opportunity to reconsider
values and instill openness, parental thinking can bring antidemocratic
impulses to the public sphere.

Chapters 1 and 2 elucidate the important and problematic role of ideas
about parenthood in foundational texts of the modern politics of virtue
and contest. Chapter 3, "Troubled Inheritance: Richard Rorty and the
Metaphysics of the Child," and chapter 4, "Deadbeat Citizens: Cornel
West and the Parent as Prophet," then consider the work of two contemporary American theorists of citizenship. Both Rorty and West rely on
ideas about parenthood in articulating conceptions of democratic citizenship that seek to balance or blend elements of virtue and contest. This is
an impulse that was not entirely absent from the work of Rousseau and
Nietzsche, and in chapters 1 and 2, I uncover some unexpected ways that
Rousseau's and Nietzsche's ideas overlap. But contemporary theorists have

been especially eager to find a way to combine the insights of these two traditions, and the chapters on Rorty and West examine the problematic role of ideas about parenthood in two accounts of how American citizens might balance these political impulses. The resulting tensions in Rorty's and West's theories of politics suggest that when the experience of parenthood is used to circumscribe the realm of political contest, the substance of political debate can become shallow and justify the status quo. When the virtuous citizenship that parenthood is meant to instill is subject to challenge, insecurities are exacerbated, and the temptation to turn to undemocratic solutions intensifies.

Chapter 3 explores the role that ideas about parenthood play in Rorty's negotiation of the competing pull of the stability of virtue and the unpredictability of contest. Rorty responded to this tension in his thinking about citizenship by positing a strong dichotomy between the two. He developed a vision of modern citizens who are uniformly virtuous for public purposes and embrace contest and contingency in private. Rorty, perhaps counterintuitively, made the experience of parenthood central to the public (and virtuous) side of this dichotomy. Parenthood is the source of the sentiments that provide roots for Rorty's public virtue. In the privacy of their own lives, Rorty believed, citizens should cultivate a sense of a contingency of their most cherished beliefs about the right way to live. But for the purposes of politics, Rorty believed that a shared hope for a better future for our children is the single disposition necessary for citizens to think about what is best for the nation.

Rorty's approach did not bring virtue and contest directly to bear on one another.[57] His dichotomy was an effort to avoid that struggle, but the effort does not succeed, and Rorty's distinctions break down. Though Rorty sought to put parenthood to use for public purposes, it is hard to imagine parenthood as a strictly public experience. In fact, as Taylor and Habermas suggest, it was the intensity of the private experience of modern parenthood, and the intensity of the scrutiny given to that experience, that made it seem a worthy subject of the conversations and debates that contributed to the development of the modern public sphere. Thus Rorty found that many citizens invoke the experience of parenthood to understand not merely their public duties and orientations but also their private sense of self. One result is that contest must be circumscribed further—not just to the private realm but to a small set of citizens. Rorty's openness to contingency was limited to inconsequential matters among a privileged group. Even among this group of "ironists," Rorty's ideas suggest that the private experience of having children can undermine one's openness to contingency and the impulse to question inherited values. These aspects of the private experience of parenthood interfere with the political uses Rorty wanted to make of our hopes for future generations. Proposed by Rorty as the root of the values that can unite Americans for politics, the private experience of parenthood introduces insecurities about one's personal worthiness that are difficult to face and corrosive to citizenship.

West's inclination is to confront the insecurities of citizens rather than deny them. In doing so, he integrates ideas about virtue and contest that Rorty attempts to separate through his public–private dichotomy. Chapter 4 uncovers the reasons why parenthood has come to play a crucial role in West's account of a citizenship in which deeply felt notions of the right way to live are balanced with a sense of fallibility and an openness to criticism. West articulates a productive tension between aspects of the virtue and contest accounts of citizenship and uses it to scrutinize several traditions in American democratic theory and practice, including pragmatism, the African American religious tradition, and socialism. In each case, West uses his dual commitment to virtue and contest to uncover useful utopian impulses and sources of hope for a more just and decent society while exposing the tendencies of such visions to indulge in fundamentalism and flirt with authoritarian arrangements in the service of their goals.

West's restless search for a political disposition rooted in love and oriented toward the future—one that might provide unity across disparate groups in American politics—ultimately culminates in a focus on parenthood as a political identity. The emotions associated with parenthood become crucial to West's hopes to ward off the nihilism that can result from the chaotic forces of the market and the impulse to authoritarianism that he believes threaten American freedom and democracy. But I show that in staking so much of his American political project on parenthood, West creates new difficulties. Nihilism can overwhelm even the altruistic feelings associated with parenthood and family. Insecurity regarding our capacities as parents can wear away at our sense of competence for citizenship, and West turns to an intrusive state for solutions. When the bastion of love and hope offered by the experience of parenthood is threatened, West is tempted by measures that court hopelessness, limit freedom, and flirt with authoritarianism. West's example indicates that placing so much importance on parenthood as a source of meaning that is useful for politics can contribute to fundamentalism regarding virtue and undermine commitments to contingency and democratic individuality.

The problems that ideas about parenthood introduce into our thinking about democratic citizenship—whether conceived in terms of virtue, contest, or some combination of the two—do not imply that ideas about parenthood and family should be excluded from politics. But in uncovering the persistence of the urge to intertwine parental and political authority and the profound insecurities, fundamentalisms, and authoritarian impulses that result, I suggest a new perspective from which political claims should be scrutinized. From this perspective, the conclusion considers several contemporary theories that invite rethinking regarding the role of parenthood in modern politics. These include William Connolly's articulations of a "pluralist" democratic citizenship that balances contest and virtue and the interest in "biopolitics" typified by Michel Foucault and Giorgio Agamben. In particular, the infiltration of ideas about parenthood into our political thinking offers a new perspective on Connolly's efforts to apply Agamben's ideas regarding "bare life" to contemporary American politics. Applying this perspective to public policy along with political theory, I then extend that analysis to the parent-centered antipoverty programs proposed by the Obama administration.

Parenthood and the Male Heterosexual

Rousseau, Nietzsche, Rorty, and West are all men. In theorizing parenthood's relationship to politics, they attend to gender and neglect it in ways that the following chapters examine.[58] In doing so, these chapters complicate the familiar story whereby masculine political theory relies on a gendered division of human functions into a feminine sphere concerned with biological reproduction and a masculine sphere centered on politics. Iris Marion Young called this "the male centeredness of modern political theory's conception of citizenship . . . [in which] the citizen virtue of mothers [entails] the virtues of caring and sacrifice necessary for nurturing children to be good citizens."[59] If this story is familiar, it is because it has been so perceptively explored and convincingly defended in previous research.[60]

Other studies that have revealed the instability of these divisions, books like Linda Zerilli's *Signifying Women* and Christine Di Stefano's *Configurations of Masculinity*, have focused on the extent to which theorists experienced anxiety at the permeability of these gendered boundaries between

politics and biology and on the manifestations of this anxiety in their political thought. The following chapters reveal ways that male political theorists have *actively* cultivated a sense of connection between these spheres
and articulated a model of political development in which the modern
citizen, as an adult, engages the procreative sphere for political purposes.
For these theorists, it is not simply a matter of associating women and the
feminine with the reproductive sphere so that men can roam freely in the
political sphere. These theorists also embrace the possibility that men's
experience of parenthood can have a transformative effect that is useful
for political purposes. Rousseau's and Nietzsche's foundational accounts
of modern virtue and contest citizenship persistently turn to ideas about
women and the feminine to tie parenthood and citizenship, including
male citizenship, more surely. This aspect of their thought helps shed new
light on the role that ideas about gender play in their theories. This is not
to say that the active cultivation of an interconnection between the realms
of politics and parenthood is not potentially just as anxiety-producing as a
subconscious awareness of permeability between these spheres, nor is it to
say that the anxieties identified by scholars like Zerilli and Di Stefano do
not exist. Perhaps nothing is more likely to produce anxiety than the idea
that it is necessary to engage the very thing that you subconsciously fear
will swallow you up.

Jacqueline Stevens suggests, "Feminist work that begins with questions
about birth and reproduction tends not to discuss the implication of such
gendered practices for citizenship."[61] This is only partly true. De Beauvoir,
for example, believed women's experience of their role in reproduction—
from menstruation through sexuality and pregnancy to mothering—was
the greatest obstacle to women's participation in the properly political activity of "transcendence."[62] From the opposite perspective, several theorists have also suggested that parenthood, especially mothering, can offer
us an intensive experience of caring for another that we might cultivate
into a broader disposition to care for our fellow citizens.[63] This particular way of thinking about citizenship could certainly fit under the rubric
of parent-based virtue citizenship and is subject to many of the problems
with this mode of thinking in ways my analysis touches upon. Joan Tronto
suggests that the association of care with parenthood stifles our ability to
appreciate care as a public value and that parents often let their care for
their children justify a lack of care for others.[64] But a focus on the capacity
to care is not the most common way that modern virtue theorists have

sought to make use of the experience of parenthood. Instead, these theorists are more commonly concerned with the passing on of a particular set
of values or qualities to one's child. These theorists focus more often on
inheritance and imitation than care itself.

Stevens offers a comprehensive and insightful account of the persistent place of ideas about gender, reproduction, and kinship in the rules
of membership in political societies. She does not address the way that
ideas about parenthood affect political theorists' figuring of the *substance*
of citizenship and political participation. Stevens demonstrates that "political societies institutionalize the relation between birth, history, and
kinship rules in ways that make concrete the attachments of parents and
children."[65] In this book, I reverse this relationship and ask how the profound and problematic attachment of parents and children determines the
citizen's relations to political society. Stevens demonstrates that democratic
societies continue to rely on birth and family, rather than on consent, in
the question of who gets to be a citizen. In this book, I explore how political theorists have thought of the parent's relationship to the child as a
measure of the quality of one's citizenship. One's child offers an answer to
the question of whether our way of life is worth consenting to.[66]

Writing about the relationship between motherhood and citizenship
and the harsh judgments often rendered upon single mothers who rely on
the state, Young suggests that citizenship requires "autonomy: within the
bounds of justice, to be able to make choices about one's life and to act
on those choices without having to obey others, meet their conditions,
or fear their threats and punishments."[67] The political theorists I explore
often imagine the child as judge of the parent—and arbiter whose judgment parents fear to face. This fear of judgment from *inside* the family—
this investment of our sense of self in a child—can have a devastating effect on a citizen's sense of autonomy.

While feminist work has helped rethink the role of the family in political theory in ways that this study will seek to build on and complicate,
queer theory has begun to reconsider the politics of the family in new
ways. Writing from a liberal-feminist perspective in "Mothers, Citizenship,
and Independence," Young defends the idea that a variety of families can
raise children with the capacities for citizenship—that liberalism's "family values can and often are realized in a plurality of family forms: gay and
lesbian families, single-parent families, blended families, nuclear families,
extended families" (553).[68] But theorists like Berlant and Edelman have

suggested ways that ideas about family might be exposed and reworked to unsettle fundamental notions regarding contemporary American citizenship. Berlant's *The Queen of America Goes to Washington City* examines how the Reagan and Clinton eras saw ideals regarding virtue in private life preoccupy citizens who were "anxious about their value to themselves, their families, their publics and their nation" (2). These anxieties can give citizens—in particular the white, male heterosexuals whose right to rule has been exposed to new challenges—the sense that they are incapable of a robust and public citizenship. Contemporary Americans, according to Berlant, have become citizens of diminished confidence and sullied virtue looking to the state to protect an intimate realm in which they heal themselves and protect the innocent, especially children. It is, Berlant suggests, in "the last few decades" that American citizens have come to feel that the "the core context of politics should be the sphere of private life" (3). Thus Berlant explores how ideas about family animate a contemporary political culture in which citizens resign from the responsibilities of citizenship. In this book, I show how modern political theorists have looked to the experience of parenthood to create our understanding of what those responsibilities are and how citizens might rise to them. So while Berlant finds that Americans turn to children and other innocents in a retreat from their inadequacy as citizens, this book suggests that the experience of parenthood is what most often dooms citizens to a sense of failure. The centrality of parenthood to the citizen's sense of self is precisely what makes that failure so devastating. Thus this study reveals that the anxieties identified by Berlant are fundamentally rooted in the relationship between the experience of parenthood and modern democratic citizenship.

Edelman's *No Future: Queer Theory and the Death Drive* also explores the ways that the "figural Child" looms over American political culture. While Berlant is most concerned with the learned helplessness produced by family-centered citizenship, Edelman uncovers how the figure of "the Child" can summon a responsibility to conserve the social order as we inherited it (11). This "reproductive futurism" renders "politics . . . at its core, conservative insofar as it works to *affirm* a structure, to *authenticate* social order, which it then intends to transmit to the future" (3). Echoing Berlant, Edelman suggests that "the figural Child alone embodies the citizen as an ideal." But while Berlant attends to the ways the ideal reflects a self-contempt that leads many to resign from assertive citizenship, Edelman looks to the way the idea of the child enlists everyone to get behind a fundamentally conservative politics—one in which "the image of the Child, not to be confused with the lived experiences of any historical children, serves to regulate political discourse—to prescribe what will *count* as political discourse"(11).

Edelman's invocation of the queer as "the side of those *not* 'fighting for the children,' the side outside the consensus by which all politics confirms the absolute value of reproductive futurism" (3) is both revolutionary and abstract. If the revolution is to do its work, it must understand the ways that modern citizens and the most influential theorists of modern politics attempt to use the relationship of the parent and child to forge and test their value as citizens. This book offers that analysis. Edelman condemns the "grimness with which a man clings to himself" and suggests we abandon "the assurance . . . of *knowing* ourselves and hence of *knowing* our 'good'" (5).[69] The chapters that follow show that parenthood is often how citizens seek both to know and to rework themselves and that they often do so with little assurance that they have made of themselves something like the good. Edelman vents his disgust with a politics focused on the recurrence of the same for the sake of children. Nietzsche considered the desire for a sort of recurrence to be the highest achievement and—despite his reservations—turned to parenthood in order to imagine how it might be accomplished. In exposing the power of ideas about parenthood to enlist a thinker as willing to contest inherited values as Nietzsche, and in showing how a reliance on parenthood persistently undermines constructions of citizenship, this book seeks to bring the critique of reproductive futurism to the heart of modern political theory and contemporary American politics.

Parenthood, Citizenship, and Failure

It was in describing parenting as a relationship of care that Stephen Macedo and Iris Marion Young wrote, "Raising children is, for most adults, a central, if not *the* central, project in their lives: a source of profound satisfaction or disappointment."[70] When the burdens of citizenship become wrapped up in this relationship, the resulting satisfaction or disappointment is not only felt deeply but has profound political effects. In considering the plurality of family forms (gay, single, nuclear, extended) that might produce good citizens, Young leaves out the plurality of ways that family life can be painful: the jealousy, anger, anxieties, rejections, failures, and betrayals—and the effects of these experiences on citizenship. Charles

Taylor addresses failure when he describes the way in which the modern sense that parenthood is central to a fulfilling life preoccupied the emerging democratic public sphere and how this idea became important to the individual citizen's feeling of competence and dignity. Our role as parent became central, according to Taylor, to whether "we think of ourselves as commanding or failing to command the respect of those around us." Thus it became central to citizenship. As Taylor writes, "The fierce competition for this kind of dignity is part of what animates democratic politics." For the citizen, the absence of dignity can be devastating. "My sense of myself as a householder, father of the family, holding down a job, providing for my dependents; all this can be the basis of my sense of dignity. Just as its absence can be catastrophic, can shatter it by totally undermining my feeling of self-worth."[71]

When our success as parent is a chief source of our dignity and feeling of competence for citizenship, the children we produce are in the best position to make us feel the devastating effects of its absence. Taylor points out in *Sources of the Self* that it is often "precisely . . . the children whose growth the householder so cherished" who rejects the parent's way of life and makes her feel like a failure. Taylor calls this "a peculiarly poignant [example] of how this aspiration to connection can motivate some of the most bitter conflicts in human life." In the face of such bitter conflicts, we might keep up the struggle in hopes of emerging with our dignity intact. Taylor notes, for example, that we might respond to our insecurities by seeking to become better parents. "But," he continues, "the issue also arises for us not just as a matter of more or less but as a question of *yes or no*. And this is the form in which it most deeply affects and challenges us" (45, emphasis added). This yes-or-no question regarding our success in our chosen way of life creates profound pressures on the parent as citizen. It is a conflict that is not dissimilar, according to Taylor, to the "Puritan [who] wondered whether he was saved" (45). And having become a parent, we can often no more escape this question of success than the Puritan can escape the judgment of God. About the citizen who has placed parenthood at the center of his life, Taylor writes, "He is deeply committed. . . . His direction is set" (46). This can be the case even for parents who do not raise their children. Chapter 1 explores Rousseau's abandonment of his offspring. Chapter 4 examines West's experience as a noncustodial parent. It is also a way of thinking about citizenship that infiltrates the imagination of nonparents like Nietzsche.

In his book *Loneliness as a Way of Life,* Thomas Dumm reflects on the role of parenthood in the way modern citizens "internalize the sovereign powers that we once could see inscribed on the bodies of kings and queens" and how citizens confront "the burdens and pleasures of inheritance." It is the burdens that hold sway. Dumm meditates on Shakespeare's Lear, the sovereign rejected by his children. Lear has two daughters ungrateful for what they have received from him, but more poignantly, he has a third whom he fears he has betrayed by asking too much of her. Lear cannot bear to ponder it: "O, that way madness lies, let me shun that! No more of that." Dumm summarizes: "His horror is that of the father who has failed."[72] Dumm finds such horror among democratic citizens as well. Arthur Miller's Willy Loman, for example, is devastated by the failure of his son Biff: "For if Biff is worthless, so is Willy" (66). Regarding contemporary American citizens in a similar vein, Michael Walzer notes, "A great deal has been written in recent years about family failure. But in truth most parents are remarkably successful in producing children much like themselves. Sometimes, unhappily, this is the sign of their failure."[73] Indeed, stagnation and failure, as the chapters that follow demonstrate, are the two problems that have most persistently haunted the parent as citizen.

Modern theorists have crafted the sovereign citizen by asking much, perhaps too much, of parenthood. Thus they describe citizens for whom failure can be devastating and incapacitating. In her defense of the politics of contest over the politics of virtue, Honig argues, "The propensity of institutions to generate expectations that they then disappoint is a feature of political life, a feature that should be engaged, not suppressed."[74] In creating our own families as political institutions, we also generate expectations that are central to our sense of ourselves as citizens. The theorists examined in this book struggle to engage the disappointment of expectations generated by the parent as citizen. That disappointment nonetheless emerges, often in unexpected ways and often in ways that undermine the use to which theorists have sought to put parenthood for citizenship.

In another book, Honig asks, "By what magic are dependent, not yet fully formed followers supposed to become the responsible, active citizens that democracy requires?"[75] Locke suggested the answer at the beginning. It is parenthood that turns dependents into adults, children into citizens. But the experience of being a parent, not just being parented, has become central to the way the theorists who followed Locke have thought about citizenship. It is parenting, not being parented, that makes them responsible adults and citizens. Those who will raise children, according to Hannah Arendt, must act as "representatives of the world for which they must assume responsibility although they themselves did not make it, and even though they may, secretly or openly, wish it were other than it is." Thus, claims Arendt, "anyone who refuses to take joint responsibility for the world should not have children."[76] As Dumm says about his and his wife's raising of their own children, "Their trajectory through childhood provided us with a measure of our own passage into adulthood.... It was simply how we became adults." Taylor claims that modern adults became citizens by thinking about and arguing about just how to pass on the right way of life to one's children. But as Dumm explains, even though "we will do anything we can to ensure that their lives will be good ones,... there is no assurance that our work will not be in vain.... It may be that only then will we learn most completely the lessons of regret."[77]

As Dumm's reflections suggest, both life and theory can uncover great difficulties that lurk in the alchemy of parenthood and citizenship. In conjuring citizens from parents, the magic that political theorists employ can darken. Where theorists of virtuous citizenship burden parental love with the demands of democratic citizenship, the result can be insecurity. Turning to the experience of parenthood to reveal our hidden strengths also threatens to expose to citizens their inadequacies—leading to despair and the abandonment of both parental and democratic responsibilities. Where theorists of a citizenship based on contingent claims and contest politics turn to parenthood as an inspiration to reexamine values, the results can be stagnation, fundamentalism, and love of the same. Turning to the experience of parenthood to inspire us to great and original responses to the circumstances of our times tempts us to insist that our vision of greatness should not be subject to revaluation. In each case, seeking solutions to make the trick work, theorists turn to undemocratic slights of hand. So to understand the antidemocratic impulses that lie within our most prominent theories of democratic citizenship, it is necessary to diagnose the pathologies of the parent as citizen.

CHAPTER 1

Monsters in the Garden:
Rousseau on Politics and Parental Virtue

When magistrature is hereditary, a child often commands men.

Discourse on Political Economy

Babies are going to lead you like a baby yourself.

Emile

THE FIRST THING JEAN-JACQUES ROUSSEAU ever did was kill his mother. Suzanne Bernard Rousseau passed away when her son was ten days old, from complications resulting from his birth. The sentiments of Rousseau's father, Isaac, helped ensure that the son would feel the loss deeply. "He seemed to see her again in me, but could never forget that I had robbed him of her; he never kissed me that I did not know by his sighs and his convulsive embrace that there was a bitter grief mingled with his affection. . . . 'Ah' he would say with a groan; 'Give her back to me, console me for her, fill the void she has left in my heart!'"[1] With such a beginning, it is particularly poignant that Rousseau would attempt to use political theory to gain mastery over the role of parent that his birth denied to his mother and ruined for his father. Despite heroic attempts in widely disparate projects, he would never succeed. Rousseau would go to his grave suspecting that the best way to salvage a worthwhile human life from the corruption of modern society was to reproduce in the right way and further convinced that he had never discovered just how it could be done.

On his way to that sad end, Rousseau would attempt to redefine the meaning that was given to the whole experience of procreation and parenthood—from the first romantic urges, through the experience of sexuality, through the experience (and spectacle) of pregnancy and nursing, and onward to the raising of a child. Throughout his oeuvre, Rousseau would aver that the proper development of passion and desire toward virtuous parenthood plays a central role in developing a life that is enchanted by virtue, and thus to a life appropriate to a republican citizen. But Rousseau's intertwined stories about parenthood and politics suggest that the extreme importance he placed on passing on a version of one's self through reproduction contributed to his despair regarding the possibility that his political vision could ever come to fruition or that he could find a practical way to contribute to the creation of a virtuous republic. Considered in whole, Rousseau's political thought suggests that modern citizens are likely to seek fulfillment in families at the expense of politics rather than in support of the virtuous democratic republic that was his ideal. This reading of Rousseau introduces the following dilemma regarding contemporary liberal democracy: On the one hand, Rousseau's earnest conception of engaged democratic citizenship continues to offer an ideal against which to identify the failings of our contemporary politics. Yet at the same time, the depth to which Rousseau's conception of fulfillment through parenthood and the sentimental family has penetrated the popular imagination might help suppress democratic engagement and contribute to political despair.

Whatever their childhood-psychological origins, the mature Rousseau's concerns about the meaning given to parenthood stemmed most prominently from his perception that by the mid-eighteenth century, the withdrawal of religious meaning had left vacant an important cultural role—a role he wanted the experience of parenthood to step into and reestablish. Many commentators have noted that, as Connolly puts it, the key to Rousseau's modernity lies "in accepting the demise of the world of miracles, divine texts, and sacred signs inscribed in custom . . . and seeking substitutes for those losses that appear too threatening."[2] Seeking a new language that would stir the sentiments and enchant the inhabitants of a disenchanted world, Rousseau turned again and again to the potential and the perils of the passions that surround "the pleasures attached to the reproduction of men."[3] In doing so, Rousseau crafted a uniquely personal and earnest mode of expression that was, as Maurice Cranston writes, "rich enough in emotional intensity to replace lost faith with new excitements."[4] Rousseau's moving exhortations "to sublimate desire into love and love into a stable union"[5] helped give birth to Romanticism and made him a cult figure in his own time. Rousseau's contemporary Georges-Louis Leclerc, Comte de Buffon, captured the unique effect Rousseau had on European sensibilities when he observed, "Others write, but Monsieur Rousseau alone commands and gets himself obeyed."[6]

As if he were a Napoleon armed only with a pen, Rousseau's commands began a transformation of Europeans' self-understanding, reorganizing priorities with a new emphasis on the nuclear family and the nurturing of children. No contemporary author was more widely or intensively read in eighteenth-century Europe, and Rousseau's readers pledged often and in earnest to remake themselves according to the ideas they encountered in his books. "Your divine works, Monsieur, are an all-consuming fire," wrote one reader in a letter typical of thousands that arrived at Rousseau's doorstep. The letter continues:

> They have penetrated my soul, fortified my heart, enlightened my mind. For a long time my reason . . . became lost in the search for truth. . . . I needed a god, and a mighty god, to pull me away from that precipice, and you, Monsieur, are the god who has performed the miracle. . . . Ever since I read your blessed book, I have burned with the love of virtue, and my heart, which I thought extinguished, beats harder than ever. Feeling has taken over once again: love, pity, virtue, sweet friendship have forever conquered my soul.[7]

Robert Darnton, having surveyed these letters, concludes that the authors ardently believed "Jean-Jacques had made them see deeper into the meaning of their lives. . . . They would now dedicate themselves to [virtue]— not virtue in the abstract, but the homespun variety, which they would work into the fabric of their family lives."[8] The warp and woof of this dedication to virtue would be a new understanding of the roles of spouse and parent. Thus it is Rousseau, more than anyone else, who is responsible for the modern development of the popular notion that human fulfillment is best sought in having and raising children. As Judith Shklar declared in her classic study *Men and Citizens*, "The child-centered family was undeniably born on the pages of [Rousseau's] *Emile* and [*Julie, or*] *La Nouvelle Héloïse*."[9] Charles Taylor, in placing conversations about the ideas found in Rousseau's books at the birthplace of the emerging public sphere, notes, "The novel which helped more than any other to define and spread the new outlook . . . was undoubtedly Rousseau's *La Nouvelle Héloïse*. . . . The impact of [the novel] when it came out in 1761 is hard to imagine in this more jaded age."[10]

But it was Rousseau's ideas about family that helped create the conditions in which democratic ages would become jaded. Rarely noted amidst the enthusiastic reception of his contemporaries were Rousseau's misgivings about the difficulty of using the experience of parenthood to transform the modern individual into a more virtuous citizen. The paradoxical effect is that Rousseau's immense popularity and the intense personal reactions that his readers had to his words resulted in a long-term legacy—a legacy whose influence on the family-centered political rhetoric we encounter today would be hard to overestimate—that reflects the opposite of what his texts imply about the actions and conditions necessary for cultivating the political potential of parenthood.

A great deal of the contemporary scholarship on Rousseau in political theory has focused on his treatment of gender, sexuality, and intimacy.[11] This approach to Rousseau often offers rich insights into the ways in which he thought passions could be used to reconfigure the sentiments for both domestic and public purposes and also the dangers the passions pose to those same goals. A number of such studies have illuminated the emphasis Rousseau placed on physical sensations, especially the most moving and visceral of those sensations, in determining the directions of a human life.[12] Rousseau believed that "the needs of the body are the foundation of society."[13] He often wondered whether the history of the corruption of man (the only history he perceived) could be reversed only if we learned "how to compel the brute functions to support the moral order they so often disturb."[14] However, to understand the role of gender and sexuality in Rousseau's thought, it is wise to take Nancy Hirschmann's advice and be "less concerned . . . with the construction of sexuality per se, or even of femininity per se, than of citizenship and freedom." According to Hirschmann, what is most interesting regarding Rousseau's ideas "about gender and sexuality is how they feed into virtue—which in turn founds freedom—rather than how virtue justifies Rousseau's construction of gender and sexuality."[15]

Studies focusing on gender and sexuality in Rousseau's thought, including Hirschmann's, have tended to neglect the extent to which Rousseau saw sexual passions most importantly as *reproductive* passions if they are to "feed into virtue" and be useful for citizenship. Thus these approaches generally neglect how it was the procreative aspects of sexuality that Rousseau found most useful in his political projects and the ways in which he saw nonprocreative sexuality as a dangerous detour from the path toward both domestic and political virtue. It is their potential culmination in parenthood that makes the sexual passions, for Rousseau, the source of the most sacred and the most politically useful sentiments.

But Rousseau was well aware that sexual pleasures could be indulged and the "natural result" avoided, that consummated desire could be decoupled from parenthood, and he seemed horrified by the possibility.[16] In both his *Discourse on the Origin of Inequality* and *Emile*, he attacked contraception and abortion with fury—remarking that these practices would help to make a desert of Europe and leave it "peopled with ferocious beasts."[17] Rousseau was careful to describe in his *Confessions* how quickly he rejected the homosexual advances he encountered as a delicate-featured teenager seeking shelter among the priests and monks of France and northern Italy. Masturbation was a constant bother to him. He thought youngsters could not be allowed to sleep alone during the critical years of sexual development for fear they might indulge in it and "suffer until . . . death the sad effects of this habit, the most fatal to which a man can be subjected" (*Emile*, 334). Rousseau periodically scolded himself in the *Confessions* for engaging in this "compensatory vice" (549). Once when Rousseau arranged an appointment with Giulietta, the most captivating prostitute in Europe (and a woman who must have known a thing or two about preventing conception), he studied her to find the flaw that revealed her to be a "worthless slut" rather than nature's perfection. Tellingly, he found that flaw right atip the nonmaternal breast:

> I perceived that she had a malformed nipple. I beat my brow, looked
> harder, and made certain that this nipple did not match the other.
> Then I started wondering about the reason for this malformation.
> I was struck by the thought that it resulted from some remarkable
> imperfection of Nature and, after turning this idea over in my head,
> I saw as clear as daylight that instead of the most charming creature
> I could possibly imagine I held in my arms some kind of monster,
> rejected by Nature, men, and love. (*Confessions*, 301)

Rousseau was even prone to find such monsters in the garden. In a letter to Mme Delessert regarding botany, he cautioned her about the plants in her kitchen plot: "These double flowers that people admire in flower-beds are monsters deprived of the faculty of producing their like which nature has endowed all organized beings."[18]

It is "producing your like" that is the crux of the matter. For Rousseau, good parents are good citizens only if they can produce good citizens in turn. Children must aspire to their parents' virtue, and if they do not, then the virtue was not there to begin with. Rousseau's lovers, if they are to be virtuous, must strive to become parents. Those lovers who do not are destined for ruin. But virtuous parenthood proves a hard test for those who take it on, and the child who scrutinizes the parent can be an unforgiving judge. Those who become parents without virtue have it worst—slavery for some, early death for the lucky ones. The virtual impossibility of entering into and sustaining the project of parenthood in the right way is the preeminent indication of Rousseau's pessimism about the possibility of virtuous citizenship in a corrupt and disenchanted world.[19]

Emile, Sophie, and the Procreative Education

Rousseau's five children were as motherless as he. But their mother did not die in childbirth, as Rousseau's had. Rather, a midwife carefully chosen for her discretion whisked them away to a Parisian foundling home, one by one as newborns. It was a decision Rousseau would defend to his death and yet one that he admitted he came to profoundly regret. Rousseau eventually felt the need to atone for this transgression. Just as his star was rising to the heights of European celebrity in the aftermath of *Julie,* he was promising his friends that he would give up writing after completing one last task. "There remains an old sin to expiate in print; after that the public will never hear of me again."[20]

The result was Rousseau's *Emile, or On Education*—a novel/treatise that chronicles the raising of the title character from infancy to imminent fatherhood by a governor named Jean-Jacques. Rousseau considered it the "best and worthiest" among his works (*Confessions,* 525). Obliquely acknowledging the project's origins, Rousseau was careful to scold himself in the text for his neglect of fatherly duties, noting that fathers should remember that each of their children "is a deposit of which he owes an account to the hand from which he receives it" and that "he who cannot fulfill the duties of a father has no right to become one. . . . I predict to whoever has vitals and neglects such holy duties that he will long shed bitter tears for his offense and never find consolation for it" (*Emile,* 53, 49). Rousseau described his efforts as a new insemination. His preface to *Emile* explains, "It is important to turn public attention in this direction; and . . . although my ideas may be bad, if I cause others to give birth to good ones, I shall not entirely have wasted my time" (33). Public attention was indeed to pivot, focusing more directly than ever before on the best ways to nurture children.[21]

But Rousseau saw *Emile* as far more than an argument for changes in the style of parenting for the sake of children's well-being. Take, for example, Rousseau's hyperbolic argument against wet-nursing near the beginning of the book. Rousseau quickly conceded that he could not come up with health-related reasons to change the current practice. "But," he pushed on, "should the question be envisaged only from the physical side?" (45). The grounds of his argument shift to the inevitably chilling effect on the mother of seeing her child become attached to another woman. Spinning out the consequences of this first "alienation" from the mother's procreative role, Rousseau insisted, "Everything follows successively from this first depravity. The whole moral order degenerates; naturalness is extinguished in all hearts; home life takes on a less lively aspect." The mother's failure quickly precipitates the father's alienation from his role as parent as well. "The touching spectacle of a family aborning no longer attaches husbands" (46). In a passage like this, Rousseau is not intent on "naturalizing" women only to tie them securely to the domestic sphere so that men may be free to engage in civil pursuits. Rousseau wants to tie fathers to the domestic sphere as well. At stake here is the question of whether mothers and fathers will be alienated from the role in life that is best suited to the permanent association of the strongest of their passions with virtue. And thus at stake also is the potential for republican citizenship, since Rousseau believed that the best means for attaining republican goals was to "make virtue reign."[22]

This goal becomes clearer in the later parts of the work, when passions begin to emerge in the young Emile. The first three books of *Emile* describe an education that is "merely negative" (57), in which the governor is constantly preventing the development in his pupil of any desires or inclinations beyond those necessary for survival. The reason for this approach is simple. "Our unhappiness consists . . . in the disproportion between our desires and our faculties" (80). But looming over these early sections of *Emile* is the unavoidable onset of new urges. As puberty approaches, Rousseau warned, "We do not have enough time to do everything which would be useful. Reflect that the passions are approaching, and that as soon as they knock on the door, your pupil will no longer pay attention to anything but them" (172).

When desire finally arrives, strategies must change. Negative education will not stop Emile's emerging passions; instead they must be channeled in the direction of virtuous parenthood. In fact, the governor's education of

Emile, which began practically at Emile's birth, is forced to virtually start over again, since "we are, so to speak, born twice: once to exist and once to live; once for our species and once for our sex. . . . It is now that man is truly born to life" (211–12). The governor must act quickly and carefully because "this moment of crisis, although rather short, has far-reaching influences. . . . Up to now our care has only been a child's game. It takes on true importance only at present. This period, when ordinary educations end, is properly the one when ours ought to begin" (212). The most important of the changes to occur in this period is the emergence of amour propre—a sort of self-love that demands the recognition of one's worthiness by others. Emile's previous motivations had been no more complicated than the simple self-regard natural to all creatures—*amour de soi*[23]—and to this point Emile has remained remarkably unattached to human society. But, "As soon as man has need of a companion, he is no longer an isolated being. His heart is no longer alone. All his relations with his species, all the affections of his soul are born with this one. His first passion soon makes others ferment" (*Emile*, 214). The governor can only react, since "whatever we may do, these passions will be born in spite of us. It is therefore time to change method" (215).[24]

This moment of suspension between the purity of *amour de soi* and the more complex and dangerous amour propre recreates the "golden age" described by Rousseau in his *Discourse on the Origins of Inequality*. There he told the story of the development of civil society, from the simple self-sufficiency of the noble savage to the wretched state of modern society in which everyone is a slave to the opinion of everyone else. In telling this story Rousseau was most nostalgic for the age when the savage had settled down into simple family life. "This period of the development of the human faculties, maintaining a middle position between the indolence of our primitive state and the petulant activity of our egocentrism, must have been the happiest and most durable epoch" (65). This era of small families living in simple huts planted the seeds of its own destruction, however. It had been born through the imitation of the strongest by the rest. "Since the strongest were probably the first to make themselves lodgings they felt capable of defending, presumably the weak found it quicker and safer to imitate them than to try and dislodge them" (62). Women and men, whom Rousseau described as having previously mated during fleeting chance encounters, began to settle down together, and "the habit of living together gave rise to the sweetest sentiments known to men: conjugal love and paternal love" (62–63).

James Martel suggests that Rousseau's affection for this imagined era stems from the self-assurance of the men of this time, which allowed a man to live with women and children without worrying about what they thought of him. Love, still in its historical infancy, was not scrutinized in this way, and thus *amour de soi* was expanded beyond the self without the corrosive effects of amour propre's dependence on the opinion of others. According to Martel, the father of the golden age "can remain intact, while all others [in the household] become 'one' with and transparent to him."[25] They imitate him rather than challenge him. But it was the father's imitation of others in building huts that made this period possible. And the continuing possibility that others were more worthy of imitation would spell the golden age's doom. As members of different families begin to live near each other and interact, "imperceptibly they acquire the ideas of merit and beauty which produce feelings of preference." Soon enough, "jealousy awakens with love, discord triumphs, and the sweetest passion receives sacrifices of human blood" (*Discourse on the Origins of Inequality*, 63–64).

Those were the beginnings of the decline that Emile's education is meant to reverse. The governor, Jean-Jacques, would accomplish this reversal by ensuring that Emile was secure in his sense of himself. Emile's new passions make him aware of others, but he must not want to imitate them. Thus Jean-Jacques will take advantage of his pupil's ignorance of the eventual object of his emerging passions. When "one desires without knowing what . . . [t]he eye becomes animated and looks over other beings" (*Emile*, 220). The governor makes sure that his pupil's eye falls only on beings who are miserable. "In order to incline a young man to humanity, far from making him admire the brilliant lot of others, one must show him the sad sides of that lot, one must make him fear it. Then, by an evident inference, he ought to cut out his own road to happiness, following in no one else's tracks" (223).[26]

But Emile will not be alone on his path. Rather, his passions must develop toward an experience in which he will be imitated—much like the fathers of the *Second Discourse*'s "happiest epoch" in the golden age. To do so, the governor adopts a new method meant to ensure that the strongest of Emile's new desires will become a passion for virtue that will guide him toward the right sort of marriage and parenthood. Jean-Jacques must make use of "nascent sensibility to sow in the young adolescent's heart the first seeds of humanity. . . . Now is the only time of life when the same attentions can have a true success" (*Emile*, 220). This passion that the governor hopes to craft is not a passion for virtue in the abstract. A purely conceptual love of virtue is insufficient to overcome more visceral desires. Rousseau offered the example of a man in the throes of "an involuntary love for the daughter or the wife of his friend." Rousseau asked skeptically, "At the moment when his intoxicated senses are ready to yield themselves to their delights, will this abstract image of virtue come to dispute over his heart with the real object which strikes it?"[27] Love of virtue itself, it appears, is not strong enough to resist the passions when they boil over. As Christopher Kelly explains, "Some additional source of strength would be needed. Virtue, by itself, may be loveable, but it is not lovable enough to supply its own strength."[28]

Emile will be taught to borrow strength from the passion of love itself. Emile learns to love virtue in a form that is not abstract but not quite corporeal either. He is kept away from women to avoid the cycle of destructive jealousy that ended the golden age. "Young people who are corrupted early and given over to women and debauchery are inhuman and cruel. . . . They knew neither pity nor mercy. They would have sacrificed fathers, mothers, and the whole universe to the least of their pleasures" (*Emile*, 220). Because it is Emile's body that is driving the changes in him, and because this period is so crucial to the development of virtue in Emile, it is important that the governor not waste this time with words and idle reasoning. One must "clothe reason in a body if you want to make youth able to grasp it" (323). Only if the governor makes his lesson felt viscerally will he "engrave it in [Emile's] memory in such a way that it will never be effaced" (321). So in order to bind Emile's first experiences of passionate love to a love of virtue, Jean-Jacques will abandon the negative education and "speak to [Emile] of love, of women, of pleasures . . . and I shall make him moderate by making him fall in love" (327). Specifically, the governor will induce Emile to conjure in his imagination a woman to desire—a woman who truly suits Emile and merits his love. The governor's description will "make agreeable and dear to [Emile] the qualities he ought to love, . . . make all his sentiments properly disposed with respect to what he ought to seek or to flee" (329). Jean-Jacques describes to his pupil all of her charms, her virtues, and even her faults, which only serve to please him more. He gives her a name, Sophie, and ensures that the vision of her will dominate Emile's imagination. Every temptation will be compared to her, and every temptation will be found wanting.

Rousseau insisted that puberty is the most important period in education, but as the passions move from nascence to this critical point in their development, the importance of each new elaboration increases. As the governor prepares to finally introduce the fire in Emile's blood to the image of a woman, Rousseau insists that he has "reflected on men's morals too much not to see the invincible influence of this first moment on the rest of his life" (318). This time in which our passions are given direction, or left to swirl chaotically, is a period of human life that is "made never to be forgotten. . . . It ought to influence the rest of his days" (321). So once Emile has fallen in love with this image of a virtuous woman in the form of the fantastical Sophie, once the most stirring of Emile's passions will have been welded to a love of virtue, the governor's work would appear to be done. At this point, Jean-Jacques asks in triumph "whether there is a young man on the entire earth who is better armed than Emile against everything that can attack his morals, his sentiments, or his principles" (331).

In fact, there is much left to be done, and the well-armed Emile will be better armed yet in the service of virtue. Emile's love of an imaginary woman must develop into a love for a wife and child. His passions must be directed toward the life project of virtuous parenthood. Sophie exists in the flesh and has long been known to the governor. She has been given an education in virtue, but her education could not be more different from Emile's. Where the young Emile has never felt constraint,[29] Sophie has felt it constantly from an early age in order to develop "a docility which women need their whole lives" (370). While no idea was introduced to Emile before he could understand it, the responsibilities of womanhood were taught to Sophie from the beginning. On the reasons for the difference. Rousseau is remarkably consistent: they derive entirely from Sophie's eventual role as mother. Not long after she is born, Sophie's destiny is guided by her potential to give birth one day. She is taught modesty because it is the best way to arouse a man to the procreative act.[30] Her gender dictates that her duties will be stricter because "the undertaking has such different consequences for the two sexes" (358). For Sophie, the consequences will be all-consuming. "Everything recalls her sex to her; and, to fulfill its functions well, she needs a constitution which corresponds to it. She needs care during her pregnancy; she needs rest at the time of childbirth; she needs a soft and sedentary life to suckle her children; she needs patience and gentleness, a zeal and an affection that nothing can rebuff in order to raise her children" (361).[31] When the first stirrings of desire took hold of Emile, the governor carefully distracted him from women and cultivated pity for his fellow man.[32] Not so with Sophie's parents. "As soon as they perceive the first restlessness of youth in her," Sophie's tender and sensible parents instruct her: "The happiness of a decent girl lies in causing the happiness of a decent man. You must therefore think about getting married. You must think about it early, for the destiny of life depends on marriage, and there is never too much time to think about it" (399). For Sophie, lectures suffice, and it is not necessary to resort to the sort of careful manipulations of emerging passion, "the clothing of reason in a body" that Jean-Jacques undertakes with Emile. Sophie's body, because of its potential to one day give birth, fulfills the job of channeling passion well enough.

> The obedience and fidelity she owes to her husband and the tenderness and the care she owes to her children are consequences of her position so natural and easily sensed that she cannot without bad faith refuse her consent to the inner sentiment that guides her, nor fail to recognize her duty if her inclinations are still uncorrupted. (382)

Sophie's education and her natural inclinations ensure that in learning to desire her, Emile will come to desire a child.

Why this single-minded obsession with Sophie's eventual motherhood? In a book about the ideal education of an individual child (or two children, once Sophie is introduced), Rousseau's reasoning regarding procreation can sometimes drift into the demographic. When he insists that though women do not always have children, "their proper purpose is to produce them" (*Emile*, 362), he goes on to worry about just how many children per woman it will take to maintain the population (about four). Rousseau worries that if women did not play their role correctly, "the human species would soon be extinguished" (361). But Rousseau is careful to demonstrate that proper development toward parenthood is as important to the success of individual women's lives as it is to the species in aggregate. To this purpose, Rousseau depicts a possible outcome for an "alternative Sophie" whose passions go awry and steer her away from a practical marriage and from having children. This Sophie, loved by her parents, loving virtue, has stumbled across a copy of *The Adventures of Telemachus*. She falls in love with the hero, just as Emile had with an image of Sophie. Seeking a man who is lovable and virtuous like the Telemachus of Fénelon's tale, she finds that every man she meets falls short. Her parents, amused at first, learn to their horror that they cannot convince their daughter to compromise the principles they taught her. Rousseau hesitated to depict the sad end of this tale: the harshness of the mother, the irritated father treating his daughter like a madwoman, and finally the death of Sophie—it is not clear whether from suicide or simply from despair—before she can be forced into a marriage with a less worthy partner (402–5). Having made his point, Rousseau regrouped. "Let us render his Sophie to our Emile. Let us resuscitate this lovable girl to give her a less lively imagination and a happier destiny. . . . I went astray myself. Let us retrace our steps" (405).[33]

Nor will Emile be well served by attempting to let his love for an ideal of feminine virtue guide him for perpetuity. Though his love of an illusion will serve him well for a time, he must develop what Rousseau calls a "true love."

> A young man must either love or be debauched. . . . Countless young people will be cited who are said to live very chastely without love. But let someone name to me a grown man who is truly . a man and who says in good faith that he spent his youth that way. In regard to all the virtues and all our duties only the appearance is sought. I seek the reality, and I am mistaken if there are other means of getting at it than those I give. (*Emile,* 470)

It does not take long before Emile, upon meeting Sophie and hearing her name, realizes that she is the true love he has been hoping for, and Sophie realizes the same about Emile. Their courtship moves quickly buts runs into some trouble when Emile and Jean-Jacques arrive later than expected for a visit. Sophie is resentful until the reason for their tardiness is revealed: they had been assisting an injured man and his pregnant wife who had gone into a painful labor at the sight of her injured husband. Hearing of Emile's noble role in this spectacle of procreative suffering, Sophie offers herself to him on the spot. "Emile, take this hand. It is yours. Be my husband and master when you wish. I will try to merit this honor" (441). In case the reader has missed it, Rousseau sends the couple back to the scene of parturition, where Sophie ministers to the couple despite foul odors and dirt. The next scene is the baptism, which finds Emile and Sophie "yearning in the depths of their hearts to give others an occasion to perform the same task. They long for the desired moment. They believe they have reached it" (442).

But they have not, and Jean-Jacques, having converted natural desires into a will for virtuous parenthood, extends the period of willing still further in order to impart a last lesson for Emile. The emergence of desires made possible an ardent love of an image of virtue, and now the arrival at marriage's doorstep makes possible a more mature orientation to the right sort of human life. But Emile is not yet fully prepared for fatherhood. "To know how to raise children, at least wait until you cease being children" (448). While Sophie's body still requires development (Jean-Jacques sees no point in marriage before she is ready for pregnancy), it is Emile's understanding of his duties that needs to be cultivated. He knows nothing of politics, and Jean-Jacques warns him, "When you become the head of a family, you are going to become a member of the state." The governor devises a long period of travel. By leaving Sophie, Emile will gain some mastery over his passion for her.[34] By studying the civil relations that characterize different nations, he will gain the perspective that will allow him to endorse the contract that binds him to his community or to renounce the contract "by leaving the country in which that community is established" (455).[35] But it is the reasons that motivate Emile's travel, not the things he will encounter, that determine the outcome of his journeys.[36] "Whoever returns from roaming the world is, upon his return, what he will be for his whole life. More men come back wicked than good, because more leave inclined to evil than to good" (455). Emile leaves with the inclination to become worthy of the role of husband and father, and it is that alone which makes his trip successful. Thus it is not worrisome that he has not found the perfect political society in his travels. "I shall not be free in this or that land, in this or that region; I shall be free everywhere on earth" (472).

What Emile achieved through his travels is an appreciation of the detachment that his governor has instilled in him from childhood. "What difference does it make to me what my position on earth is? . . . If I were without passions, I would, in my condition as a man, be independent like God himself; for I would want only what is and therefore would never have to struggle against destiny" (472). What keeps Emile from achieving this lofty orientation toward fate is the one passion that has taken hold of him. "At least I have no more than one chain. It is the only one I shall ever bear, and I can glory in it. Come, then, give me Sophie, and I am free" (472–73). This failure to achieve complete detachment hardly displeases the governor. Jean-Jacques is quick to emphasize the parental aspects of the solitary bond that ties the godlike Emile to human society:

Dear Emile, I am very glad to hear a man's speeches come from your mouth and to see a man's sentiments in your heart. This extravagant disinterestedness does not displease me at your age. It will decrease when you have children, and you will then be precisely what a good father of a family and a wise man ought to be. (473)

But it is quite notable how little Rousseau offered on this last point. After spending hundreds of pages expanding on Emile's development toward virtuous parenthood, he had almost nothing to say about what will happen to the couple once they have had a child. After advising Sophie on how to keep Emile's passion alive,[37] Jean-Jacques admits:

Nevertheless, do not believe that even this art can serve you forever. Whatever precautions anyone may take, enjoyment wears out pleasures, and love is worn out before all others. But when love has lasted a long time, a sweet habit fills the void it leaves behind, and the attraction of mutual confidence succeeds the transports of passion. Children form a relationship between those who have given them life that is no less sweet and is often stronger than love itself. When you stop being Emile's beloved, you will be his wife and friend. You will be the mother of his children. (475)

And that is all Rousseau had to say in *Emile* about the effect on the parents of actually having a child. The announcement of Sophie's pregnancy ends the novel. Rousseau conceded the temptation to depict their union further, but he chose not to because "these details might be pleasing without being useful" (475).

The Matter of the Child (If the Child Matters)

Without being useful? Has the child no importance in this? It is remarkable how little time Rousseau spent, in *Emile* or elsewhere, actually discussing the pleasures that parents might take in their children after they are born. Emile, for all appearances, has no mother or father once he has been handed over to his governor. Perhaps the most Rousseau offers in this regard are his depictions in the *Confessions* of himself as a child reading with his father or of the two of them discussing Rousseau's mother—though they knew they were "sure to cry" (19). This is hardly a cheerful scene, and Rousseau's attempts to depict Isaac as "the best of fathers" despite his leaving Rousseau behind at a young age and making only halfhearted attempts to locate him later, only add a poignancy to Rousseau's loneliness. Even his *Julie*, Rousseau's novel of letters, filled with so many moving descriptions of domestic bliss, hardly engages the children of the household. Julie's children are barely named, and when the characters bother to refer to them, they say "the children," "the eldest," and "the younger one" (and, morbidly, "the one costing her her life") (583). At the end of the novel, when a dying Julie writes to St. Preux, the lover of her youth and tutor of her children by another man, "you know whether [my children] were dear to me," the reader, frankly, does not (610).[38] It is not obvious, then, how much it mattered to Rousseau that a child is the likely result from these "pleasures attached to the reproduction of men" which he made so central to his ideal education (619).

Perhaps it mattered too much. Martel believes it reveals Rousseau's "true democratic colors" that he "subverts his own utopias."[39] Eventually, in an unfinished and unpublished sequel entitled *Emile and Sophie, or the Solitary Ones*, Rousseau even subverted the marriage of Sophie and Emile—which is ultimately destroyed when Sophie becomes pregnant by another man. But while we hear of the death of their son and their daughter, the reader never meets them. We never see the virtuous parenting itself—the relationship of parent to child—or see it come apart. It seems parenting was the one utopia Rousseau could not bring himself to depict in ruins. One exception is *Julie*, in which the title character is torn between her father and her lover. But Julie, as I explore later, figures in the novel less as a daughter than as a potential parent.

Children do seem to matter to Rousseau even if he does not depict them. As mentioned earlier, Rousseau was hostile to any sexuality divorced from procreation—contracepted, aborted, gay, masturbatory, or floral.[40] While nonreproductive sexuality did not appeal to Rousseau, a commitment to celibacy hardly struck him as a better option. In *Emile*, Rousseau praised the practice of the Abbè de Saint Pierre, who "took the vow, like all priests of his communion, not to have a wife of his own; but, being more scrupulous than the others about adultery, he is said to have chosen the course of having pretty servants with whom he did his best to atone for the outrage he had committed against his species by this rash commitment" (198). The country priest who offers "The Profession of Faith of the Savoyard Vicar" in *Emile* suggests his suffering in life was due to his vow of celibacy, which meant "obliging myself not to be a man." It is hard, he explains, to forbid oneself "what well-ordered nature permits us, and all the more so for what it prescribes to us" (267).

If a lifelong commitment to celibacy in the name of God is not a good option, there is always celibacy in the name of a passion for virtue specifically rooted in desire. Remember that Emile and Sophie had learned to channel their passions into a love of virtue long before they had reached the marital bed. Must things be consummated in cases like these?[41] *Julie* suggests an answer. The title character's young tutor, St. Preux, praises passion without consummation in one of his first love letters to his pupil, exclaiming, "My flame and its object will together preserve an incorruptible purity. I would shudder to lay a hand on your virgin charms, more than I would at the vilest incest, and your surety is not more inviolate with your father than with your lover" (34).[42] But the tutor soon realizes that even in the name of love, one should not entertain priestly vows. "I feel I have assumed an obligation that exceeds my strength. Julie, take back your own guardianship; ... I have made a rash commitment. I wonder how I have been able to keep it so long." (40).

The youngsters play out their commitment to chastity like a game of hot potato—passing it back and forth in order to keep it alive. Julie does take back the trust she had given St. Preux and discovers a strength she did not believe she had: "Two months' experience have taught me that my too tender heart needs love, but that my senses have no need of a lover. Imagine, you who love virtue, with what joy I made this happy discovery" (41). But the dialectic must continue, and Julie's newfound strength inspires her lover to attempt to raise himself to her level, to love the perfection of her soul above her more tangible charms. Even as he does so, he believes that Julie's self-assurance cannot be so well justified and insists that "though wisdom speak through your mouth," nature and natural desire speak through Julie's eyes (43).[43] One can well imagine the effect of St. Preux's fresh pledge to protect her purity. Julie confesses that she feels "a thousand times more affected by your respect than by your transports, and I greatly fear that in making the more honest choice, you may ultimately have chosen the more dangerous one" (44). This proves to be the case, and when St. Preux persists in his commitments to virtue, Julie admits to him that "the most dangerous of your seductions is to use none." Feeling the need for an "eternal attachment," she entertains thoughts of "being able one day to make you as happy as you deserve to be" (50) and makes plans for a first step in that direction—the granting of a kiss.

That chaste kiss, of course, is the point of no return, the beginning of a synthesis to this dialectic of desire and virtue. Julie faints on the spot; St. Preux is transformed forever. He declares to Julie, "I can no longer live in my present state, and sense that I must ultimately expire at your feet . . . or in your arms" (52). In a desperate effort to forestall what must inevitably follow, the lovers separate, and St. Preux travels through the countryside. Julie learns that her aristocratic father will not approve her match with a lowly tutor, and St. Preux suggests that they run off together. It is too much, and soon the reader is confronted with "sweet Julie [at] death's door [with] perhaps not two days to live" (76). Fearing for Julie's life if she is separated from St. Preux any longer, her cousin Claire beckons the young man to Julie's bedside. In the few moments after he arrives, they enact in person all the tensions explored in their letters, and the path to Julie's arms turns out to begin at her feet after all. Julie reports:

> He would throw himself headlong at me in a blind transport; suddenly he would stop; an insurmountable barrier seemed to have surrounded me, and never would his impetuous but honest love have crossed it. I dared observe too long this dangerous spectacle. . . . I shared his torments, thinking I was just being compassionate. I saw him in convulsive agitation, about to faint at my feet. Love alone might have spared me; O my Cousin, it was pity that undid me. . . . I had to deliver the death blow to those who gave me life, to my lover, or to myself. Without knowing what I was doing I chose my own demise. I forgot everything and remembered only love. So it is that a moment's distraction has undone me forever. I have fallen into the abyss of infamy from which a maiden can never return; and if I live, it is only to be more unhappy. (78–79)

But somehow, out of the midst of all these death blows, demises, and undoings, an affirmation of life begins to emerge. Julie's despair is real, but her health returns, and her mood improves. Having forfeited her virtue, she resolves to merge her being entirely with her lover's so that whatever honor and virtue he possesses will be hers as well. And a means is perhaps in gestation that might grant all this spiritual talk of merged souls a worldly manifestation—their child. "Ah! If only my faults could give birth to some means of atoning for them! The sweet hope of being some day . . . but inadvertently I might say more than I mean to about the plan I have in mind." Immediately St. Preux seizes on her hints. Though fearing that her plans might be "founded on fantasies," he recognizes her pregnancy as their best hope of deliverance and urges her, "Let us at least begin to make them come true" (88). Caught up in these reproductive hopes, the couple emerges from their debasement to find their passions purified again. "True love is the most chaste of all bonds. It alone with its divine flame knows the art of purifying our natural inclinations. [Lovers like Julie and St. Preux] do not desire, they love. The heart does not follow the senses, it guides them; it throws over their ecstasies a delightful veil" (113).

In the remarkable events that follow, it is always the possibility of a child that is associated with the lovers' chance for a happy life. As the tangible effect of their love, the child takes all the concepts they have batted back and forth—virtue, love, passion—and transforms them into something that is undeniably "real" and "true," something that demands a way of life beyond transports and regret. One never expects illicit lovers to hope for pregnancy, of all things, and yet Julie insists:

> Our love's first fruit was to confirm this tender bond. I begged
> it of Heaven as token of my return to virtue and of our common
> happiness; I desired it as another in my stead would have feared it;
> the spell of tender love . . . consoled me for my weakness through
> the result I was expecting from it, and made of such a cherished
> expectation the charm and hope of my life. (283)

Her pregnancy promises to makes the ineffable livable—it resolves all tensions, or at least it demands that a way be found to resolve them. The tension between virtue and desire is transformed in a tender and true love. The tension between Julie's love for St. Preux and her father's plans to marry her to his friend Wolmar will be resolved by this expediency as well. Julie decides that when she can no longer hide her condition, she will make a public declaration of her love before her preacher and her family. "I knew my father would give me death or my lover . . . and, one way or the other, I anticipated that this step would put an end to all my woes" (283).

So central to her hopes is the expected child that when Julie realizes she is not pregnant, she plans a "reckless tryst"—and sneaks her lover into her room under her parents' noses (119). Just as the back and forth of desire and virtue were enacted all at once at the scene of their first lovemaking, this second attempt will enact the new tension the first pregnancy created. Julie has conceived of a plan that will end in conception or in the lovers' demise. Their moment of happiness,

> is surrounded by the horrors of death; . . . I know my father too well to doubt that I would see your heart instantly pierced by his hand, if indeed he did not pierce mine first. . . . If we are caught my design is to throw myself into your arms, to wrap you tightly in mine, and thus receive the fatal blow so as never again to be separated from you, happier in my death than I ever was in life.
>
> I hope a sweeter fate is reserved for us; I feel at least, that it is due us, and fortune will tire of being unjust to us. (284)

Both stealthy and fecund, Julie and St. Preux avoid the paternal sword, and soon Julie finds herself again in the condition that promises their worldly salvation. Of course, the threat of the father still looms, and the tension may still end in a sudden death rather than a contented life. The means found to keep this tension from achieving its resolution too early (we are still in the first of six volumes) is classic Rousseau. Julie's father flies into a rage when he is confronted by her love for St. Preux and her plans to abandon the commitment to Wolmar. Though he is still unaware of her pregnancy and never suspects that his daughter would have sunk so low as to have slept with her tutor, he nonetheless beats Julie "mercilessly," forcing her to stumble, fall, and finally miscarry. That spells the end of hope for Julie and St. Preux. Julie despairs that "all is finished for me; all my expectations abandon me at the same time . . . the accident . . . destroyed, along with the seed I bore in my womb, my hopes' last foundation" (146, 284). St. Preux recognizes as well that Julie and he have lost the chance to give their otherworldly passion a foundation in the real world. On hearing that Julie is no longer carrying their child, St Preux's hopes are deflated. "Thus . . . there will remain on earth no monument to my happiness; it has disappeared like a dream that never had any reality" (152).

Many commentators have depicted the story of *Julie* as a conflict between fatherly patriarchy, associated with aristocracy and monarchy, and youthful affections crossing divisions of class, associated with democracy. In fact, the conflict is between the parent and potential parents. When the pregnancy ends, the conflict does too—at least until Julie becomes a mother by another man, as I explore shortly. If *Julie* offers an allegory about democracy, it is a democracy in which citizens must be parents to succeed. Tony Tanner, impressed by the power of Julie's father in comparison to other characters in the book, suggests, "There is never any real chance of her abandoning her father for the lover."[44] In fact, there was a chance, but St. Preux could win his lover only by becoming a father himself. Once Julie and St. Preux are potential parents no more, they simply give up. St. Preux goes away.

Children, Hatred, and Betrayal

The first half of *Julie* reveals one way in which the child may figure in the centrality that Rousseau gives to parenthood in his vision of citizenship. The possibility of a child represents for the lovers the tangible synthesis in their dialectic of virtue and desire. The promise of a birth forces the tensions between duty and love to find a resolution—either in a contented and virtuous way of life or in death. But Rousseau has obviously constructed a dramatic set of circumstances in *Julie*.[45] What role might the child play in the deployment of the procreative passions in the absence of the sort of life-and-death crisis introduced by Julie's father—and what role might a child play if it was born? One place to turn for an answer is Rousseau's account of his own disastrous fatherhood (the impetus for *Emile*), and the related role that passion played in his own life.

Rousseau describes many loves in his *Confessions*. At one point, he refers to falling in love with nearly every woman he encountered as his "usual custom" (254). In fact, despite the flowery phrases employed in parts of *Emile* and *Julie*, Rousseau was not always a great believer in a single love everlasting. In *Julie*, Claire maintains that once passion is fulfilled, it then proceeds to "feed only on itself. The whole world has never seen a passion weather this test, what right have you to hope that yours would have?" (263). And though Rousseau was so often enamored, his *Confessions* (and his subsequent biographers) nowhere describe a love affair that was both happy and long. The long ones were not particularly happy, and the happy ones quickly came to ruin. Rousseau's longest affair—with the sometime laundry maid Thérèse Levasseur—never became, for Rousseau anyway, an affair of love.[46] Nevertheless, their union produced what Julie and St. Preux could not: a child, or rather five.

What happened to those five children hardly matches Julie and St. Preux's vision of parenthood in which love is made material and brought back to earth, transforming the lovers' relationship by giving them a "new world" to hold in common.[47] Instead, Rousseau cajoled his mistress into allowing each of their children to be delivered straight to the Parisian foundling home. Rousseau argued that given his circumstances—he was poor and entangled with Levasseur's hopelessly corrupt family—the state would provide a better upbringing for his children than he would.[48] But evidence supports the common opinion in Rousseau's time that the foundling home was no safe place for newborns.[49] No one knows what became of Thérèse and Jean-Jacques's five children.

The point of telling this sad story is not to scold or deride Rousseau. Rather, the darkly obscure fate of his and Levasseur's children is emblematic of the way Rousseau made parenthood central to his political thought. The most important reason Rousseau's stories about having children, the one he lived and the ones he wrote (and the ones he wrote about the one he lived), are so messy and conflicted is that he saw so much at stake in parenthood. It is because procreative concerns also carry political burdens that in an age of corruption they could be all but unbearable. Near the beginning of *Emile,* Rousseau was already fielding objections that the responsibilities he assigns to those who would have children are beyond what any parent can accomplish. Rousseau did not deny it: "This objection is strong and solid. But did I tell you that a natural education was an easy undertaking? O men, is it my fault that you have made everything good difficult? I sense these difficulties; I agree they are difficulties. Perhaps they are insurmountable" (*Emile,* 94–95).

One of the most important obstacles that Rousseau diagnosed in corrupt times was that it could be impossible to meet and develop feelings for the right kind of spouse. Indeed, the steps to which Emile's governor must go to find and cultivate a girl for Emile, and the steps he takes to have the young people meet and court at the right time and in the right way, are implausibly remarkable. But with the wrong spouse, passions can become corrupted to such a point that instead of instilling the right sort of political sentiments, marriage becomes the paradigm of moral and political corruption. The nadir, as always for Rousseau, was Paris:

> One would say that marriage in Paris is not of the same nature as everywhere else. It is a sacrament, at least that is what they pretend, and this sacrament lacks the force of the most minor civil contracts:

it seems to be no more than the consent of two free persons who
agree to live together, to bear the same name, to recognize the same
children; but who have, other than that, no sort of claim to each
other. (*Julie*, 222)

It is hardly surprising, then, that Rousseau did not pursue matrimony during his own years in Paris.[50] During those years, ensconced with Thérèse,
Rousseau began to think differently about love. Far removed from his
youthful fancy where love was his usual custom, Rousseau began to believe
that he would never truly experience this emotion—despite that he felt he
was born to feel it. "How could it be that with such inflammable feelings,
with a heart entirely molded for love, I had not at least once burned with
love for a definite object? Devoured by a need to love that I had never been
able to satisfy, I saw myself coming to the gates of old age, and dying without having lived" (*Confessions*, 396–97).

How did Rousseau come to this? The *Confessions* offers some suggestions that shed light on the questions about parenthood and citizenship
raised by *Emile* and *Julie*. The obvious place to look is Rousseau's relationship with Thérèse—the relationship that he insisted "determined my
moral being" (*Confessions*, 385). Rousseau never failed to describe her ten-
derly, and the moments he spent alone with her, eating simple meals on a
windowsill or walking in the countryside, are some of the most poignant
in the *Confessions*. At least for a time, Rousseau and Thérèse "enjoyed the
most perfect domestic happiness that human frailty permits. Thérèse had
the heart of an angel; our affection grew with our intimacy, and we felt
more strongly every day that we were made for each other" (330). But
Rousseau never qualified his insistence that despite that "the most inextin-
guishable of all my needs was entirely one of the heart," during his years
with Thérèse, nothing was able to fulfill that need, and thus he "always felt
a void" (386).[51]

It is apparent that Rousseau hoped at one point to achieve with
Thérèse true love and a virtuous domestic contentment. "I believed that
the moment had come when I should feel [the void] no longer. This
young person . . . would have absorbed my whole existence within herself
if I could have absorbed hers in me, as I had hoped" (*Confessions*, 386).
But the Levasseur family continually got in the way, unsettling Rousseau
and Thérèse with their greed and their nefarious advice. Still, hopeful and
stubborn, Rousseau struggled on. He tried to protect Thérèse from these

baser influences and thus salvage the potential of their relationship, but her family always managed to "hinder in great part the effect of the good maxims I made efforts to inspire in her" (387). This struggle continued, in one way or another, for all of Rousseau's productive years and for the better part of his life.

Like any struggle, this one had its decisive moments: moments when Rousseau had to confront the probability that the void in his heart would never be filled. Once again, children were at the center of the problem. More specifically, the reason Rousseau could never abandon himself to unite his soul with Thérèse's was his belief that her family would prevent the peaceful and virtuous domestic order needed for raising children. It was not simply love that might have filled the hole in Rousseau's heart but the channeling of that love, through the experience of parenthood, into a virtuous way of life appropriate to republican citizens.[52] As Rousseau describes it, "Children came, who might have filled [the void in my heart]; but that made things even worse. I trembled at the thought of entrusting them to that badly brought up family, to be brought up even more badly" (*Confessions*, 387). These were Faustian moments for Rousseau. Looking back, he described the decision to deliver that first child to the foundling home as "fatal conduct" that would impose itself "in my way of thinking and also in my destiny" and have consequences that "were as cruel as they were unforeseen" (322).[53]

According to the *Confessions*, Rousseau did not bring his conduct to bear on his way of thinking until Thérèse became pregnant for a third time. It was then that Rousseau really concentrated his mind and his sentiments on the significance of his "expedient" for these "inconveniences" in terms of his ideas on morals and politics (322). He describes the disposal of their first two children as if it were almost thoughtless.[54] When Rousseau finally subjected his conduct toward his children and his mistress to the judgment of his morals and his sentiments, the precipitating incident was not the famous tear-filled moment of illumination on the road to Vincennes to visit Diderot—the moment when Rousseau said he conceived all at once of his system of philosophy and decided to write his *Discourse on the Sciences and the Arts*.[55] Rather, these reflections caught up with Rousseau only when he was informed that his essay had won the prize at Dijon. Rousseau testified that it was this symbol of public affirmation, this gratification of amour propre, that "reawakened" his ideas from that essay and "endowed them with fresh vigor" (*Confessions*, 332). As fate would have it, Rousseau's moral and philosophical insemination was accompanied by a physical one for Thérèse—her third pregnancy.[56] This coincidence of pregnancy and philosophy led to a self-examination that is remarkable enough to quote at length:

> Too sincere with myself, too proud in my heart, to be willing to belie my principles by my actions, I began to consider the fate of my children and my relationship with their mother, by reference to the laws of nature, justice, and reason, and of [religion]. . . . If I were one of those low-born men, deaf to the gentle voice of Nature, a man in whose breast no real feeling of justice and humanity ever arose, this hardness of heart would have been quite easy to explain. But my warm-heartedness, my acute sensibility; . . . my innate goodwill towards my fellow men; my burning love for the great, the true, the beautiful, and the just; my horror of evil in every form, my inability to hate, to hurt, or even to wish to; that softening, that sharp and sweet emotion I feel at the sight of all that is virtuous, generous, and lovable: is it possible that all these can ever dwell in the same soul along with depravity which, quite unscrupulously, tramples the dearest obligations underfoot? No, I feel, and boldly declare—it is impossible. Never for a moment in his life could Jean-Jacques have been a man without feelings or compassion, an unnatural father. I may have been mistaken, but I could never be callous. (333)

In truth, this declaration seems less than bold. Nor is Rousseau being particularly intrepid when he goes on to provide the "general statement" that by giving his children over to the state to be raised for lives as "workers and peasants," he believed he was "acting as a citizen and a father, and looked upon [himself] as a member of Plato's Republic" (*Confessions,* 333). Cranston opines that this explanation is "one of the least compelling passages in that book."[57]

Still, it is a remarkable list of personal qualities and convictions that Rousseau had to reconcile with that decision, made five times over, to have his child taken away to who knows what fate. It indicates that parental questions lead directly to an examination of the qualities most crucial to virtuous citizenship. While Rousseau strongly implies the "most decisive" (*Confessions,* 334) issue was Thérèse's family, he refused to elaborate on his precise reasoning at the time. He claimed, "If I were to state my reasons, I should say too much. For since they were strong enough to seduce me, they would seduce others" (333). Furthermore, Rousseau never claimed to be anything but conflicted about the decision he made—with his heart telling him he was wrong but his reason continuing to affirm his actions (333).

Rousseau offered one justification for his decision in the *Confessions*— the last one he mentioned—that stands out because it is so speculative that one wonders why he would bother to include it. Rousseau wondered what might have happened if he had kept his children, and "at a later date," one of his rich friends, Mme d'Epinay or Mme de Luxembourg, had offered to take care of his children for him. Rousseau could then have had regular contact with his progeny without condemning them or himself to the ravages of financial hardship. He might even have played the role of governor, the role in which he would later cast himself in *Emile*. Rousseau seemed to harbor a fear, however, that he would have been unable to impart to his children the value of the ideas, principles, and sentiments— the love of virtue—that he held most dear and to which he had devoted his life. In fact, Rousseau was "sure that [my children] would have been led to hate, and perhaps betray, their parents. It is a hundred times better that they have never known them" (*Confessions*, 333). Rousseau imagined this betrayal as an annihilation of his sense of self. In *The Reveries of the Solitary Walker*, Rousseau elaborated, "What Mahomet did to Séide would have been nothing compared to what would have been done to them with regard to me" (139). In the play by Voltaire to which Rousseau referred, Séide is persuaded to murder his father.

Here was Rousseau, at the moment of birth, at the inception of new life, the moment for which Emile and Sophie were carefully prepared, the moment that Julie and St. Preux prayed to reach, and he was haunted by the image of himself hated, betrayed, and destroyed by the child he helped to create. Faced with a child of his own, Rousseau could only think of that child imitating his enemies and others less worthy than he. How could this be? Was Rousseau's "innate goodwill towards [his] fellow men" not more compelling than the greed and manipulation that he associated with Thérèse's family? Was his "burning love for the great, the true, the beautiful, and the just" not a more shining example than the shallowness and dishonesty that one encountered in the social circles of his patrons Mme d'Epinay and Mme de Luxembourg? Rousseau would write books and create characters that inspired thousands to re-create themselves—yet he suspected that his own way of living would not inspire one child to imitate him. Like those monstrous flowers one finds in kitchen gardens, Rousseau believed he could not produce his like.

The Circle of Imitation: Virtuous or Vicious?

Rousseau's decision reveals a suspicion of his own unworthiness—a failure to have been successfully transformed through the development of his passions toward virtuous parenthood. His relationship with Thérèse failed to epitomize the union of desire with virtue and to channel that synthesis into a true and stable love. Thus this love could not be embodied in a child that would give it a worldly manifestation and enchant the rest of their days. It is the dual aspects of this failure that inspired his two great novels. Rousseau said it was the inability to achieve a love that would fill the void in his heart that "precipitated me into the land of chimeras; and seeing nothing that existed worthy of my exalted feelings, I fostered them in an ideal world which my creative imagination soon peopled with beings after my own heart" (*Confessions,* 398). The result was *Julie,* and Rousseau cast himself in the novel. "I identified myself as far as I could with [St. Preux]. But I made him young and pleasant, whilst endowing him also with the virtues and faults that I felt in myself" (400–401). *Emile,* of course, was Rousseau's response to his decision regarding his children, and he placed himself in that novel quite explicitly in the role of the governor Jean-Jacques.

It is interesting to reconsider these two books from this perspective, starting with *Emile* and paying special attention to what the novel implies about the governor. Jean-Jacques is, foremost, what Emile must become. "Remember that before daring to undertake the formation of a man, one must have made oneself a man. One must find within oneself the example the pupil ought to take for his own." Petty relatives and gossipy friends will not be a problem for the fictional Jean-Jacques as they were for Rousseau: "Make yourself respectable to everyone. Begin by making yourself loved so that each will seek to please you. You will not be the child's master if you are not the master of all that surrounds him; and this authority will never be sufficient if it is not founded on the esteem for virtue" (95). By giving the fictional governor qualities that he felt he did not possess, Rousseau ensures that there is no chance that Jean-Jacques will face hatred and betrayal at the hands of Emile.

The governor is not himself a father (as far as we are told), and this makes him a special case. Rousseau believed that it was the development toward parenthood that allows for the forging of a virtuous life, and he reminds readers, "In truth, to make a man, one must be a father or more than a man oneself" (50).[58] But Emile's governor, starting off as more than a man, will end as a father after all. When first he receives the infant Emile, they are pupil and governor and nothing more. So it remains until Emile reaches puberty and the development of his passions can be diverted no longer. At this critical juncture where Emile's desire must be bound tight to the ideal of virtuous femininity—the chimera given the name Sophie—the language of paternity must be adopted. The shift is dramatic, and Rousseau carefully sets the scene, describing "the rocks, the woods, and the mountains" that will mark the spot for the first fatherly conversation.

> What surprise, what agitation I am going to cause him by suddenly changing language! . . . I shall say to him "You are my property, my child, my work. It is from your happiness that I expect my own. If you frustrate my hopes, you are robbing me of twenty years of my life, and you are causing the unhappiness of my old age." (323)

At this point Jean-Jacques is setting scenes and taking on the role of father for instrumental reasons. But while conjuring an imaginary Sophie is one thing, preparing Emile for the real Sophie and a virtuous life as father and husband is another. The former may be done by a governor masquerading as a father, but the latter calls for true paternity. And so at the moment when Emile is ready to encounter his spouse, Jean-Jacques finally declares in earnest: "*I am Emile's true father; I made him a man.* I would have refused to raise him if I had not been the master of marrying him to the woman of his choice—that is, of my choice. Only the pleasure of making a happy man can pay for what it costs to put him in a position to become happy" (407, emphasis added). Emile could hardly disagree, embracing Sophie eagerly and thereafter referring to Jean-Jacques as "my father."[59]

Rousseau counseled that in order to be a governor, one must "find within oneself" the example that would guide the pupil. And so in navigating his pupil successfully through the virtuous development of his procreative passions to the verge of fatherhood, Jean-Jacques has made himself worthy of the name father. The ultimate proof is Emile's words to his governor/father in the speech that closes the book: "My master, congratulate your child. He hopes soon to have the honor of being a father. . . . As long as I live, I shall need you. I need you more than ever now that my functions as a man begin. You have fulfilled yours. *Guide me so that I can imitate you*" (480, emphasis added).

In this system imagined by Rousseau, a man transforms himself into a model worthy of being followed through the long process of creating and crafting a person to follow it. The true test of your worthiness of imitation comes when your child is grown and ready for parenthood. Despite Rousseau's claim that Emile would "cut out his own road to happiness, following in no one else's tracks," Emile must imitate Jean-Jacques by becoming worthy himself of imitation by his own child; and so on, ad infinitum (223). Some version of this works for women as well. For Sophie and other virtuous mothers, their dearest wish and greatest reward will be "the pleasure of seeing themselves one day imitated by their own daughters" (46).[60]

In describing this pleasantly (maddeningly?) circular system, Rousseau seeks to re-create in his corrupt times the spirit of the ancient festivals of Sparta, which he described in his *Letter to D'Alembert* as a model for a more virtuous alternative to the theater. In these festivals, there were

> always three dances in as many bands, divided according to the differences in age; and they danced to the singing of each band. That of the old began first, singing the following couplet:
> *We were once young, Valiant and hardy*
> There followed that of the men who sang in their turn, beating their arms in cadence:
> *We are so now, ready for all comers*
> And then came the children, who answered them singing with all their force:
> *And we will soon be so, we who will surpass you all.*
> These Sir, are the entertainments which republics need. . . . May [Geneva] transmit to its descendants the virtues, the liberty, and the peace which it has inherited from its fathers! This is the last wish with which I end my writings; it is the one with which my life will end. (136–37)

This sort of public spectacle recasts the circularity of *Emile*'s cycle of imitation in a more explicitly political context. It was the context in which Rousseau most dearly imagined himself. His obsession with his political inheritance as a "citizen" of Geneva made it even more painful to bear his personal feelings of unworthiness for a fatherhood that would pass on that inheritance. Political hopes complemented the dreams of a virtuous domestic union with Thérèse that Rousseau maintained in the years during which he wrote *Julie* and *Emile*. Rousseau not only entertained the possibility of leaving France to return to his patria Geneva, he was fairly obsessed with the idea.[61] His pride in his citizenship there would be hard to exaggerate, as demonstrated in the dedication he wrote for *The Discourse on the Origins of Inequality*, the *Letter to D'Alembert*, and throughout his correspondence. The complications that poisoned this plan for Rousseau were the same that convinced him to give away his children—especially Thérèse's family and their "corrupting" influences.[62]

In fact, the personal politics presented in *Emile* were intended to have public consequences as well. When Emile returns from his travels and boldly declares that he does not care where he lives as long as he is with Sophie, Jean-Jacques praises his detachment but offers a correction. He reminds Emile that he does owe something to his homeland and he should stay there, even if he must live in opposition to the dominant values of his country. Jean-Jacques reminds Emile that in becoming a worthy father, he has become a worthy example to his fellows and someone they might imitate. He tells Emile to "go and live in [his countrymen's] midst, cultivate their friendship in sweet association, be their benefactor and their model. Your example will serve them better than all our books, and the good they see you do will touch them more than all our vain speeches" (474).

With reference to "our books" and "our vain speeches," Rousseau was getting in a dig at himself, whom he had interjected earlier in the paragraph. The caveat he inserted reads, "There are circumstances in which a man can be more useful to his fellow citizens outside of his fatherland than if he were living in its bosom. Then he ought to listen only to his zeal and to endure his exile without grumbling" (474). In the case of Rousseau, we have discovered what the most important of those circumstances was: his inability to transform his burning passion into a project of virtuous procreation. He thus was worthy neither of the role of father—the only role worth having for a man in his "best and worthiest" work—nor the role of citizen of Geneva. So while Emile can achieve a sort of effective citizenship (as did Jean-Jacques before him, whose magically transformative effect on those who meet him Rousseau is careful to note),[63] Rousseau is left to the diminished role of social critic.

And this caveat should remind us that even in striking an optimistic note Rousseau is still aware of the difficulties and elusiveness of a virtue grounded in parenthood. In his *Letter to D'Alembert,* Rousseau depicts Emile's doppelganger, a young man whose passions have not been channeled toward virtuous procreation, and who has therefore fallen victim to the "disorder of women." This young man "makes himself . . . into a public enemy by the seduction of his accomplices, by the example of the effect of his corrupted morals and, above all, by the pernicious moral principles he cannot fail to disseminate in order to authorize his deeds. It would have been better had he never existed" (110). While Emile is unique, and his education perhaps impossible, this sort of young man is all too common. Even within *Emile,* long before Rousseau has developed the charming story of governor and pupil transformed into father and son—the one determined to inspire imitation in imitation of the other—Rousseau has already traced this circle's negative image. Despairing of there ever being found a governor in his corrupt times who is truly up to the task he is about to describe, Rousseau mused, "The more one thinks about it, the more one perceives new difficulties. It would be necessary that the governor had been raised for his pupil. . . . It would be necessary to go from education to education back to I know not where. How is it possible that a child be well raised by one who was not well raised himself?" (50).

Shklar believed this darker tone was closer to Rousseau's heart. She argued, "The happy end of *Emile* is false, especially to the tone of its opening pages, so full of dark foreboding."[64] She preferred the ending offered in *Emile and Sophie, or the Solitary Beings,* Rousseau's unfinished sequel to *Emile.*[65] In it, Rousseau describes the dissolution of the perfectly cultivated domestic virtue that had promised to enchant the rest of the couple's lives. But no matter how dire the situation becomes for Emile and Sophie—and things get pretty dire when their daughter dies and the couple moves to the capital city, where their passion for each other and for virtue chills— Emile maintains two hopes for the rebirth of their love and the recovery of their charmed life. One is to rekindle their virtuous love by overcoming Sophie's chaste resistance and reestablishing "the rights of a husband" (*Emile and Sophie,* 205). The other source of hope is their son, for Emile believed that "this connection would always prevent her from being a stranger to me, that children form a truly indissoluble bond between those who gave them being" (215). Sophie kills both those hopes with one blow when she stops Emile's forceful embraces by revealing that she is pregnant by another man. She becomes, in Emile's eyes, like the prostitute Giulietta in Rousseau's, "the most odious of monsters" (209). It is not Sophie's having been unfaithful but rather her pregnancy that decides the matter.[66] The idea of Sophie giving birth to a child not his own "alienated me from her more than everything that had tormented me up until then; from that moment I was irrevocably decided" (215). Emile says he would rather see his son dead than see Sophie mother another man's child. He leaves them to travel abroad and ends up a slave. He comes to realize slavery is his proper place.

Parenthood and Citizenship

Emile's failed fatherhood and citizenship reflect upon the concepts developed in the political treatise *The Social Contract*, which describes how modern men—slaves themselves and "everywhere ... in chains"—might be made free through political arrangements.[67] Rousseau worked on it in the same period as the original *Emile*, and a version of *The Social Contract* appears at the end of the book, when Emile is ready to marry Sophie and Jean-Jacques intercedes to send him on a political journey. Emile examines several foreign political systems in order to decide which is best for the sort of virtuous family he and Sophie will create. He returns having discovered a set of principles that characterize the best sort of government— principles that closely resemble those developed in *The Social Contract*— but also convinced that there was no society that successfully embodied them. He concludes that he can best serve as citizen by being an example in his own land.

Emile might be the sort of individual who is ready for the right sort of laws, but this is only thanks to his miraculous governor. This mirrors a dilemma embedded in *The Social Contract*. The lawgiver, the foreigner who must bestow the proper laws upon the people, must be either a genius or a god—a man whose "great soul is the true miracle" (87). His presence must be capable of accomplishing for the whole of society what Emile's might for his neighbors: to "change human nature, to transform each individual" (84). The lawgiver can "employ neither force nor argument, he must have recourse to an authority of another order, one which can compel without violence and persuade without convincing" (87). The lawgiver does this by acting with such wisdom that the people believe him to be touched with the divine. Rather than seeking to comprehend him on the level of reason or interest, they are inspired to transfigure themselves thanks to his presence.

Of course, such men must be as hard to find as the sort who might serve as Emile's governor, and their origins just as mysterious. There is the additional complication that if the lawgiver is to succeed, he must find the people already prepared to receive what he has to offer. "The wise lawgiver begins not by laying down laws good in themselves, but by finding out whether the people for whom the laws are intended is able to support them" (*The Social Contract*, 88). Failed lawgivers, like Peter the Great, are as common as failed tutors. "[Peter] urged his subjects to be what they were not and so prevented them from becoming what they might have been. This is just how a French tutor trains his pupil to shine for a brief moment in his childhood and then grow up into a nonentity" (90). The work of crafting authentic citizens or raising one citizen both founder on the same difficulties—a lack of transformative resonance between leader and people, adult and child. It is a lack of resonance that reflects most poorly on the leader and the parent—who are exposed by their failure as unworthy of deep imitation.

For the social contract to succeed, the people must be ready to embrace not just laws but something deeper—a faith and civic religion that feel as natural to them as if they were born with it. The lawmaker must speak wholly in terms of this faith, in terms of "simple dogmas" rather than in terms of the complex political principles laid out by Rousseau. The effort to make the right sort of laws feel natural is just what Jean-Jacques sought to do with Emile from the beginning. So "Rousseau's foreign-founder is like the good father,"[68] as Honig notes, but his work also requires that good fathers have preceded him.

Thus *The Social Contract* is faced with the dilemma of the backward-looking circle of imitation that Rousseau presented regarding Emile's governor—in which the governor must have been perfectly raised himself, by another perfectly raised, ad infinitum. The lawgiver simply cannot succeed in convincing a people of the rightness of the laws by reason if the people were not already prepared by faith: "The effect would have to become the cause; the social spirit which must be the product of social institutions would have to preside over the setting up of those institutions; men would have to have already become before the advent of the law that which they become as a result of the law" (87). Connolly suggests it is this aspect of Rousseau's *The Social Contract*, that the general will can only preside "over a fortunate people whose basic traditions already dispose them to it," that makes Rousseau's theory "a nihilistic theory" that "devalues the political dimension of life."[69] Connolly values the political dimension of life in that he believes democratic politics might transform citizens rather than require a particular sort of citizen. Thus it frustrates him that Rousseau's citizens must be transformed *before* politics, to have somehow achieved virtue if they are to engage in virtuous politics. Connolly prefers the Nietzschean lessons of contest that I turn to in the next chapter. But as we will see, Nietzsche will mimic Rousseau in turning to the experience of parenthood as an impetus for self-transformation. Nietzsche and Rousseau have more in common than contemporary appropriations of Nietzsche would suggest, and this should offer pause to theorists like Connolly who seek to apply Nietzschean lessons to democratic politics.

Hirschmann believes the appearance of the principles of *The Social Contract* on the eve of Emile's marriage to Sophie indicates that the experience of being husband and father will provide Emile with the virtue that prepares him for the social contract and motivates his part in "the general will." Rousseau wrote that marriage is a partnership that produces "a moral person of which the woman is the eye and the man the arm . . . the man learns from the woman what must be done" (*Emile,* 377). In *Julie,* he maintained, "One does not marry in order to think solely about each other, but in order to fulfill conjointly the duties of civil life" (306). Hirschmann interprets that "Rousseau does not mean that husbands and wives will discuss political issues. Rather, 'the duties of civil life' entail the production of children" as well as the creation of an ordered life at home. She believes Rousseau hoped that "the citizen who comes home from the assembly, battered by the corruption of particular interests, sees his wife and child at the hearth, and knows what the general will is."[70] This is an upbeat vision of the role of family in *The Social Contract,* and in Rousseau's thought in general, which Hirschmann uses to defend Rousseau against some of his feminist critics.

But once again, Rousseau seems to invite a darker interpretation. A wife and child can undermine rather than confirm a father's sense of virtue—his confidence that he can be a good citizen and capably ascertain the general will. Emile abandoned Sophie and citizenship because of his horror at the idea of her bringing another man's child into their home. This same possibility comes up in the *Discourse on Political Economy* in which Rousseau suggests that the only substantive reason fathers "ought to command in

the family" is because "the husband has to be able to review his wife's conduct: for it matters to him that the children he is forced to recognize and
to raise belong to none other than himself" (4). Rousseau was careful in
that essay to note that political economy is not like domestic economy,
and a family is not like a state. The main difference involves that faculty
for review. In "domestic government . . . the father can see everything for
himself," whereas in civil government, "the chief sees almost nothing but
through someone else's eyes" (3). The perfect state takes an interest in the
legitimacy of marriage, however, and Rousseau's final thought in *The Social
Contract*[71] regards his reasons that the rules of marriage are a crucial concern for the state. "Marriage . . . has civic consequences without which it
would be impossible for society itself to subsist. . . . [I]t could not endure
if composed only of bastards" (187).[72]

While many bastards might ruin a state, it took only one false child
to ruin Emile, despite how well his governor had prepared him. The false
child (whether a symbol of Sophie's betrayal, Emile's failure to protect her,
or both) reveals that Emile had never been prepared after all. *Becoming* a
father, even in the right way, did not prove Emile was ready for citizenship.
The test of worthiness continues, and one must raise a child whose will
is to imitate the parent. It was only the mature Emile's readiness to dedicate his life to imitating Jean-Jacques that once and for all confirmed the
worthiness of Jean-Jacques for his task. So Emile too, while he seemed to
possess all the necessary qualities for citizenship, must carry the burden of
uncertainty until his children are grown and can decide to dedicate themselves to imitating him in turn. In the meantime, one's parenthood must
be scrutinized and reviewed, and one's worthiness as a citizen is always
in doubt. Emile never earns the final judgment of virtue because his children do not live to render it, and Emile ends not as a citizen but as a slave.
He realizes about himself that "in order not to be destroyed, I need to be
driven by the will of another" (*Emile and Sophie,* 225). As father, Emile
might have been affirmed by the will of his child to imitate him. As a failed
father, he rejects his own father, whom he once sought to imitate, telling
Jean-Jacques, "You have done me more harm than you have ever done me
good" (206).

Similar fates await even those citizens that Rousseau's interpreters
have taken to represent his ideal. Hirschmann believes "Julie *is* Rousseau's
ideal citizen."[73] Shklar thought Rousseau's ideal was represented by Julie's
husband Wolmar, who is "omnicompetent and perfect."[74] Yet the difficult

burdens that parenthood places on citizenship overwhelm even Julie and Wolmar. The common understanding is that Rousseau's *Emile* is about education, and his *Julie* is about love. But the question of how Julie's children will be educated and whom they might come to imitate becomes central to the second half of the novel. In the first half of *Julie,* she and St. Preux are worthy of imitation by dint of their passionate virtue. Because they are "souls of a certain temper; they so to speak transform others into themselves ... one cannot know them without wanting to imitate them" (167). By introducing the question of the education of Julie's children into the second half of the novel, Rousseau revisits the dilemma of fatherhood and imitation, the dilemma suggested by the story he tells about his own fatherhood in the *Confessions* and resolved in the figure of Jean-Jacques in *Emile* (if not in its sequel).

When the second half of the novel begins, Julie has married her father's friend Wolmar and borne several children. Meanwhile, St. Preux has spent years traveling the world by sea—the fate Rousseau seems to have favored for failed fathers. Wolmar and Julie appear to have created the perfect domestic arrangements. In their house, one manages to find "comfort, freedom, gaiety in combination with order and attention to detail" (434). Wolmar offers his children not merely comfort and care but, more importantly, an exemplar to imitate. In this way, Wolmar proves himself far superior to

> these slave fathers [who] do not live for themselves, but for their children; forgetting that they are not fathers only, but men, and that they owe their children the example of the life of man and of the happiness that goes with wisdom. ... One of the main duties of a good paterfamilias is not only to make his home cheerful so that his children will thrive [there], but to live himself in an agreeable and easy life, so that they will feel that one is happy living as he does, and will not be tempted to adopt for that purpose a conduct opposed to his. (434–35)

Cheerful and happy sounds nice, and even worth imitating. But as we know from *Emile,* the indispensable part of education deals with the passions, and this is where Wolmar and Julie run into trouble. Julie's father stifled her passions, and though she believes she has calmed her love for St. Preux, she develops none for Wolmar. In fact, she tries to embrace love's absence, musing, "The thing that long deluded me . . . is the idea that love is essential to a happy marriage. My friend this is an error" (306). Wolmar himself is depicted as a passionless man, with "a tranquil soul and a cold heart" (402). In marrying Julie, he did not need to change much. "I perceived I was alone," he reflects on his decision to marry, "though I had not lost my coldness I needed an attachment" (404). Seeing Julie's tears of joy on embracing her father, Wolmar felt "the first or rather the only emotion I have experienced in my life. Though this impression was slight, it was unique, and in order to act the sentiments require strength only in proportion to those that oppose them" (404). Obviously, this is hardly the language of a St. Preux.

And so, though every character in the novel praises Wolmar's qualities nearly every time they speak of him, no one believes he should educate his own children. The proper cultivation of the passions, the channeling of them toward a love for virtue, can hardly be a job for a man whose only passion is "slight." Problems inevitably emerge, and we find Julie complaining to her cousin: "We cherish our children long before they can sense it and love us in return; and yet, one has so great a need to tell how much one loves them to someone else who can understand us! My husband understands me; but he does not respond enough to me for my fancy . . . his tenderness for them is too reasonable" (328). Wolmar is far too perceptive not to recognize his own shortcomings. So he turns to the man who nearly fathered Julie's first child:

> [My] plan is to charge [St. Preux] with my children's education. I am not unaware that these important responsibilities are a father's first duties; but when it is time to undertake them I shall be too old to fulfill them, and being placid and contemplative by temperament, I was never active enough to be able to govern the activity of youth. . . . [St Preux] appeared to me to possess in combination all the suitable qualities, and if I have well compassed his soul, I imagine no greater felicity for him than to accomplish their mother's in these dear children. (416)

If only Wolmar had read those letters from the first half of *Julie*, he would understand that there *is* a much greater felicity and that Julie and St. Preux have already tasted it—and though this felicity had been aborted, it could never be fully forgotten.[75] Soon enough, we find Julie practically begging

St. Preux to have sex: "Man is not made for celibacy, and it is very unlikely that a state so contrary to nature will fail to lead to some public or
hidden disorder. How can one forever escape the enemy one constantly
carries within? . . . Because [the celibate] have disdained humanity, they
debase themselves beneath it" (548). Of course, she is not asking St. Preux
to sleep with *her* but rather to marry Claire. Still, the reader senses that
though she claims to want to protect St. Preux from himself, her deepest
concerns are for her own resolve.

And so, a few letters further, Julie is dead. Half-drowned after rescu-
ing her son from the lake, she seems to resign from life and fades away.
She is not sorry to die because she realizes that she had deluded herself in
thinking her passion for St. Preux had faded. "Aye, however much I wanted
to stifle the first sentiment that brought me alive, it crystallized into my
heart." How could she have borne the spectacle of the man, who by right
of his passion should be the father of her children, performing a "father's
first duty?" If her sons became St. Preux's children, as Emile became the
son of Jean-Jacques, how could she not become St. Preux's wife? "Who
knows whether seeing myself so near the abyss, I would not be drawn into
it? . . . One more day, perhaps, and I was a criminal!" (608–9). And so by
dint of having the wrong father, her children must lose their mother.

Resignation

In describing a path to virtuous parenthood so difficult to negotiate and
political burdens so difficult to bear, Rousseau offers a warning against the
uses of parenthood for citizenship. He occasionally gave up on parenthood
altogether—praising citizens who provided examples of political virtue
their children would not live to emulate. In his "Letter to Franquières," he
recalled "Brutus causing his children to be put to death. . . . Brutus was
a tender father, to do his duty tore up his insides, and Brutus was virtuous" (281). In *Emile,* he praised "a Spartan woman [who] had five sons in
the army and was awaiting news of the battle. A Helot arrives; trembling,
she asks him for news. 'Your five sons were killed.' 'Base slave, did I ask
you that?' 'We won the victory.' The mother runs to the temple and gives
thanks to the gods. This is the female citizen" (40).

Or, Rousseau speculated, children might be taken from their parents in
the name of political virtue. In the *Discourse on Political Economy,* Rousseau
concluded the essay "at a deeper level . . . where I should have begun it"—

with the subject of raising children. "You will have everything if you form citizens, if you do not, you will have nothing but nasty slaves, beginning with the chiefs of state" (20). In that essay, he suggested that children be raised (as Rousseau's were, *if* they were) in common by the state—"surely the state's most important business"—rather than "abandoned to their father's lights and prejudices" (21–22). By taking education from the hands of parents, Rousseau suggested, we might also eliminate the vagaries of virtue that plague those in the midst of citizenship. Children being raised to be virtuous citizens should be exposed only to the most praiseworthy of aged citizens—whose paths in life are known and fixed and whose virtue is unassailable. The "sublime office" of educator should be reserved for only the best citizens, as "the sweet repose of their old age, and the culmination of all their honors." They will teach children virtue by "example," not by "precept," because "virtue itself is discredited in the mouth of one who does not practice it." In this way, Rousseau believed, the best citizens might by their example "form virtuous successors and transmit from age to age unto succeeding generations . . . the courage and the virtue of citizens, and the emulation common to all of them to live and die for the fatherland" (22).

Rousseau thought it would be a just reward to these virtuous citizens to be watched and imitated at the end of their lives. Christopher Kelly argues that for Rousseau, in order for virtue to nourish amour propre and thus be worth the struggle, a witness to our virtue must always be supposed.[76] When virtue seemed most difficult and most unrecognized, Rousseau could fall back on the existence of God to provide this witness. As Rousseau wrote in his "Letter to Franquières," "Even the mere idea of [God's] existence would be for man an encouragement to virtue and consolation in his miseries. . . . It is at least one solace in adversity to have a witness to one's not having deserved it" (282). But, Kelly goes on to argue, even this is not always enough, and Rousseau ultimately concedes that in some cases, without the further expectation of a life to come, virtue would have no rewards. Rousseau's politics of parenthood, the aspect of his thought about which his contemporaries most obsessed, works along analogous lines. In *Emile, Julie,* and the *Confessions,* Rousseau explores a formula for the cultivation of virtuous lives in corrupt times. The characters in these works attempt to forge enchanted lives by binding the love of virtue to the development and realization of the passions culminating in parenthood. This process by its nature creates witnesses in the form of the children that result. These witnesses may even promise some version of a life to come—but that's the rub. Only those parents who have negotiated the development of their passions correctly will be worthy of imitation, and only they will have the pleasure of seeing the essence of themselves projected into the future. In Rousseau's depiction, this result is profoundly difficult to achieve. Citizenship conceived on this basis is haunted by self-doubt rather than animated by the confidence of virtue. St. Preux and Julie have their hopes for a virtuous love and their potential for happiness sacrificed to her father's aristocratic values. Emile, for whom everything was perfectly arranged, loses his way when his tutor leaves him. The *Confessions* depicts Rousseau's own coming to grips with the role that failed parenthood played in his life. Rousseau strove to transform his passions into a virtuous love, but he could not face the witnesses he and Thérèse produced. For reasons he never fully revealed, he judged himself and found himself wanting. This is ultimately the trouble with Rousseau's politics of parenthood: it is hardly difficult to produce a witness, but it is likely you will produce a witness for the prosecution.

· CHAPTER 2 ·

The Tragedy of Birth:
Nietzsche on Parenthood and Political Contest

The bond between man and man depends on the transmission and elaboration of . . . fictions; while fundamentally the real bond (through procreation) goes its unknown way.

from Nietzsche's notebooks

Procreation is the real achievement of the individual and consequently his highest interest, his highest expression of power (not judged from the consciousness but from the center of the whole individuation).

from Nietzsche's notebooks

A S NIETZSCHE DESCENDED INTO MADNESS, he insisted that there had been only one true love in his life—his love for Cosima Wagner. That love had been born twenty years earlier during an evening at Wagner's home, the night when a very pregnant Cosima and her future husband Richard first sat down with young Friedrich Nietzsche and really got to know him. At the end of the conversation, Cosima went upstairs and gave birth. The Wagners believed Nietzsche's presence in their home that particular evening was a good omen for both the newborn child and the newborn friendship.[1]

In the years that followed, few themes would appear more persistently in Nietzsche's writing than procreation. In fact, procreation is introduced in the first sentence of Nietzsche's first book. *The Birth of Tragedy* begins: "We shall have gained much for the science of aesthetics, once we perceive . . . that the continuous development of art is bound up with the Apollinian and Dionysian duality—just as procreation depends on the duality of the sexes, involving perpetual strife with only periodically intervening reconciliations."[2] In nearly every work that followed ideas about procreation and parenthood would play a prominent role. Parenthood would strike Nietzsche as an impetus to rise to the challenges of "perpetual strife" that mark the politics of contest. But parenthood would also tempt Nietzsche to indulge in the comforts of those "reconciliations" that intervene to provide relief from such strife, and to make such reconciliations permanent. The political uses of parenthood would tempt Nietzsche to withdraw from the challenges of contest.

In this chapter, I explore Nietzsche's preoccupations with parenthood and in so doing find unexpected connections between Nietzsche's ideas and the place of parenthood in Rousseau's political thought. For Rousseau, it was the distinctive qualities of the experience of parenthood—its associations with transformative passions and the tangible, worldly manifestation of those passions—that made it uniquely suitable to inscribe a love of virtue onto the souls of secularized moderns. One hundred years hence, Nietzsche reacted violently to the enduring popularity of Rousseau's conception of virtue. But even as he did so, he appealed to many of the same aspects of parenthood in his attempt to create a compelling account of what he took to be humanity's fundamental task, and the sort of person who might undertake it. That fundamental task, as he put it in one early essay, was to *"promote the production of the philosopher, the artist and the saint within us and without us,"* or, couching the idea in more procreative terms, "to prepare within themselves and around them for the birth of the genius."[3] The more Nietzsche explicated the work that would go into this "fundamental task," the more the "within us" and the "without us" became conflated in a complex relationship centering on becoming a parent.

Of course Nietzsche was no democrat. He was among the harshest critics of Rousseau and the tradition of democratic thought of which Rousseau was a part. Nonetheless, Nietzsche's attacks on democratic society—his unflinching exploration of the human shortcomings and weaknesses that he saw flourishing under the symbol of political equality—have been incredibly useful to subsequent theorists interested in improving on the democratic project. Honig, for example, values the democratic possibilities of "Nietzsche's call for a shifting of perspectives and habits as part of a practice of perpetual self-transformation."[4] Other theorists of democracy, in particular theorists who figure democratic citizenship in terms of political contest, have found inspiration in Nietzsche's ideas about self-transformation, the interrogation of inherited values, and the creation and communication of new values.[5] In this chapter, I argue that it was in working out just those ideas that democratic theorists of contest have found most useful that Nietzsche most often relied on the notion that parenthood provides the opportunity to craft the best—and most politically useful—sort of life.

But he often did not deploy those ideas in a way that theorists who advocate the politics of contest might wish. Nietzsche believed that the possibility of passing on a way of life to one's child could inspire a person to reconsider and recraft his or her fundamental values—which is perhaps a useful notion for the politics of contest. But Nietzsche also found in the experience of parenthood many temptations to forgo the openness of *perpetual* contest and self-overcoming and to settle down into a spiritual existence that is more fixed and comforting. Parenthood can help inspire in us the qualities best suited to the politics of contest, but it can also lure us to cling to fundamental commitments and take respite from the rigors of citizenship.

Thus this chapter identifies and explores an aspect of Nietzsche's work often neglected in contemporary scholarship. In doing so, it offers an interpretation of Nietzsche's thought, centered on his ideas about parenthood, that cuts against the grain of many recent efforts to appropriate Nietzschean ideas for democratic theory. Attention to Nietzsche's ideas about procreation and parenthood—especially to their origins in his early thought—reveals different aspects of Nietzsche than we are used to seeing. Compared to the ecstatically self-creating Nietzsche we often encounter, this examination uncovers a Nietzsche who is daunted by the task of dealing with what we have inherited from our culture, our parents, our ancestors, and our educators. This Nietzsche is much less confident about our ability to transform that inheritance in a way that matters. This is a Nietzsche who was deeply attracted to the idea that parenthood is useful in confronting the overwhelming difficulty of undertaking the task of a deep self-transformation that involves, to use Connolly's description, "tactics or artistry applied by the self to corporeal layers of being not sufficiently susceptible to direct conscious control."[6]

For this sort of work on the self to be useful to the politics of contest, a person must communicate the results in a way that might have an impact on his or her community. Honig notes how Nietzsche's refiguring of virtue as *virtù* "does not unite men or bespeak their commonality" and that "it individuates . . . it is uncommunicative."[7] To express matters of such depth through words, Nietzsche believed, often trivializes them beyond usefulness. But Honig also notes Nietzsche's openness "to the project of ordering a contingent world as part of an attempt to maintain a community and its form of life." She suggests that Nietzsche's gestures in this direction, in which a new form of life, once crafted, seeks to "situate and maintain itself, . . . is an important (and underrated) strand in Nietzsche's thinking."[8] It certainly is. In this chapter, I explore the ways that Nietzsche thought of parenting as crucial to efforts to order a part of the contingent world in a way that maintains—and passes on—the form of life a person creates for himself or herself. Nietzsche believed a child's imitation of her or his parents has the potential to reach beyond the surface of consciousness and communicate a sense of what we have made of ourselves at the deepest layers of our being.

Attention to Nietzsche's ideas about parenthood suggests that this "underrated strand" in his thinking raises complications regarding just those strands that theorists of the politics of contest rate most highly. Nietzsche's concerns about how to maintain and pass on a form of life through parenthood lead him to indulge in dreams of rest, desires for fixity and control, habits of generalization, and reluctance to interrogate inherited "truths." Nietzsche's politics of parenthood also provides valuable context for understanding those aspects of Nietzsche's thought that are most troubling to those who find his work valuable: his ideas about women and his discussions of projects of "breeding."

To the extent that a consensus has emerged among Nietzsche scholars regarding his ideas about procreation, the consensus goes something like this: Nietzsche was so persistent in writing about procreation because it provided the concepts and images he chose to help him think about, explain, and affirm what was of paramount importance to him—the host of attitudes and behaviors that fall under the rubric of a sort of life-affirming creativity and generativity. In other words, according to this consensus, Nietzsche's ideal individual would be involved in a constant or semiconstant process of "self-creation," or of "giving birth" to himself or herself, and Nietzsche persistently employed metaphors of procreation and pregnancy in order to develop and drive home this point. This interpretation of Nietzsche's imagery of pregnancy in particular is central to a great deal of insightful work that confronts the issue of gender in Nietzsche's thought.[9] I argue, however, that close attention to Nietzsche's ideas about procreation and parenthood makes it necessary to complicate this scholarly consensus. This is not to say that other scholars have gotten Nietzsche "wrong" on this point. Rather, it is to say that there is not a single answer regarding the prominence of ideas about procreation in Nietzsche's thought. Fredrick Appel suggests that it is a mistake to give Nietzsche's ideas about procreation a "strictly metaphorical interpretation" and maintains that Nietzsche's "positive stance toward childbearing and child rearing" is one of the "best kept secrets" about his ideas.[10] This chapter brings those secrets to light. In doing so, I show that Nietzsche's ideas about procreation and parenthood *are* useful in thinking about the sort of openness to self-transformation required by the democratic politics of contest. However, Nietzsche's ideas about parenthood also took him in directions that should give theorists of contest pause. These ideas suggest that while parenthood might offer an opportunity to refigure our most closely held values, it also creates attachments to new values that citizens are reluctant to abandon.

Hating Rousseau

Nietzsche liked to remind readers, "I still hate Rousseau."[11] He referred bitterly to "the moral tarantula Rousseau," whose bite had infected the souls of modern men.[12] Rousseau had discovered, particularly through his depictions of the sentimental family, a way to make a love of virtue feel real and important to modern Europeans, and in doing so, he earned Nietzsche's disdain. As Nietzsche noted in *Ecce Homo,* he only attacked "causes that are victorious."[13] He was well aware of Rousseau's victories and the importance of Rousseau's vision of domestic virtue to the modern self-understanding. Nietzsche credited Rousseau with the creation of an "image of man . . . which will no doubt long inspire mortals to a transfiguration of their own lives." Comparing Rousseau to Goethe and Schopenhauer—men whom Nietzsche greatly admired—he was forced to admit that it was Rousseau who "possesses the greatest fire and is sure of producing the greatest popular effect" ("Schopenhauer as Educator," 150–51). Nietzsche included Rousseau among the writers with whom he "had to come to terms" and from whom he would "accept judgment" (*Human, All Too Human,* 299).

Just what was it about Rousseau that caused Nietzsche to take him so seriously and yet treat him so venomously? Perhaps it was because Rousseau's solution to the question of how secularized modern men could be inspired to live virtuously hit Nietzsche a little too close to home. One way to understand why Nietzsche regarded Rousseau as the "first modern man" is that Rousseau was among the first to accept that the withdrawal of religious belief as an unquestioned source of meaning in people's lives had changed the entire context of European culture and politics.[14] What this development meant foremost to Nietzsche was an opportunity to cast aside Christian notions of morality, a morality he believed was hostile to life.

> The greatest recent event—that "God is dead," that the belief in the Christian god has become unbelievable—is already beginning to cast its shadows over Europe. . . . One [cannot] suppose that many people know as yet *what* this event really means—and how much must collapse now that this faith has been undermined because it was built on this faith, propped up by it, grown into it; for example, the whole of our European morality.[15]

Nietzsche detested the ingeniousness with which Rousseau managed to push back this shadow and to reinscribe a love of virtue onto the souls of semisecularized Europeans. "It cannot be denied that from the beginning of the last century a stream of moral awakening has flowed through Europe. It was only then that virtue again became eloquent; . . . If we seek the source of this stream we find first of all Rousseau" (*Human, All Too Human*, 365). What set Rousseau apart in Nietzsche's eyes was not simply that he advocated a return to virtue but the popularity and efficacy of Rousseau's particular approach to the problem. Rousseau's efforts to bind desire and parenthood to virtue had co-opted what was to be one of the most important tools in the immoralist's toolbox. For Nietzsche believed that the sexual passions, in their association with the profound mysteries surrounding the creation of new life, were crucial to his own very different account of the best way to live. By harnessing these passions to a quasi-Christian conception of virtue, Rousseau created a new and unique moral dilemma that Nietzsche had no choice but to face directly. Thus Nietzsche found himself treading so often upon ground already marked by Rousseau's footsteps despite his determination to ultimately lead his readers to a very different destination. Sounding much like Rousseau, Nietzsche believed that "The man who has overcome his passions has entered into possession of the most fertile ground. . . . To sow the seeds of good spiritual works in the soil of subdued passions is then the most immediate urgent task" (323). As with Rousseau, Nietzsche's goal was not simply to subdue passions but to harness them for other purposes.

One of these purposes was a sort of progress. Many interpreters of Nietzsche have noted his hostility to the progress narratives that modern Europeans used to explain their place in history and to justify their way of life—narratives in which unenlightened cultures (organized on the basis of deceptions, prejudices, and superstitions) develop into enlightened ones (organized according to the principles of reason).[16] Nietzsche indeed criticized these progress narratives.[17] He disliked the idea that there is a force outside of human history, something over and above the substance of people's actual lives (like God, or "enlightenment") that determines the direction in which societies and civilizations develop.[18]

But Nietzsche's critique of this sort of progress narrative should not obscure his attraction to another sort of human progress—achieved through the slow accumulation of individuals transforming some aspect of themselves for reasons and through means that are grounded in the specificity of their own lives rather than in abstractions like "history," "society," or "species." One way to explore the difference between these two conceptions of progress is to look at Nietzsche's discussions of the Enlightenment. Nietzsche was hostile to many of the ideas we have come to associate with Enlightenment thinking, but in *Human, All Too Human,* he indicated he might have been pleased had the Enlightenment been "left to itself" and therefore had "long been content to address itself only to the individual: so that it would have transformed the customs and institutions of nations only very slowly." But the Enlightenment was not left to itself. Rousseau got his hands on it, and "this creature [Rousseau] then went on with perfidious enthusiasm to set the Enlightenment too on its fanatical head, which thereby began to glow as though in a transfigured light" (367). Nietzsche counseled his readers to reject any sense of historical progress illuminated by otherworldly or historical forces. Rather, he urged the reader "to *continue* the work of the Enlightenment *in himself.*" (367). The difficult work that Nietzsche hoped might be continued by an individual on whatever is "within himself" was *progressive* work. Rousseau's "passionate follies and half-lies . . . called forth the optimistic spirit of the Revolution" and thus "for a long time banished *the spirit of the Enlightenment and of progressive evolution:* let us see—each of us within himself—whether it is possible to call it back!" (169).

Through these jabs at Rousseau and engagements with the Enlightenment, Nietzsche sought to reclaim the spirit of progress for his own project. Based on Nietzsche's criteria, this would not be a progress predetermined by a god whose vision for humanity would emerge as history unfolded; and it would not be a progress toward an abstract ideal whose luminous beauty might tempt some group to try to achieve it all at once through revolutionary change.[19] Rather, it was a progress that was internally driven. This progress would occur through the organization and enrichment of the instincts, energies, and talents possessed by the individuals in a culture. Though it was important to Nietzsche that human beings focus on what was close—the substance of their present lives—this progress *would* be inspired by a vision of what the future could hold for both the individual and the larger culture. Nietzsche realized it could be a delicate balance to find a vision of the future that would inspire people to examine without distortion their present way of life. It was Nietzsche's early efforts to articulate a way to find and maintain this balance that led his thinking about progress toward ideas about parenthood.

Exemplar as Parent

Nietzsche's early steps on this path are evident in the essay "Schopenhauer as Educator" in which he confronts the question of how individuals can be inspired by an external vision without losing view of the substance and circumstances of their own lives. Finding the right sort of exemplar, as Nietzsche had found in Schopenhauer, makes a sort of progress possible. The young Nietzsche valued Schopenhauer for his rare greatness and his unprecedented honesty. Yet a person should not forget himself even in beholding a Schopenhauer. So in describing Schopenhauer's greatness, Nietzsche emphasized how important it was not to lose oneself in the "intoxicating vision" Schopenhauer provided ("Schopenhauer as Educator," 156). The important question therefore became, "To ask the definite question: is it possible to bring that incredibly lofty goal so close to us that it educates us while it draws us aloft?" (156).[20] The purpose of bringing an exemplar close was practical and involved hard work. A good exemplar, brought close enough to educate, makes it possible to find a "circle of duties" and "practical activity" that allow one to "proceed toward so extravagant a goal" (156). The goal is not to become a mere imitation of the exemplar but rather to be inspired to think back on ourselves and to realize that "each of us bears a productive uniqueness within him as the core of his being" (144).

   Nietzsche believed that procreative metaphors[21] provided a useful way of thinking through how individuals might be "productive" with their "uniqueness"—how individuals might discover and develop what is unique in themselves in such a way that it can be divided or communicated. For example, the point of identifying a set of practical duties and activities was to "promote an evolving culture and the procreation of genius" ("Schopenhauer as Educator," 142). The alternative was that a person become too caught up in himself or herself and lose sight of how to contribute to the evolving culture. The result in such a case was that "he ceases to be fruitful, to propagate himself . . . ; in a cultural sense he becomes feeble or useless. The uniqueness of his being has become an indivisible, uncommunicating atom, an icy rock" (144).

The essay on Schopenhauer shows Nietzsche's early engagement with the issues that would lead him from a metaphorical consideration of procreation to an increasingly literal engagement with the role parenthood might play in his vision of an "evolving culture." Nietzsche moved into this territory when he addressed the question of how the work the individual does on himself or herself could become "productive" for the larger culture. On one level, the Schopenhauer essay seems like a call for a purely personal transformation. Nietzsche was concerned with describing how the example of the life of a man like Schopenhauer might help individuals to look inside themselves, be true to what is unique in them, be "responsible to themselves for their own existence," and "live according to [their] own laws and standards" (128). Yet he mentioned repeatedly that in doing so, they might contribute to the development of a culture that promotes the production of the genius, "the reproduction of Schopenhauer."

Only in the final sections of the essay did Nietzsche address directly the question of how the "productive" uniqueness of individuals in the present might help culture proceed toward the lofty goals he had described. Nietzsche did so by introducing a new problem: the way the effect of genius can become so diluted that his or her influence on the future of a culture is negligible.

> How dull and feeble is the effect [nature] generally achieves with the philosophers and artists! How rarely does it achieve any effect at all! . . . It achieves its aims in a broad and ponderous manner: and in doing so it sacrifices much too much energy. The artist is related to the effect of his art as a heavy cannon is to a flock of sparrows . . . Just think of the true greatness of Schopenhauer—and then of how absurdly small his effect has been! (177–78)

The crucial question, then, is how the effect of the genius can be *concentrated* so that it can have an influence on the future.[22] In an effort to answer this question, Nietzsche began to think in ways that would lead him to a father's relationship to a son.

First, for the effect of a genius to remain sufficiently concentrated, it is not enough for a multitude to read his or her works—rather someone must know and learn from the genius's way of living. As Nietzsche put it, "I profit from a philosopher only insofar as he can be an example.... But this example must be supplied by his outward life, and not merely in his books—in the way, that is, in which the philosophers of Greece taught, through their bearing, what they wore and ate, and their morals, rather than by what they said, let alone by what they wrote" (137).[23]

Second, knowledge of the exemplar is not sufficient—there has to be a relationship of love. "How can man know himself?... Let the youthful soul look back on life with the question: what have you truly loved up to now, what has drawn your soul aloft, what has mastered it and at the same time blessed it?" (129). The need for love raised a host of complications in getting an individual to do the sort of work on himself or herself that might eventually contribute to culture.

> It is hard to create in anyone this condition of intrepid self knowledge because it is impossible to teach love; for it is love alone that can bestow on the soul, not only a clear, discriminating and self-contemptuous view of itself, but also the desire to look beyond itself and to seek with all its might for a higher self as yet still concealed from it. Thus only he who has attached his heart to some great man receives thereby the *first consecration to culture.* (163)

In describing this experience of love, Nietzsche was thinking about exemplars and the sort of attachment that he felt to Schopenhauer. In seeking to illustrate this attachment, Nietzsche gravitated toward the metaphor of father and son.

Upon discovering Schopenhauer, Nietzsche recalled, "I trusted him at once.... Though this is a foolish and immodest way of putting it, I understand him as though it were for me that he had written" (133). But in explaining his trust for Schopenhauer, Nietzsche pointed out that Schopenhauer had written with a complete lack of artifice because he had no audience in mind. "Schopenhauer never wants to cut a figure: for he writes for himself and no one wants to be deceived. . . . Schopenhauer speaks [only] with himself" (134). How should one imagine this relationship—how can Schopenhauer write only for himself and yet write for Nietzsche as well? If it is because he writes for himself that Schopenhauer achieved greatness, how can his work make the transition from the "within" to the "without," from himself to Nietzsche, and not lose what is great in it? Parenthood provided the answer. If one feels "obliged" to imagine Schopenhauer writing for an audience, Nietzsche explained, "one should think of a son being instructed by his father. It is an honest, calm, good-natured discourse before an auditor who listens to it with love" (134). In other words, in finding an educator and an exemplar—the person who would inspire him to think back on his own uniqueness and find what is productive within it— Nietzsche found a father.[24] And while writing only for himself was a measure of Schopenhauer's strength and genius, writing for a son as well (or writing as if for a son) will not dilute that strength and genius too much.[25] The effect of the genius will remain sufficiently concentrated and not lose what is great about it in dispersion. Furthermore, by appealing to the father–son relationship, Nietzsche incorporated both the requirements mentioned previously: knowledge of an exemplar's way of living and the element of love.

So the father–son relationship struck the young Nietzsche as a useful analogy in thinking about the dual project of promoting "the production of the philosopher, the artist and the saint within us and without us" (160)—of working toward the evolution of the culture "at first only for yourself, to be sure; but through yourself in the end for everyone" (142). The question remains as to whether Nietzsche, fatherless himself after his fourth year, was interested in more than the analogy and hoped that in ideal circumstances biological sons might get from their fathers what metaphorical sons could get from exemplars. The Schopenhauer essay contains several nods in this direction.

For example, while Nietzsche admired Schopenhauer because he wrote for himself, Nietzsche intended his own essay for the person with a particular kind of parent. One of Nietzsche's concerns was to describe the dangers that threaten to distract certain "free spirits" from the cultivation of their potential for genius (179). But while their spirits were free, their potential was tied to their origins: "I now seek the conditions with the assistance of which a born philosopher can in the most favourable case at least avoid being crushed by the perversity of our times" (180).

The pages that follow seem to confirm that in saying free spirits are *born* philosophers, Nietzsche meant that they have the potential they do because of who happens to be their parents. Nietzsche immediately turns to the case of Schopenhauer's parents—in particular, he claimed it was "the proud, free, republican character of his father... that bestowed on [Schopenhauer] the first thing a philosopher needs: inflexible and rugged manliness" (180).[26] Fourteen years later in *Ecce Homo*, Nietzsche praised his own father in similar terms.[27]

Without dismissing the influence of Schopenhauer's actual father, Nietzsche went on to note how important it was that Schopenhauer had found his own exemplar, his own spiritual father, in Goethe. It seems both were necessary—the inborn genius and the outside influence that shows one how to be true to it. "Schopenhauer... had the indescribable good fortune to be able to see genius from up close not only in himself, but also outside himself in Goethe" (181). Nietzsche was eager, however, to emphasize that Schopenhauer had managed to learn what Goethe had to teach while Schopenhauer was still very young. It is almost as if he were born with Goethe's qualities inside him as well as his father's: "[We] can well believe he had already seen [life from Goethe's perspective] as a child. Everything he subsequently appropriated to himself from life and books, from the whole wealth of the sciences, was to him hardly more than colouring and means of expression" (182).

In the final section of the essay, Nietzsche revisited the topic of literal fathers and sons. He suggested that the essay might serve as a sort of education manual for fathers—a new *Emile* of sorts. "From what we have discussed perhaps some father or other may be able to learn something and apply it in some way to the private education of his son" (183). But while Rousseau feared the project he presented in *Emile* would strike fathers as too difficult, Nietzsche feared that fathers would be inclined to reject the premises of his project altogether.

> Fathers in every age have put up the most determined resistance
> to their sons' being philosophers, as though it were extremely perverse; ... Plato for that reason considered it necessary to institute
> a whole new state if the existence of the philosopher was not to be
> imperiled by the unreason of fathers. (183)

In fact, Nietzsche believed that the modern state had been too successful in taking over from fathers the task of producing philosophers. In the essay's conclusion, Nietzsche explains in vituperative terms how the state had failed at this task.

So perhaps it was time for fathers and fatherly exemplars to take back the responsibility for the creation of the philosophers of the future. Perhaps it was necessary that they undertake "what has never been taught at universities"—that they provide to those they love, through the example of their way of living, "the only critique of a philosophy that is possible and that proves something, namely trying to see whether one can live in accordance with it" (187). One can gather from this essay a set of concerns that Nietzsche would carry forth into his later work to a more direct engagement with the role parenthood played in the lives of modern Europeans. Nietzsche was interested in a sort of progress that was inspired by a vision of what the future could hold—a slow progress that developed from and was grounded in the substance of people's actual lives. He believed that individuals who would contribute to this progress needed to think back onto themselves, discover what was productive about their own uniqueness, find a way to make that uniqueness divisible, and communicate it. He thought that the only way for the effect of such an accomplishment to be passed on in sufficient concentration, without losing its power in dispersal, was through a relationship of love that was combined with an intimate knowledge of the exemplar's way of living. Reinforcing this perspective, Nietzsche suggested that for the effect of a genius to be passed on, the recipient needed a sort of "inborn" genius of his or her own and an intimate knowledge of the exemplar from childhood. He thought the best metaphor for this relationship was the relationship between a father and his child and speculated that actual fathers were the ideal audience for his ideas. Finally, while Nietzsche suspected actual fathers were unlikely to heed the advice he offered, he seemed to like the alternative approaches for the production of genius even less.

Heredity, Self-Transformation, and Procreation as Achievement

In the years after the Schopenhauer essay Nietzsche intensified his approach to the problem of encouraging "genius" through ideas about procreation. Tracy Strong remarks that "after leaving Basel, [Nietzsche] conspicuously stops using [the word] *erziehen*, which has connotations of 'bringing up' and 'educate.'" Instead, Nietzsche "repeatedly uses the word *zuchten*, which means to breed, raise, rear, grow or cultivate."[28] *Zeugung* (procreation) also emerged as a more important concern for Nietzsche. In

Daybreak, Nietzsche summarized the relationship this way: "Education is a continuation of procreation, and often a kind of supplementary beautification of it" (173).[29]

The central reason for the shift in focus toward procreation over education was foreshadowed in the Schopenhauer essay: Nietzsche came to believe the most important human qualities were impossible to convey or pass on through words but might be passed on from parent to child in unconscious ways. In *The Gay Science,* Nietzsche explained that any feeling, reaction, or evaluation that has risen to the level of thoughts or words has already shed the qualities that made it truly individual in the sense of being unique in a way that has the potential to be "productive": "Fundamentally, all our actions are altogether incomparably personal, unique, and infinitely individual; there is no doubt of that. But as soon as we translate them into consciousness *they no longer seem to be*" (299).[30] If one were to focus solely on influencing culture at the level of consciousness, it would convey to others precisely what it was least important to pass on: "Man, like every living being, thinks continually without knowing it; the thinking that rises to *consciousness* is only the smallest part of all this—the most superficial and worst part" (298–99).

Working the same idea out in his notebooks, Nietzsche suggested that procreation might provide a way around this limitation by making it possible to pass on what is truly individual—what exists below the level of consciousness. Nietzsche urged himself to explain "how all our words refer to fictions . . . and how the bond between man and man depends on the transmission and elaboration of these fictions; *while fundamentally the real bond (through procreation) goes its unknown way*" (*The Will to Power,* 358, emphasis added).[31] He worked to describe just how "the real bond"—procreation—managed to pass on what words could not in aphorism after aphorism, particularly in *Human, All Too Human* and *Daybreak,* the books that followed *The Untimely Meditations.*

In Nietzsche's view, the important aspects of heredity were not biological.[32] Rather than being born with talents, feelings, and inclinations, Nietzsche believed, children picked them up by imitation.

> He who was a child is aware of the existence of manifold and strong feelings . . . and thus used up the best of his energy and time in the imitation of feelings: he will as an adult remark in himself that every new thing, every new person, at once arouses in him liking or dislike

or envy or contempt. . . . Towards [the experience of these evalua-
tions] he feels himself powerless. (*Daybreak, 66*)

These feelings and evaluations come to feel "natural." People will be inclined
to "trust their feelings" without realizing that "behind feelings there stand
judgments and evaluations which we inherit in the form of feelings. . . . To
trust one's feelings means to give more obedience to one's grandfather and
grandmother and their grandparents than to the gods which are in *us:* our
reason and our experience" (25).

This context makes it easier to understand what Nietzsche meant by
saying that procreation provides the "real bond" between people, though
it is a bond that tends to distract a person from the "productive" potential
of his or her uniqueness.[33] Elsewhere, Nietzsche took a different tone in
describing procreation not simply as the most fundamental of bonds but
as something even more—an *achievement* above all others. He wrote:

> The tremendous importance the individual accords to the sexual
> instinct is not a result of its importance for the species, but arises
> because *procreation is the real achievement of the individual and
> consequently his highest interest,* his highest expression of power (not
> judged from the consciousness but from the center of the whole
> individuation). (*The Will to Power,* 360, emphasis added)

This assessment of procreation as an individual's greatest accomplishment is harder to comprehend given what the previous quotations indicate about Nietzsche's understanding of the operations of inheritance.
Individuals inherit inclinations and automatic reactions from their parents
as children and are basically stuck with what they have inherited. When
they have children, they will pass on these inclinations in just the way that
they themselves acquired them. How can this be seen as the "real achievement" of the individual? This process could be so unconscious, Nietzsche
believed, that it was not uncommon for a person never to be aware of a
personal quality yet still pass it on to his or her children. "What was silent
in the father speaks in the son; and often I have found in the son the un-
veiled secret of the father."[34]

It is just these difficulties—the automatic and unconscious nature of the
normal operations of heredity—that made Nietzsche believe that procreation, if achieved in the right way, might be the individual's greatest work.

The first problem is how a person can create something that he or she has *willed* for himself or herself rather than merely inherited—what was already chosen for the person when he or she was a child:

> Active, successful natures act, not according to the dictum "know thyself," but as if there hovered before them the commandment: *will* a self and thou shalt *become* a self.—Fate seems to have left the choice still up to them; whereas the inactive and contemplative cogitate on what they *have* already chosen, on *one* occasion, when they entered into life. (*Human, All Too Human*, 294)

But it is difficult to create a self that is different from the self we are born into. For Nietzsche, those things that we inherit from our parents, and through our parents from our ancestors—the energy, talents, feelings, and inclinations that we acquire through imitation when we are children—are the most important aspects of who we are. In the normal course of life, it is profoundly difficult to change this aspect of ourselves in a permanent way.[35] No matter what education we encounter and what passions we engage in our youth, eventually we will find that "our fundamental feelings and outlook have come to dominate them" (*Human, All Too Human*, 194).[36] It is not enough to merely rebel against those things that come naturally to you or to refuse to act on certain inclinations. This sort of superficial triumph will not matter when you face the crucial test of parenthood. Suppress what qualities you will, they will be sensed by your child and passed on despite your efforts.

But Nietzsche believed a self-transformation of an entirely different quality is possible, and is necessary, if the effects of that conversion are to be passed on to the next generation. The problem was that we would pass onto our children, and through them to the future of our culture, those aspects of ourselves that seem a part of our nature, that are closest to the core of our being—in other words, just the qualities *we* inherited as children. So the solution was to find a way to create a sort of second nature for ourselves—to transform the core of our being in a way that encourages the "procreation of genius" within us and through us to our children. In another of *The Untimely Meditations*, Nietzsche emphasized the profound difficulty of the task facing those who would overcome their past and transform themselves:

> For since we are the outcome of earlier generations, we are also the outcome of their aberrations, passions and errors, and indeed

of their crimes; it is not possible to wholly free oneself from this chain. If we condemn these aberrations and regard ourselves as free of them, this does not alter the fact that we originate in them. The best we can do is to confront our inherited and hereditary nature with our knowledge of it, and through a new, stern discipline combat our inborn heritage and implant in ourselves a new habit, a new instinct, a second nature, so that our first nature withers away. (76)[37]

Nietzsche did not think the chances for success were good. But it is just this rare person, who has achieved this self-transformation and has managed to give his or her second nature—a self-willed nature—this quality of firstness, who is ready to pass on something new. And so Nietzsche's language once again takes a procreative turn. Regarding such individuals who had transformed their nature in this way, Nietzsche said, "Even if they themselves are late-born . . . coming generations will know them only as first-born" (106–7).

Such a person has to remake herself or himself at a level that is deeper than consciousness. As Nietzsche would put it many years later, "States of consciousness, any faith, considering something true, for example—every psychologist knows this—are fifth-rank matters of complete indifference compared to the value of the instincts" (*The Antichrist*, 613).[38] States of consciousness are communicated primarily through words, and Nietzsche was convinced that "all our words refer to fictions." He was frustrated that so often "the bond between man and man depends on the transmission and elaboration of these fictions" (*The Will to Power*, 358). The fruits of a self-transformation that reaches the level of instinct, on the other hand, can be transmitted through a superior sort of bond, "the real bond" of procreation. It was precisely in thinking about a human life "not [in terms of] consciousness, but from the center of the whole individuation" that Nietzsche declared "procreation is the real achievement of the individual and consequently his highest interest" (360).

What misgivings Nietzsche had about the possibility of a person achieving this sort of self-transformation only pushed him further in the direction of thinking about parenthood and procreation—and how they might allow an individual to contribute to the gradual *progress* of an "ongrowing" culture. For example, there is a caveat offered in *Beyond Good and Evil*: Nietzsche, the teacher of self-overcoming, self-transformation, and transfiguration reflected that "at the bottom of us, 'right down deep,' there is, to be sure, something unteachable, a granite stratum of spiritual fate, of

predetermined decision and answer to predetermined selected questions"
(162–63).[39] It is difficult to grasp how this idea fits together with Nietzsche's
ideas about self-transformation, as presented in the essay on history and
elsewhere. Nietzsche seemed to be of two minds about whether the fundamental character of an individual is fixed or changeable—ambivalence
on display in the following aphorism from *Human, All Too Human:*

> *The unalterable character.*—That the character is unalterable is not
> in the strict sense true; this favorite proposition means rather no
> more than that, during the brief lifetime of a man, the effective
> motives are unable to scratch deeply enough to erase the imprinted
> script of many millennia. If one imagines a man of eighty-thousand
> years, however, one would have in him a character totally alterable:
> so that an abundance of different individuals would evolve out of
> him one after the other. The brevity of human life misleads us to
> many erroneous assertions regarding the qualities of man. (35)

This aphorism, in ostensibly suggesting that the character is alterable,
strongly implies that for any given individual, it is not. Nietzsche implied
that certain individuals, for example Goethe, can transverse as much as
"four successive generations" in a lifetime (128).

But while the rare individual might be able to achieve many generations worth of change in one lifetime, Nietzsche more often talked about
an incremental type of change that would literally span generations: "An
ongrowing culture at once needs for its salvation another new generation,
which in its turn, however, does not get very far: for to *overtake* the culture
of his father the son must consume almost all the inherited energy the father himself possessed at the stage of life at which he begot his son; it is
with the little bit left over that he goes past him" (*Human, All Too Human,*
128). This language of incrementalism seems to get away from the sense
of radical change that is often associated with Nietzsche and is suggested
by the language of "self-transformation" and "exchanging a first nature for
a second one." But a transformation of the self does not necessarily mean
that a person has developed qualities that are the opposite of those they
had before. Nietzsche suggested that important change would resemble
mutation more than a complete transformation of that sort. "However
vigorously a man may develop and seem to leap over from one thing into
its opposite, closer observation will nonetheless discover the *dovetailing*

where the new building grows out of the old" (359). This suggests that the most important changes humans can make would span generations and reinforces the idea that parenthood would be the best way to pass on the product of a hard-won self-transformation and make it worthwhile. While Nietzsche's early concerns with finding a way both to inspire a self-transformation and to pass the results of that effort on led him toward thinking about procreation, this caveat regarding the limits of self-transformation only pushed him farther in that direction. The implication is that the results of this sort of self-transformation are most useful precisely when they accumulate across generations.

The Parent and the Culture

So despite Nietzsche's professions of hatred for Rousseau, each found it useful to bind self-transformation to ideas about parenthood. Rousseau hoped the promise of parenthood would channel the development of desire into a love of virtue—a self-transformation confirmed if our virtue inspires others to imitate us in turn. Nietzsche counseled the young to find an exemplar, and in coming to think of the exemplar as a parent, to be inspired to look within oneself and embark on one's own self-transformation. This would allow individuals to develop what was unique in them into an individuality that was worthy of passing on—something that could be passed on most effectively by becoming parents (or at least parental) themselves. Expressed more succinctly: "He who has founded something great . . . takes pains to rear heirs for himself" (*Human, All Too Human,* 188). These parallels do not mean that Rousseau's and Nietzsche's approaches to these matters were just the same. Rousseau hoped the promise of parenthood might inspire a person to acquire a particular and exacting quality of virtue. Nietzsche hoped that our self-transformation would accomplish something more individual and unique but also something we could pass on to a child.

Nietzsche's valorizations of the unique, the new, and the unpredictable are central to his appropriation by contemporary theorists of political contest. But so should be his ideas about how to communicate these qualities. New values and new interpretations are useless to the politics of contest if they are not communicated. The individual must relate to her culture if her efforts at self-creation are to have any effect, and the smallness of the typical effect of "genius" was one of Nietzsche's chief frustrations. So

Nietzsche wrestled with this question, as Rousseau had before him. In her appropriation of Nietzsche to explicate the politics of contest, Honig recommends special attention to this aspect of Nietzsche's thought. As mentioned earlier, she acknowledges that Nietzsche's politics "individuates" modern citizens more than it brings them together. But Honig suggests renewed attention to Nietzsche's interest in communicating what is profoundly difficult to communicate and creating communities around shared values and meanings. In this vein, Honig calls for scholars to "critically reconstruct an account of Nietzschean institutions."[40] She notes Nietzsche's claim that "for institutions to exist there must exist . . . solidarity between succeeding generations backwards and forwards ad infinitum."[41] In fact, this is where Honig leaves off her engagement with Nietzsche in articulating the politics of contest.

If we are to take Honig's advice and come to grips with this "underrated" aspect of Nietzsche's thought, it is necessary to examine the role of parenthood in overcoming the isolation of our uniqueness, in fostering solidarity between generations, and in helping make what is most individual in us "productive" and passing it on. Rousseau suggested we might broaden our individuality in the context of a small family-centered community in which one avoids the lonely isolation of the natural savage but will not become a slave to status and opinion like "the man accustomed to the ways of society [who] is always outside himself and knows how to live only in the opinion of others."[42] There are certain aphorisms in which Nietzsche's formulations on these matters sound much like the "the moral tarantula." For example, in *Human All Too Human,* he claimed:

> If a man has no sons he lacks full right to a voice in discussion of public affairs. . . . To possess a just and natural interest in the fate of institutions one has to have in view the happiness of one's posterity, and thus of course to possess posterity. The evolution of a higher morality in a person depends upon his having sons; the fact makes him unegoistic, or, more correctly, it broadens his egoism in respect of duration and enables him seriously to pursue objectives that transcend his individual lifespan. (167)

Egoism is broadened, yet one still remains most concerned with what is close. In this quote, it is the child who makes it possible to negotiate the bridge between the individual and community without losing oneself.

The role that having children can play in nudging the individual away from egoism is of particular interest because Nietzsche, particularly in thinking about "institutions," was deeply interested in the problem of how to strike a balance between individual and cultural meanings. It is a question he began exploring with his examination of the tension in ancient Greece between the Apollinian spirit of individuation and a countervailing Dionysian spirit in which "nature seems to . . . [heave] a sigh at her dismemberment into individuals" (*The Birth of Tragedy*, 40).[43] The crucial question, put musically, was "how the individual can be adapted to the enormously diversified demands of culture without being distracted by them and his individuality dispersed—in short, how can the individual be set in place within the counterpoint of private and public culture, how can he play the main theme and at the same time play the subordinate theme as well?" (*Human, All Too Human*, 116).

These concerns about the "dispersion" of "individuality" recall the preoccupations of the Schopenhauer essay. For example, speaking of the "practical activity" of self-transformation that the exemplar is meant to inspire, Nietzsche wrote,

> One thing above all is certain: these new duties are not the duties of a solitary; on the contrary, they set one in the midst of a mighty community held together . . . by a fundamental idea. It is the fundamental idea of *culture,* insofar as it sets for each one of us but one task: *to promote the production of the philosopher, the artist, and the saint within us and without us and thereby to work at the perfecting of nature.* ("Schopenhauer as Educator," 160)

In the Schopenhauer essay, it is precisely the commitment to critical self-examination and self-transformation that creates the community defined by a particular culture. "By coming to this resolve he places himself within the circle of *culture;* for culture is the child of each individual's self-knowledge and dissatisfaction with himself" (162–63). But if "culture is the child" of this work of self-transformation, one contributes to this culture in large part through one's child. Procreation bridges the work that goes on "within us" and our efforts to influence what is "without us." Parenthood, therefore, might serve as a bridge between the individual and culture.

While Nietzsche speaks in terms of a "mighty community," he more often sought this balance by considering how individuals could begin to consider themselves as members of small communities united by shared meaning. Just as Nietzsche thought it was more productive to entertain a personal rather than a metaphysical notion of progress, he would also en-courage his readers to think about their community in narrower terms—in terms of what is closest to them. Though Nietzsche hoped it was possible to find a balance between the demands of our individuality and the demands of community, he was wary that in the search for connectedness, individu-als might lose themselves—fail to think back on themselves, fail to find what was unique in themselves that might be made productive. He believed that people were far more likely to neglect the demands of their individual-ity, the call to find what was productive in their uniqueness, than they were to neglect the tug of community, particularly in a culture dominated by a morality of pity. In *The Gay Science,* he asked in frustration, "How is it at all possible to keep to one's own way?" (270).[44] The temptations were so great, in fact, that Nietzsche sometimes suggested the only answer might be soli-tude. "Live in seclusion so that you *can* live for yourself" (271).

But more often Nietzsche seemed to believe that a life of total seclusion tipped too far in the other direction. He allowed, therefore, that a person engaged in the great task may help others, "but only those whose distress you *understand* entirely because they share with you one suffering and one hope—your friends—and only in the manner in which you help yourself" (271).[45] You can think in terms of community, but you should still think in terms of what is very close. So close, in fact, that the members of your community share what is most central to your being—those very aspects of yourself that, as Nietzsche said elsewhere, cannot be communicated through words but might be passed on through procreation. Perhaps by having a child, a person could make such a friend rather than find one. As Zarathustra says, "Companions the creator once sought, and children of his hope; and behold, it turned out that he could not find them unless he first created them himself" (*Thus Spoke Zarathustra,* 273). But procre-ation, even if it represents "the real achievement of an individual," is not something that the individual can achieve on his or her own.[46] Thus one needs to find such a friend before making one—a possibility that would turn Nietzsche's mind to the small community of the family and the rela-tionship between men and women.

Marriage, Children, and Rest

When Nietzsche wrote in *Beyond Good and Evil* about the fixed and un-changeable "granite stratum of spiritual fate" that exists within each of us, he gave only one example: "About man and woman, for example, a thinker cannot relearn but only learn fully—only discover all that is 'firm and set-tled' within him on this subject." It was only after providing this caveat that Nietzsche felt he could be "permitted to utter a few truths about 'woman as such': assuming it is now understood from the outset to how great an extent these are only—my truths" (162–63). It was, of course, an aspect of Nietzsche's "spiritual fate" that had a profound impact on his ideas regarding the way in which a person can accomplish the "real achievement of the individual"—procreation. The passage is followed by a series of aphorisms about women and to a great extent about the role women play in procreation. "Man and woman" was one place where Nietzsche allowed his ideas to rest undisturbed and excused himself from the task of challenging his fundamental values.[47] This impulse to rest on the given, to resign from the politics of contest, to forgo openness to new interpretations, to cling to the same, also pervades Nietzsche's ideas about the project that man and woman take on together: family and parenthood.[48]

Nietzsche blamed this impulse to rest mostly on women. He worried that women would interfere with men's resolve to undertake the diffi-cult and unpredictable task of self-transformation as well as with their ability to pass it on to a child. He suggested, "The natural tendency of women towards a quiet, calm happily harmonious existence, the way they pour soothing oil on the sea of life, unwittingly works against the heroic impulse in the heart of the free spirit" (*Human, All Too Human,* 159). And he believed this was particularly a problem among wives: "Wives secretly intrigue against the higher being of their husbands; they desire to deprive them of their future for the sake of a quiet, comfortable pres-ent" (159).[49]

All this sounds dismissive of women as timid or complacent, but in *Human All Too Human,* Nietzsche offered a more thoughtful (though no less misogynistic) formulation that suggests more complex ties between his association of women with a satisfaction with the comforts of the given and his concerns with men's capacity for self-transformation.

Woman fulfils, man promises.—Through the woman nature shows the point it has by now reached in its work on the image of man-kind; through the man it shows what it had overcome in attaining to this point, but also what its *intentions* are with respect to mankind.— The complete woman of every era is the idleness of the creator on that seventh day in the creation of culture, the repose of the artist in his work. (278)

This notion of woman as repose, as rest, as a relief from the challenges of contest and self-transformation is part of what makes women compelling to men, Nietzsche believed. In *Daybreak,* he suggested that a reverence for custom and a hesitancy to challenge it is the source of women's beauty (20).

Perhaps to avoid the way woman's conservatism might interfere with man's "achievement" through procreation, Nietzsche often, notoriously, described woman as a mere vessel for the production of children. He suggested her "first and last profession . . . is to bear strong children" (*Beyond Good and Evil,* 168). Zarathustra remarks, "Man is for women a means: the end is always the child." Zarathustra then asks, "But what is woman for man?" (*Thus Spoke Zarathustra,* 178). He offers no answer. The larger context of Nietzsche's thought suggests it is more often the woman who is a means for man. The "end" in this case is a child who inherits the qualities that result from the man's hard work of self-transformation. The woman's role was to somehow give birth to and parent a child and yet leave this transmission undistorted.[50]

But Nietzsche worried that in modern times a woman might assert her own will and in doing so affect the child too much. He thought modern women "need children and wish for them in a way that is altogether different from that in which a man may wish for children" (*The Gay Science,* 71). In particular, he thought due to the shame that women can never quite divorce from sensuality, they experience their child as "an apology and an atonement" (71).[51] Of course, experiencing a child as atonement for moral failure is precisely the opposite of the idea that Nietzsche had developed of procreation as a person's most important achievement, one in which it is the ability to overcome and revalue morality that is crucial. Summing up his fears that the union of man and woman might somehow interfere with the transmission of the fruits of an individual's self-transformation, he wrote that if a "benevolent god" looked over mankind, it would be the marriages that frustrated this god most. The god would be pleased to see that there are individuals who manage to "go far" in their lifetime.

> But when one sees how he takes the legacy and inheritance of this struggle and victory, the laurel wreath of his humanity, and hangs it up at the first decent place where a little woman can get at it and pluck it to pieces: when one sees how well he knows how to gain but how ill to preserve, that he gives no thought to the fact, indeed, that through procreation he could prepare the way for an

even more victorious life: then, as aforesaid, one grows impatient and says to oneself: "nothing can come of mankind in the long run, its individuals are squandered, chance in marriage makes a grand rational progress of mankind impossible." (*Daybreak*, 97)

Nietzsche asked whether most marriages entered into on the "whim" of love would not turn out to be the "kind one would prefer not to be witnessed by a third party? But this third party is almost always present—the child" (151).

One way that Nietzsche dealt with the problems he saw inherent to marriage—its potential to discourage the hard work of self-transformation or to interfere with the communication of a man's accomplishments to his child—was to valorize an estrangement between the sexes—the "perpetual strife" he identified in the first sentence of his first book. Nietzsche subsequently made frequent and rarely critical references to the "eternal estrangement" of men and women and gave it central importance to his notion of the best sort of individual.

To blunder over the fundamental problem of "man and woman," to deny here the most abysmal antagonism and the necessity of an eternally hostile tension, . . . this is a *typical* sign of shallowmindedness, and a thinker who has proved himself to be shallow on this dangerous point—shallow of instinct!—may be regarded as suspect in general, more, as betrayed, as found out: he will probably be too 'short' for all the fundamental questions of life, those of life in the future too, incapable of *any* depth (*Beyond Good and Evil*, 166).[52]

To be wrong on this crucial matter, to Nietzsche, meant to give in to the temptation to abstain from the hard work of self-transformation that marked great individuals, from the sort of work that Honig describes as the "perpetual process of self-overcoming." Nietzsche noted that a man, as he dedicates himself to his own plans and projects, "is apt . . . to see quiet, magical beings gliding past him and to long for their happiness and seclusion: *women*." But Nietzsche urged men not give in to this promise of repose, to appreciate this vision from afar. He warned men not to search for their "better self" among women. "The magic and the most powerful effect of women is, in philosophical language, action at a distance, *actio in distans;* but this requires first of all and above all—*distance*" (*The Gay Science,* 124).

As a model of such distance, Nietzsche admired the marriages of the ancient Greeks. In describing why, Nietzsche revealed his attraction to a different sort of rest from the difficult work of questioning and refiguring inherited values. In Greek marriages, he thought, men paid very little attention "to commerce with women." Instead, "considerations of child-begetting and sensual pleasure—that was all that counted here; there was no spiritual commerce, not even an actual love affair" (*Human, All Too Human,* 121–22). Nietzsche appreciated the effect this arrangement had on procreation. It meant that Greek women were better able to pass on, without interfering with, what was important about the father. "The women had no other task than to bring forth handsome, powerful bodies in which the character of the father lived on as uninterruptedly as possible" (122). Such a contribution was crucial to everything that Nietzsche saw as great about the Greeks. "The Hellenic woman as mother had to live in obscurity, because the political instinct together with its highest aim demanded it."[53]

What the Greek woman offered to "the political instinct" and "its highest aim" was a place to rest and seek refuge from the challenge and continual contest of politics. According to Nietzsche, the Greek woman, because she was "obscure" and did not challenge the man, allowed for a sort of cultural respite from the demands of politics, contest, challenges, and self-overcoming. "In her nature lies the healing power, which replaces that which has been used up, the beneficial rest in which everything immoderate confines itself, the eternal same, by which the excessive and the surplus regulate themselves. In her the future generation dreams."[54]

In this vision of Greek women and Greek marriage, Nietzsche indulges in the attractions of a resting place, a shelter from the "immoderate" and ever-challenging aspects of political life among the Greeks. Nietzsche would also put the idea of marriage as a resting place and a respite from the challenges of self-overcoming into the mouth of the character Zarathustra. Zarathustra indulges in some hopes for the best sort of marriage and the children such a marriage would produce but ultimately rejects both for fear of falling into stagnation and a love of the same.

Zarathustra suggests we can judge "how deep" a person is if we know whether he is "a man entitled to a child." You are not entitled to this wish if "the animal and need" or "loneliness" or "lack of peace with yourself" is behind your desire for a child. But you are entitled if you are "the victorious

one, the self conqueror." Then you should "let your victory and your freedom long for a child" (*Thus Spoke Zarathustra*, 181). So while Zarathustra
was dismissive of modern marriage—marriages of the "all-too-many . . .
this filth of the soul in pair! Alas, this wretched contentment in pair! . . .
What child would not have cause to weep over its parents?" (182)—he
seemed to hope for the right sort of marriage for those who longed for a
child in the right way. "You shall build over and beyond yourself. . . . You
shall not only reproduce yourself, but produce something higher. May the
garden of marriage help you in that!" (181).[55]

But Zarathustra ultimately turns away from the idea of marriage and
children, even of the best kind. He repeats seven times the mantra: "Never
yet have I found the woman from whom I wanted children, unless it be this
woman whom I love: for I love you, O eternity" (340). Zarathustra prefers
"the nuptial ring of rings, the ring of recurrence" to a wife and child (341).
For much of the four volumes that bear his name, Zarathustra dreams
above all of one thing: "a genuine son and perfect heir" (395). His children
can be the spur for Zarathustra to do the work on himself that Nietzsche
valorizes—"for his children's sake, Zarathustra must perfect himself" (273).
But he also harbors a fear that his desire for an heir will be the very thing
that prevents his own perfection. He is afraid to be "chained to the love for
my children: desire set this snare for me—the desire for love that I might
become my children's prey and lose myself to them. Desire—this means
to me that I have lost myself. *I have you my children!* In this experience
everything shall be security and nothing desire" (274). By the end of the
book, Zarathustra seems to have rejected the idea of fatherhood altogether,
as anathema to the doctrine of eternal recurrence. "'I want heirs'—thus
speaks all that suffers; 'I want children, I do not want myself.' Joy, however,
does not want heirs, or children—joy wants itself, wants eternity, wants
recurrence, wants everything eternally the same" (434).

Such moments of Zarathustrian ecstasy, however, did not wipe away
Nietzsche's interest in the role of parenthood in his political vision even as
they suggest his fear that parenthood might induce a person to seek respite
from the difficulties of perpetual contest and revaluation. In considering
how it could be done, how marriage and parenthood might allow one to
pass on the fruits of one's hard work at self-transformation, Nietzsche indulged in his impulse to rest yet again—resting himself upon his "Dionysian
dowry" of underexamined "truths" about women.[56] When thinking opti-
mistically about marriage and parenting, Nietzsche frequently maintained

that the best sort of woman gives herself away completely and in doing so transforms herself all at once. For such women, according to Nietzsche, love means "total devotion with soul and body, without any consideration of reserve . . . [an] unconditional renunciation of rights of her own." This woman's way of loving "presupposes precisely that on the other side there is no equal pathos, no equal will to renunciation; for if both partners felt impelled by love to renounce themselves, we should then get—I do not know what; perhaps an empty space?" (*The Gay Science*, 319). Any woman who brings her own character into contact with the already transformed instincts of a man—the second nature he has managed to create for himself—can only diminish or muddle that accomplishment. So to participate in this sort of marriage, a woman must lose her own first nature and gain another, second nature that resembles the man's. But Nietzsche demanded that a woman accomplish all at once, due to love for a man, what a man needs a long time, or even a lifetime, to accomplish—"truly, a hard law for women," he admitted (*The Gay Science*, 126). According to Nietzsche, a woman's "spiritual power" was "best demonstrated by her sacrificing her own spirit to that of a man out of love for him and of his spirit but then, despite this sacrifice, immediately evolving a new spirit within the new domain, originally alien to her nature, to which the man's disposition impels her" (*Human, All Too Human*, 277). This sort of immediate self-transformation contradicts everything that Nietzsche said about the long and difficult struggle of transforming one's first nature into a second nature in *The Untimely Meditations*.[57]

Procreation as Symbol, and Faith in the Future

In the face of these difficulties and contradictions, Nietzsche pushed his ideas about how best to encourage "the procreation of genius" away from individuals and toward higher levels of aggregation and abstraction—toward discussions of the best sources of meaning for cultures broadly conceived. While Nietzsche had seized on procreation under very particular circumstances as a difficult "achievement" possible for a few rare individuals, he also came to generalize about the worthiness of whole cultures based upon their attitudes toward procreation. This was true when Nietzsche chose to condemn cultures en masse ("In all pessimistic religions the act of procreation is felt as being bad in itself" [*Human, All Too Human*, 76]), when he chose to endorse them as a group ("The act of procreation is the mystery as such of all nonascetic religions: the sort of symbol of perfection and of the mysterious design of the future: rebirth, immortality" [*The Will to Power*, 94]), and when he chose to single out particular cultures for praise ("The basic fact of the Hellenic instinct finds expression ... by the word Dionysus: ... the way of life, procreation, as the holy way" *Twilight of the Idols*, 561–62).

There is a different quality to Nietzsche's ideas about procreation when he was generalizing about cultures rather than working out the concerns with individual transformation (and the small communities of shared meaning that individuals create) that preoccupied him elsewhere. In Nietzsche's writing about cultures, a reverence for procreation takes on the qualities of a sort of magic formula for the affirmation of life rather than a part of a process that would be long and arduous and would require fierce self-examination. This is in part because Nietzsche seemed to want to get across that the effort to live his ideal would be moving, stirring, or enthralling, not just difficult. For example, among the ancient Greeks, a cultural reverence for procreation and sexuality represented

> the future promised and hallowed in the past; the triumphant Yes to life beyond all death and change; *true* life as the overall continuation of life through procreation, through the mysteries of sexuality ... , [is] the real profundity and the whole of ancient piety. Every single element in the act of procreation, of pregnancy, and of birth aroused the highest and most solemn feelings. In the doctrine of the mysteries, *pain* is pronounced holy: the pangs of the woman giving birth hallow all pain. (*Twilight of the Idols*, 561)

Such a cultural attitude contrasts with the Christian one in which hostility to sexuality and suspicion of procreation is indicative of a culture that does not accept pain and suffering as part of life but suffers *from* life and grasps onto the promise of redemption from life. For the Dionysian, as indicated by a reverence for procreation, life itself "is counted as *holy enough* to justify even a monstrous amount of suffering" (*The Will to Power*, 543).[58]

Nietzsche made attitudes toward procreation a blunt heuristic in his analysis of cultures past and present. His generalizations regarding cultures of the past were often paired with invocations regarding our orientation toward the future. While procreation, as the "real achievement" of the individual, meant passing on a form of life to the next generation, it did so through a focus on what was close by, whether physically, spiritually, or temporally. But Nietzsche's invocations of the future often became more expansive. Honig suggests that Nietzsche's thought "challenges man . . . to find within himself the capacity to reclaim (in transvalued form) the present moment."[59] But Nietzsche's invocations of the future obscure the importance of the hard work of self-transformation that he articulated elsewhere.

Nietzsche would pursue his ideas about the importance of the future in two problematic directions. In one case, he invoked increasingly abstract visions of a future salvation for modern man—often in ways that seem to violate his many warnings about the dangers of the metaphysical view in which the driving force of progress is something that exists over and above the substance of individual human lives. If the problem in that case is a creeping toward abstraction, the problem in the second case is with the specifics—in particular Nietzsche's exploration of how his objectives could be achieved through social control and of the disturbing concept of breeding as a political strategy to achieve the sort of future he envisioned.

Nietzsche made references to the importance of a belief in a better future throughout his work. As he jotted in one of his notebooks, "Fundamental thought: we must consider the future as decisive for all our evaluations— and not seek the laws of our actions *behind* us!" (*The Will to Power*, 519). Looking back all the same, Nietzsche made it clear that a profound faith in the future, like a profound reverence for procreation, was among the most important qualities of the ancients that was missing in modern times.

> —Bold and daring undertakings are rarer in the modern age than they were in ancient times, or in the Middle Ages—probably because the modern age no longer believes in omens, oracles, soothsayers or the stars. That is to say: we have become incapable of *believing in a future* determined for *us,* as did the ancients: who—in this quite different from us—were far less skeptical in regard to what was *coming* than they were in regard to what *is.* (*Daybreak*, 98–99)

Perhaps in an effort to counteract this modern quality, Nietzsche often expressed a faith in the possibility of creating a better future despite his frequently dismal assessments of his fellow moderns and their way of living. In the first two essays of *The Genealogy of Morals,* Nietzsche explained how, through the turning inward of ressentiment, there had developed over two millennia in Europe a morality "through which the present was possibly living at the expense of the future." (20) But even as he described how the future was being diminished, Nietzsche looked to it for salvation. At the end of the second essay, Nietzsche declared: "This man of the future, who will redeem us not only from the hitherto reigning ideal but also from that which was bound to grow out of it, the great nausea, the wheel to nothingness, nihilism; . . . this Antichrist and antinihilist; this victor over God and nothingness—*he must come one day*" (96).

Despite the tone of such a passage, Nietzsche's ideas on self-transformation and procreation suggest that Nietzsche's faith in the future was *not* a belief that a great man or a savior would arrive from on high, like a quasi-Christian second coming, to redeem the species.[60] Rather, the faith in the future that Nietzsche envisioned as the proper source of meaning for modern man was a specialized version of faith in oneself. But this faith could be hard to hold. Nietzsche did not seem optimistic about the possibility of a vision of the future being conjured in a way that was tangible and compelling enough to inspire individuals to the difficult task of transforming themselves. He thought that those who undertook the task of organizing the chaos within themselves, "that first generation of fighters and dragon-slayers which will precede a happier and fairer culture and humanity," would have to do so "without itself having more than a presentiment of this future happiness and beauty" ("On the Uses and Disadvantages of History," 121).

But at the same time, Nietzsche seemed remarkably optimistic about the existence of contemporaries who might respond to this call despite the difficulty of the task and the diaphanous quality of the vision of future happiness. He expressed confidence that there was a group of "hopeful young people" who would "understand all these generalities from close personal experience and will translate them into a teaching intended for themselves" ("On the Uses and Disadvantages of History," 121). Eventually, Nietzsche grew less confident on this point. Revisiting his early books with new prefaces, Nietzsche would entertain the idea that "perhaps" he had deceived himself "over the Germans and their future." The sort of readers he had hoped for "do not exist, did not exist" (*Human, All Too Human*, 6). But having failed to find those who might be inspired to transform themselves by a vision of the future, Nietzsche clung to a faith that the future would bring them. So necessary is a faith in the future to Nietzsche's vision that he grasped at *a faith in a future faith in the future*. Thus even as he acknowledged his self-deception, Nietzsche absolutely insisted "that our Europe *will* have such active and audacious fellows among its sons of tomorrow and the next day, physically present and palpable and not, as in my case, merely phantoms and hermit's phantasmagoria. . . . I see them already coming, slowly, slowly" (6). While digesting this condition of antepenultimatism, Nietzsche looked for signs that "a more virile, warlike age is about to begin. . . . For this age shall prepare the way for one yet higher, and it shall gather the strength that this higher age will require some day" (*The Gay Science,* 228)[61]

Derrida offers a reading of this aspect of Nietzsche's thought in *The Politics of Friendship.* He suggests that in "feigning to record" the coming of the philosophers of the future, Nietzsche was seeking a way to create a feeling of community that nonetheless allows for distance and isolation. The figure of the philosopher of the future, in other words, was another way for the individual to relate to the culture without getting lost in it, to communicate and also keep to one's own path. In Nietzsche's call for philosophers of the future, suggests Derrida, "the invitation comes to you from those who can *love only at a distance, in separation . . .* who love only in cutting ties." The resulting friendship would be bearable to Nietzsche because in its distance it is "without familial bond, without proximity . . . therefore without resemblance."[62] Derrida suggests that such philosophers of the future, isolated even in friendship, are "capable of enduring the intolerable."[63] But Nietzsche, as I discuss later, found cutting ties to be especially difficult, even unendurable, in the context of parenthood where proximity and resemblance are most closely felt.

Whether it was born of frustration with his contemporaries or a desire for friendship that maintained distance, Nietzsche was not long satisfied to simply hope for a future in which individuals might undertake the sort of work on the self he envisioned. He noted that hope for future redemption had been one of the most powerful tools of Christian morality and that hope was considered by the Greeks to be "the evil of evils, the truly insidious evil" because of "its ability to keep the unfortunate in continual suspense" (*The Antichrist,* 591). Nietzsche wanted his vision of the future, even the distant future that the antepenultimates would never see themselves, to motivate his contemporaries to forge a better way of life. But he also warned, "When one places life's center of gravity not in life but in the 'beyond'—*in nothingness*—one deprives life of its center of gravity altogether" (618).

Nietzsche originally examined parenthood and procreation as an impetus to set to work on what was central to our lives and our selves and to pass the fruits of our accomplishments on to the future. Parenthood was a way to not simply hope for but to *build* the future out of the substance of our own lives, to place life's center of gravity at least somewhere partway between our own lives and the beyond. But because it was hard to bring that beyond quite close enough—to imagine that the future would really inspire a generation of antepenultimates to take on the hard work of self-transformation—Nietzsche occasionally engaged in a variety of thought that moved in the opposite direction from his invocations of increasingly abstract and distant sources of "hope." In these moments, Nietzsche indulged visions of exerting a more direct control in the development of the sort of culture he hoped for. This path took Nietzsche in the direction of his imagery of "Züctung"—breeding.[64]

Breeding, Domination, and Ressentiment

Nietzsche's interest in breeding was the bitter amalgam of the Nietzsche who liked to generalize about cultures of the past and future and the Nietzsche who wanted to remind individuals to undergo the slow, difficult work of transforming themselves. For Nietzsche, breeding became a way to think about the work that would go into using reproduction on a cultural level to create the conditions in which the great man, the genius, was more likely to emerge. In giving so much importance to a vision of the future and a connection to the future through procreation, Nietzsche gave rise to, and sometimes gave in to, a desire to exercise control over the uncontrollable over an extended period of time. The idea was built into Nietzsche's very definition of breeding: "Breeding, as I understand it, is a means of storing up the tremendous forces of mankind so that the generations can build upon the work of their forefathers—not only outwardly, but inwardly, organically growing out of them and becoming something stronger" (*The Will to Power*, 215). Marriage and parenthood were central to Nietzsche's vision of breeding. So in listing the qualities that distinguish "good Europeans," Nietzsche included "preparation for becoming the legislators of the future, the masters of the earth, at least our children. Basic concern with marriages" (81).

Nietzsche's interest in breeding, with its ties to marriage and parenting, seems rooted in his conviction that people should take on the difficult work

of questioning their fundamental values and transforming their lives—
and should pass on the results of that hard work through parenthood.
Nonetheless, ideas about breeding became another place where Nietzsche
indulged in the desire to escape from the challenges of openness to self-
transformation—to betray the aspect of his thought that democratic theorists have come to admire most. Nietzsche himself praised aristocratic
communities that "breed and cultivate" a few specific qualities—"these
qualities it calls virtues"—through close attention to "the measures it
takes with respect to women, in marriage customs" (*Beyond Good and
Evil*, 200). The result was not change, openness, or variety but rather "a
type with few but very marked traits . . . firmly fixed beyond the changes
of generations" (200).

The point of breeding was control rather than openness to contingency. Nietzsche called for a "new philosopher" who would "prepare for
great enterprises and collective experiments in discipline and breeding
so as to make an end of that gruesome dominion of chance and nonsense
that has hitherto been called 'history'" (*Beyond Good and Evil*, 126).[65] This
would mean, most importantly, control over parenthood. It would be super-
vised and, in some cases, encouraged:

> *On the future of marriage:* . . . advantages of all kinds for fathers
> who bring many boys into the world: possibly a plural vote; a
> medical certificate preceding every marriage and endorsed by the
> communal authorities, several definite questions must be an-
> swered by the couple and by the doctors ("family history"—); . . .
> every marriage warranted and sanctioned by a certain number of
> men in the community, as a matter of concern to the community.
> (*The Will to Power*, 388)

In other cases, it would be discouraged:

> In numerous cases, society ought to prevent procreation: to this
> end it may hold in readiness, without regard to descent, rank or
> spirit, the most rigorous means of constraint, deprivation of
> freedom, in certain cases castration.—The biblical prohibition
> "thou shalt not kill!" is a piece of naiveté compared with the
> seriousness of the prohibition of life to decadents: "thou shalt
> not procreate." (389)[66]

It is hard not to be disturbed by Nietzsche's images of the political or ideational control of marriage and reproduction. But a certain element of control and domination existed in his emphasis on parenthood from the beginning. After all, while Nietzsche spoke a great deal about individuals transforming themselves, rarely did he encourage parents to help their children to transform themselves in turn. For Nietzsche, like the Greeks, the child was there to preserve the character of the father. Nietzsche thought a parent's desire to dominate often supplemented a child's efforts to learn by imitation.

> Parents involuntarily make of their child something similar to themselves—they call it "education"—and at the bottom of her heart no mother doubts that in her child she has borne a piece of property, no father disputes his right to subject it to *his* concepts and values. Indeed in former times ... it seemed proper for fathers to possess power of life or death over the newborn and to use it as they saw fit. (*Beyond Good and Evil*, 117–18)[67]

This most "natural" form of domination served as the model for more "civilized" forms. "And as formally the father, so still today the teacher, the class, the priest, the prince unhesitatingly see in every new human being an opportunity for a new possession. From which it follows...." (*Beyond Good and Evil*, 118).

That is Nietzsche's ellipsis that follows "follows." What does follow the ellipsis raises an intriguing question about Nietzsche's use of images of breeding. What comes next is an aphorism about the Jews—describing Jews as a people considered by "the whole ancient world" as "born for slavery" (118). The aphorism traces Nietzsche's alternative history of morality in which the Jews were able to achieve a "miracle of inversion of values," which began "the *slave revolt in morals*" (118). This is the story of the triumph of ressentiment, which Nietzsche would later describe in detail in *The Genealogy of Morals*. What is the significance of Nietzsche's introducing the slave revolt in morality after hanging that intriguing ellipsis off an aphorism about the ways parents control and dominate their children?

It could point toward the possibility that both Nietzsche's vision of the political uses of parenthood and his related ideas about breeding would feed into a cycle that would continually re-create the conditions for ressentiment—failing to take us beyond good and evil but leaving us trapped between them in a condition of stagnation. Regarding the sort of person he hoped would result from projects of breeding, Nietzsche wrote, "The higher form of being . . . needs the opposition of the masses, of the leveled, a feeling of distance from them! He stands on them. He lives off them" (*The Will to Power,* 464).[68] It is hard not to hear echoes of the ancient idea of the race "born for slavery" in these words. So it is hard not to think of the inversion of values that Nietzsche believed those "born for slavery" achieved. Perhaps breeding cannot help but breed ressentiment in turn. Perhaps the domination inherent to parenthood cannot either.[69]

It might be for these reasons that Nietzsche expressed his resignation regarding the prospects of breeding a stronger type of human in his notebooks. "If only we *could* foresee the most favorable conditions under which creatures of the highest value arise! It is a thousand times too complicated and the probability of failure very great: so it is not inspiring to look for them!—Skepticism—" (*The Will to Power,* 480). Such skepticism convinced Nietzsche to focus on the individual, on what is immediate and close, and the work that the individual must undertake to craft something new from her inheritance with no certainty of the outcome. "On the other hand: we can increase courage, insight, hardness, independence and the feeling of responsibility; we can make the scales more delicate and hope for favorable accidents" (480). In other words, the answer is a turning back toward the work on the self, the creation of the genius *within us,* that Nietzsche had explored since the essay on Schopenhauer. As he restated it in *The Will to Power,* "The actual *creation* of such conditions as are created by chance presupposes iron men who have never yet lived. The immediate task is to make the personal ideal prevail and become real!" (480–81).

Betraying the Child

In these moments of abandoning breeding for the cultivation of the personal ideal, was Nietzsche also turning away from procreation as a way to pass on the fruits of one's self-mastery—away from procreation's role in the effort to foster the genius not only within us but also "without" us? The answer is not clear. It often seems as if Nietzsche's ideal human was actually divided into pairs of types.[70] What is most important in any pair is the ability to move between those types, to experience them both, to switch perspectives. In many of those pairings, procreation and parenthood are central to the way of life of just one of those types in the pair.

But it is precisely because procreation is central to one of these types that moving back and forth within each pair can be difficult.

Nietzsche began developing the importance of dual perspectives with his exploration of the Apollinian and Dionysian in *The Birth of Tragedy*. But he most directly developed the importance of an individual being able to switch perspectives in regard to himself in his last book, the auto-biographical *Ecce Homo*. There he discussed the opposing perspectives he had inherited from his mother and father, which allowed him to experience life from "the highest and lowest rung on the ladder of life, at the same time a decadent and a beginning . . . I know both, I am both" (222). Nietzsche suggested this one point was the key to understanding his importance. "Now I know how, have the know-how, to *reverse perspectives*: the first reason why a 'revaluation of values' is perhaps possible for me alone" (223). As a child of these parents Nietzsche can reverse perspectives, but only because each parent embodied that perspective completely. What happens when a person who can reverse perspectives acts as a parent in turn? Nietzsche does not offer an answer.

Mother and father are not the only pair of human types in which procreation plays a key role in forming the pair. Another pair that Nietzsche considered was those who store up energy or capacities and those who expend them—usually figured as the ancestor and the heir. The central activity that marks the ancestor in this pairing is the living of a "preparatory life," or the "storing up" of energy. Any energy or capacity that has "gradually been accumulated . . . waits for an heir that might squander it" (*The Gay Science*, 298). Thus it is only the sacrifice of ancestors and parents that makes great individuals and great deeds possible.

> The great capabilities of the individual are utterly out of proportion to what he himself has done, sacrificed, and suffered for them. But if one considers his family history, one discovers the history of a tremendous storing up and capital accumulation of strength through all kinds of renunciation, struggle, work and prevailing. . . . One's forebears have paid the price for what one is. (*The Will to Power*, 508)

Nietzsche sometimes wrote as if one is fated to take on one of these roles or the other. Thus, in answering the question "How do men attain great strength and a great task?" Nietzsche offered two answers. One sounds like hard work—much like the work Nietzsche associated with self-transformation inspired by the possibility of passing the results on as a parent. "All the virtues and efficiency of the body and soul are acquired laboriously and little by little, through much industry, self-constraint, limitation, through much obstinate, faithful repetition of the same labors, the same renunciation" (*The Will to Power*, 518). Some, however, are fortunate enough to have the opportunity for another sort of life—more like an heir than a parent. Nietzsche continued,

> But there are men who are the heirs and masters of this slowly-acquired manifold treasure of virtue and efficiency—because, through fortunate and reasonable marriages, and also through fortunate accidents, the acquired and stored up energies of many generations have not been squandered and dispersed but linked together by a firm ring and by will. In the end there appears a man, a monster of energy, who demands a monster of a task. (518)

The important question is whether it is possible to attain the perspectives of both one who stores and one who expends, both parent and heir, in one lifetime.

Nietzsche suggests that it is possible, if difficult, to move in one direction across this pair. A person could take whatever quality of energy he or she has inherited and undertake the laborious efforts necessary to channel that energy into the "virtues and efficiency" that allow a person to take upon himself or herself a great task.

> The highest and most illustrious human joys, in which existence celebrates its own transfiguration, come, as is reasonable, only to the rarest and best-constituted men; and even to these *only when they themselves and their ancestors* have lived long preparatory lives toward this goal. Then an overflowing wealth of the most multifarious forces . . . dwell amicably together in one man. (540, emphasis added)

But it does not seem possible to move the other way. Those great individuals who emerge thanks to the tremendous storing up of energy across generations will expend that energy and leave little to pass on. The wealth of creative energy does not merely overflow but is poured out upon the great task. As such, great individuals do not make good ancestors, and persons of the highest type do not make good parents.[71] Nietzsche noted,

> The meager fruitfulness of the highest and most cultivated spirits and the classes that pertain to them, the circumstance that they are frequently unmarried and are sexually cool in general, is essential to the economy of mankind: reason recognizes and makes use of the fact that at the outmost point of spiritual evolution the danger of a *nervously unsound* posterity is very great: such people are the great peaks of mankind—they must not taper off into little peaks. (*Human, All Too Human*, 359)

So while an individual can move from the perspective of one who stores to one who expends, it is much harder to move in the opposite direction and lead an effectively preparatory life for the next generation. Such a person becomes useless for the task of procreation and parenthood and for the progress of culture.

That is perhaps a small price to pay to taste the highest sort of existence. For Nietzsche, a single great human can justify a great deal, even some useless progeny. So perhaps the more important question is whether individuals who have lived a preparatory life and gone the additional step to procreate (with a fortunate marriage, et cetera) in such a way that they pass on the crucial qualities or energy that they managed to attain can then switch perspectives and engage in the highest sort of activities. One way to think of this is in terms of another pair: the father and the philosopher. This pair was introduced in opposition to each other in the Schopenhauer essay, where Nietzsche noted that fathers generally do not want their sons to be philosophers. In *Human, All Too Human*, he suggested that fathers are not suited to be philosophers themselves:

> It is laughable . . . when the childless participate in a country's practical lawgiving. For they have insufficient ballast in their ship to be able safely to set sail into the ocean of the future. But it appears equally absurd when he who has chosen for his task the most universal knowledge and the evaluation of the totality of existence burdens himself with personal considerations of family, nutrition, security, care of wife and child, and extends before his telescope that dark veil through which scarcely a ray from the distant firmament is

able to penetrate. In affairs of the highest philosophical kind all married men are suspect. (160)[72]

It seems that marrying and parenting make it impossible to switch perspectives. What is it about the veil introduced by family that makes it so impenetrable?

Nietzsche thought that important experiences required a willingness to be veiled for a time and blind to alternatives. *"Do not want to see prematurely.*—For as long as one is experiencing something one must give oneself up to the experience and close one's eyes: that is to say, not be an observer of it while still *in the midst* of it" (*Human, All Too Human,* 385–86). Even an experience that was on its surface a distraction from the work of self-cultivation could actually be useful toward the overall goal.

> From this point of view, even the *blunders* of life have their own meaning and value . . . forgetting oneself, *misunderstanding* oneself, making oneself smaller, narrower, mediocre, become reason itself. Morally speaking: neighbor love, living for others and other things *can* be a protective measure for preserving the hardest self-concern. This is the exception where, against my wont and conviction, I side with the 'selfless' drives: here they work in the service of *self-love, of self-discipline.* (*Ecce Homo,* 254)

Why would having children not be an instance of this sort of living for others that ultimately works in the service of self-discipline?

It seems that Nietzsche thought it could be too hard to get away from the perspective of being a parent once a person had begun to raise a child. It was important to Nietzsche that the blunders and sicknesses of life, though valuable, not become the *substance* of a person's life. He thought a person could afford sickness only if he or she were not a fundamentally sick person—a point he developed regarding himself: "As *summa summarum,* I was healthy; as an angle, as a specialty, I was a decadent. . . . I took myself in hand, I made myself healthy again: the condition for this . . . is *that one be healthy at bottom.* . . . For a typically healthy person . . . being sick can even become an energetic stimulus for life, for living *more*" (*Ecce Homo,* 224). Nietzsche seemed to worry that a person could not be a parent without being a parent *at bottom* and losing themselves in the process.

Nietzsche preferred that if a person lose himself or herself, it be temporary. He wrote, "I love brief habits" (*The Gay Science*, 236). Honig highlights this aspect of Nietzsche's thought—the idea that Nietzsche accepts "some measure of constancy" and does not demand "perpetual improvisation"— in her account of the uses of Nietzsche for a democratic politics of contest. This is an important part of what Honig calls Nietzsche's "recovery of responsibility"—to impose some order on a part of the world, to make a claim about how to live and to *believe in it*, but also to know that such claims are contingent and subject to change or abandonment. Though Nietzsche calls these habits "brief," the love he expressed for them was earnest and deeply felt. He did not mean that we should take these experiences lightly simply because they will end. "I always believe that here is something that will give me lasting satisfaction—brief habits, too, have this faith in eternity. . . . But one day its time is up; the good thing parts from me" (*The Gay Science*, 236). Such partings are not easy because the love we feel for a particular idea of the good, a particular value or way of life, is earnest and deeply felt.[73]

As we have seen, Nietzsche often conceived of these claims in terms of parenthood. We can be inspired to transform our values and craft a new way to live by the idea of passing on the results of our hard work to a child. But raising a child, loving a child, and passing on a form of life to a child is a habit that is not brief. A child will part from his or her parents eventually, but the parting might not come quickly or thoroughly enough for Nietzsche. "*Enduring* habits I hate . . . constant association with the same people, a permanent domicile, or unique good health" (*The Gay Science*, 236). But more importantly, the love for a child can be something felt so deeply that the parting can be too painful. When Nietzsche argued that only fathers have "full right to a voice in discussion of public affairs," he explained: "One has to have staked, with the others, that which one loves best" (*Human, All Too Human*, 167). Nietzsche wrote about the good things in his life that had taken their leave of him, but what is the effect of losing that which "one loves best"?

Harder still is taking the active role in parting—of leaving, even betraying, what you had cared about. These betrayals that we author ourselves are the most painful but also necessary if we are not to stagnate. "We cannot advance from one period of our life into the next without passing through these pains of betrayal and then continuing to suffer them" (*Human, All Too Human*, 199).[74] And what we have to betray is precisely those earnest and deeply felt new values and accounts of the good that we craft in our lives, the ones we hope to pass on to our children. "That a man must, in subsequent cold sobriety, continue to adhere to what he has said, promised, resolved in passion—this demand is among the heaviest burdens that oppress mankind. To be obliged to recognize the consequences... of an enthusiastic devotion, for all future time" (198). Nietzsche found this unacceptable. "Are we advised to be faithful to our errors, even when we realize that through this faithfulness we are injuring our higher self?—No, there exists no law, no obligation, of this kind; we *have* to become traitors, be unfaithful, again and again abandon our ideals" (198–99). If the children we raise are the result of a sort of promise resolved in passion, perhaps Nietzsche believed parents must become traitors to their children as well.

In elliptical ways, Nietzsche suggested as much. He wrote, cryptically, that "fathers have much to do to make amends for having sons" (*Human, All Too Human*, 150). And he allowed the child to imagine that the parent should have been a traitor of sorts: "In the maturity of his life and understanding a man is overcome by the feeling that his father was wrong to beget him" (150). Nietzsche suggested it is because the "free spirit... has to learn to love what he formerly hated and the reverse" that he is not "created for a happy marriage" (158).[75] But why the indirect approaches? Perhaps it was simply too painful for Nietzsche to suggest the necessity of betraying the project embodied in one's own child. Nietzsche knew "it is so hard to hurt people" (*The Gay Science*, 249) but insisted no one "will attain anything great if he does not find in himself the strength and the will to *inflict* great suffering" (255). But to inflict such suffering on a child, the thing one "loves best," might be too much. Is this why the free spirit cannot become a parent, and a parent cannot become a free spirit—why in this case it is impossible to reverse perspectives and transvalue the values wrapped up in one's experience of parenthood? Rousseau encountered such suffering in abandoning his children and felt his life was never the same. Nietzsche never had children but gained perspective on such suffering through his own family drama.

In Rousseau's family drama, as discussed in chapter 1, he was afraid that his children would grow up to betray him. Looking at things from the child's perspective, Nietzsche feared he had betrayed his father.[76] In 1882, Nietzsche's mother told him that his writings were so shameful as to defile the tomb of his father. At the time, Nietzsche packed his trunk and left her house immediately. Six months later, he was still enraged and wrote to a friend that he had not "for one moment gotten away from the thought" of what his mother had said. Compared to the betrayal of which his mother accused him, "a pistol shot is a relatively welcome thought."[77] Strong traces Nietzsche's rage at this incident to a passage meant for *Ecce Homo* in which Nietzsche denies his relation to his own parents. Nietzsche suggested that he is not related to his mother and sister ("to believe myself related to such *canaille* would be a blasphemy on my godliness") nor even to his father: "One is least related to one's parents: it would be the surest sign of commonness, to be related to one's parents. Higher natures have their origins much farther back. . . . I don't understand it, but Julius Caesar could have been my father—or Alexander, this embodied Dionysus."[78] The tone of this passage is quite different from the one it was meant to replace, in which Nietzsche's father is praised heavily ("I consider it a great privilege to have had such a father") and his mother is given no worse treatment than that she is "something very German" (*Ecce Homo*, 225).

Here we are dealing with the reverse situation from the one discussed previously. It is the son who has changed his perspective and in doing so betrayed his parents. Strong gives the passage from *Ecce Homo* a suggestive reading. He says that for Nietzsche to feel that he has truly escaped from one form of life into another, to truly feel that he has transformed himself, he must "annihilate" his genealogy, become "his own progenitor on earth," be "chthonically reborn, this time of himself alone."[79] But, Strong believes, psychologically this is perilous for Nietzsche to attempt: "The discovery of his new self, nonfamilial in character, coincides with the onset of his insanity. . . . To live without Heimat [homeland], as Nietzsche knew himself to be doing, is to live in the end in a dangerous and world historical gamble."[80] Strong refuses to draw a specific conclusion from all this. "We admire Nietzsche that he dared to go into it with a full sense of what lay behind. We do not say if the possible outcomes are endurable. If not, however, then we will have to revise the wisdom of Marsyas: it will be a far better thing not to have been born, than to have been born of oneself."[81]

Strong's reading of the difficulties, perhaps the unbearable difficulties, of Nietzsche's sense of abandoning and betraying his parents can help clarify the stakes involved in betraying a commitment to procreation—betraying one's child. In developing his reading, Strong calls attention to Nietzsche's reflections in *The Birth of Tragedy* on the myth of Oedipus, who killed his father, married his mother, and solved the riddle of the Sphinx. Nietzsche interpreted the Oedipus myth to mean that where prophetic and magical powers have broken the spell of present and future, the rigid law of individuation, and the real magic of nature, some enormously unnatural event—such as incest—must have occurred earlier, as a cause. How else could one compel nature to surrender her secrets if not by triumphantly resisting her, that is, by means of something unnatural. . . . Indeed, the myth seems to wish to whisper to us that wisdom, and particularly Dionysian wisdom, is an unnatural abomination; that he who by means of his knowledge plunges nature into the abyss of destruction must also suffer the dissolution of nature in his own person. (*The Birth of Tragedy*, 69)

The "dissolution of nature in our own person" could be recast to include the betrayal of the child to whom we have passed on our nature. Oedipus started life as a victim of an attempted infanticide. If incest and parricide can force wisdom from nature, then perhaps infanticide could as well. In the last year of his sanity, Nietzsche scrawled into his notebooks, "Dionysus cut to pieces is a *promise* of life: it will be eternally reborn and return again from destruction" (*The Will to Power*, 543). Dionysus was cut to pieces as an infant.[82]

Nietzsche had said that procreation was the real achievement of the individual. This was because procreation represented individuals' best means to communicate *outside* themselves the fruits of their achievement *within* themselves—to pass on the second nature with which they had replaced their first. So perhaps the person who attempts to betray his or her child, who attempts to revalue the values embodied in the project of procreation, risks the dissolution of his or her own nature. Who knows if its outcomes are endurable either? The problem that Rousseau endured his whole adult life is the one question from which Nietzsche seemed to shrink. Nietzsche's thought suggests that while the idea of parenthood might inspire us to the politics of contest, the *experience* of parenthood can have the opposite effect.

The young Nietzsche of *The Untimely Meditations* hoped to inspire his readers to give themselves a goal, a possible achievement, that would inspire them to re-create themselves. As he urged in the essay on history, "Do ask yourself why you, the individual, exist, and if you can get no other answer try for once to justify the meaning of your existence as it were *a posteriori* by setting before yourself an aim, a goal, a 'to this end,' an exalted

and noble 'to this end'" ("On the Uses and Disadvantages of History," 112).
Parenthood represented one way to think about this goal. It represented
a tangible experience in which individuals could feel that they were passing on the essence of themselves—and allowing the personal transformation they had accomplished to contribute to the work of progress. But the
problem with figuring the goal this way, with calling procreation "the real
achievement" of the individual, is that a person is likely to become deeply
attached to this particular accomplishment. In passing on a form of life to
a child, the person could render himself or herself unable to revalue the
values embodied in that way of life.

The issue here is one of responsibility. Honig made the notion of
responsibility—the need to take responsibility for the values we articulate
and also to continually challenge ourselves to reconsider our convictions—
central to her reclamation of Nietzsche for the democratic politics of contest. But a parent's sense of responsibility seems to undermine the aspects
of Nietzsche that are most useful to Honig and other theorists of agonal
politics. By making procreation a goal, by figuring procreation as the individual's "real achievement," Nietzsche ran into the problem that we feel a
different sort of responsibility for the goals we set for ourselves when we
achieve them through *embodying that achievement in another person.* It is
hard not to feel responsible for our children and for the instincts, values,
talents, and habits that we pass on to them, if only by their witness of our
way of living. Emerson, the contemporary whom Nietzsche most admired,
wrote, "Every spirit makes its house, but afterwards the house confines the
spirit."[83] For Nietzsche, it was the way we populate our house that mattered most, and it was through parenting that we take the active role and
confine ourselves. Perhaps that is why, in *Twilight of the Idols,* he denied
the very relationship between parents and children that he had sought to
explain in so many of the aphorisms that came before. Nietzsche, who had
written "one pays a price for being the child of one's parents" (*The Gay
Science,* 290), later wrote:

> What alone can be *our* doctrine? That no one *gives* man his
> qualities—neither God, nor society, nor his parents and ancestors,
> nor he himself. . . . No one is responsible for man's being there at
> all. . . . That nobody is held responsible any longer . . . that alone is
> the great liberation; with this alone is the innocence of becoming
> restored. (*Twilight of the Idols,* 500–501)

This resistance to responsibility is not in itself problematic for those who would enlist Nietzsche's ideas for the democratic politics of contest. Honig suggests that "Nietzsche's recovery of responsibility" incorporates, rather than denies or punishes, our tendency to resist even those responsibilities we assume. Nietzsche's view of the self, she suggests, is of

> an original multiplicity that is enabled by, but also resistant to, its formation into a responsible subjectivity. Nietzsche's alternative ethic values not the construction and maintenance of any single form of subjectivity, but a commitment to a perpetual process of self-overcoming that offsets and (artistically) engages the tendency of sedimented identities and forms of life to engender remainders.[84]

Explaining further, however, Honig reduces that multiplicity to a duality, one reminiscent of Nietzsche's persistent use of pairs. She suggests we consider Nietzsche's ideal, the overman, as a "part of all selves," which will "democratize the figure and its effects." The other half of the pair is the "herd," which represents "those parts of the self that prefer the familiar, predictable routines of the subjectivity that constitutes them to the unknowns of a Nietzschean self-overcoming."[85]

Honig's dual self is certainly a productive way to reconfigure Nietzschean ideas for democratic purposes. But in a democratic society that privileges parenthood as a political identity, we should attend to the difficulties that parenthood introduced to Nietzsche's own efforts to think in pairs and move between them. For Nietzsche, our "formation into a responsible subjectivity" was often wrapped up with our becoming a parent.[86] That particular approach made it difficult to abandon "the construction and maintenance" of the identity we construct for ourselves and reengage with the "process of self-overcoming." Nietzsche's ideas suggest reasons why parenthood tempts us to settle and control rather than challenge and reconfigure: settle on our ideas about ourselves, about gender, about our culture, and control our children and the influences they might encounter.

Turning to contemporary political theory, the next chapters explore two theorists, Rorty and West, who create their own dualisms in an attempt to strike a balance between the challenges of contest and the comforts of virtue. In doing so, they re-create and reconfigure the pathologies of the parent as citizen for contemporary times.

CHAPTER 3

Troubled Inheritance: Richard Rorty and the Metaphysics of the Child

We can never embrace . . . a single person, but embrace the whole of her or his family romance.

Harold Bloom

To the devil with the child, the only thing we ever will have discussed, the child, the child, the child.

Jacques Derrida

A s A TEENAGER, the American philosopher Richard Rorty liked to hike through the mountains of northwest New Jersey searching for wild orchids. On these hikes, Rorty began to invest deep significance into an intoxicating admixture of sexuality, evolutionary superiority, and the avoidance of pain. Just being alone in nature helped Rorty avoid pain, since bullies from his high school often beat him up when they could find him. It was the orchids that added the other ingredients. As Rorty put it,

> I was not quite sure why those orchids were so important, but I was convinced that they were. . . . I was also convinced that there was a deep significance in the fact that the orchids are the latest and most complex plants to have been developed in the course of evolution. Looking back, I suspect that there was a lot of sublimated sexuality involved.[1]

That amalgam of superior complexity, sex, and the avoidance of cruelty went on to play an important role in the thought of the adult Richard Rorty. If it was in "looking back" that Rorty perceived the sublimated sexuality involved in his love of orchids, it is through the importance he placed on looking forward that procreation and parenthood, where sexuality and evolution meet, became central in his thinking about citizenship and his notions of politics as the management of cruelty and humiliation.

In offering his account of democratic citizenship at the turn of the twenty-first century, Rorty incorporated elements of both Rousseau's politics of virtue and Nietzsche's politics of contest. In doing so, Rorty crafted an enormously popular version of contemporary American citizenship— one that seemed hopeful, practical, and progressive. It was also an account of citizenship that engaged the ideas of Nietzsche and his contemporary interpreters regarding contest, self-transformation, and openness to questioning and transforming values. It was an important part of Rorty's success that in his work from the 1980s through the turn of the century he was able to incorporate the insights of postmodern and critical theorists. He repackaged postmodern ideas into something that could coexist with a form of American patriotism, affirm citizens' practical ability to improve society and our politics, and offer a hopeful version of citizenship. Rorty made it possible to engage the new and preserve the old, to acknowledge that "Nietzsche, Heidegger, Foucault and Derrida—are largely right in their criticisms of Enlightenment rationalism," and still claim that "traditional liberalism and traditional humanism are entirely compatible with such criticisms. We can still be old-fashioned reformist liberals."[2] In doing so, Rorty reinvigorated interest in the American tradition of pragmatist political thought. The question of developing accounts of the right, the true, or the good that are deeply felt yet open to contest is one of the central themes of the pragmatist tradition.

But in giving parenthood a central place in his efforts to strike this balance in the American context, Rorty inherited versions of the difficulties that faced the theorists of virtue and contest who had done so in the centuries before. Rorty staked his hopes for political change on parental sentiments more likely to reinforce the status quo than inspire reform. This antifoundationalist made the experience of parenthood foundational to his politics. Seeking to insulate political virtues rooted in the experience of parenthood from the challenges of democratic variety and contest, he ultimately undermined what is compelling in each.

In borrowing elements of virtue and contest politics, Rorty rarely, at least purposefully, brought their different standards and values to bear on each other. Rather, his ideas depended on a clean and well-ordered division between public concerns and private ones—between politics and what he sometimes called "self-perfection." He believed that a hope for a better future for our descendants—our own children and grandchildren and, by extension, those of other members of our community—is the only disposition necessary or appropriate to citizenship and to thinking about how to improve American politics. To the extent that contest occurs in Rorty's ideal politics, it is a limited contest of ideas that occurs in a public arena circumscribed by a family-centered virtue. It is only outside this public arena, in our private lives, that we might engage in a deeper sort of contest, one that acknowledges the contingency of our way of life, our doubts about whether we are living the right way, and the possibility of self-transformation. But Rorty's own ideas, when examined in their totality, implied that the private experience of having children is likely to interfere with the political uses he wanted to make of our hopes for future generations. Furthermore, the public burdens he places on parenthood interfere with the democratic self-creation we undertake in our private existence.

As mentioned in the previous chapter, Honig suggests we "radicalize" Nietzsche's ideas for democratic purposes by thinking of the self in terms of a coexistence of the "overman," who can tolerate and embrace the unknown and contingent, and the "herd" that prefers the familiar and predictable. Rorty also reconfigured the herd and the overman in several ways. In one sense, he, like Honig, conceived of them as different aspects of a single individual. But for Rorty, unlike Honig, these two parts of the self are appropriate to two different spheres of life.[3] In private, a person should entertain "radical doubts" about his or her beliefs and should endlessly reconfigure them. In public, a person should refrain from such complications and discuss common problems in terms that are "banal, familiar,"[4] and also sentimental and familial—something reminiscent of the simple dogmas recommended by Rousseau for a society of equals united by the social contract.

But Rorty was like Nietzsche in that he saw important differences between an elite few and the masses. It is actually a small group of intellectuals, whom Rorty referred to as "ironists," who are capable of enduring or enjoying the difficulties of contingency and doubt. The majority prefers to cling to their beliefs rather than open them to challenge and contest. Luckily, the beliefs that people in our society take to be fundamental, Rorty thought, also tend toward the virtuous: these beliefs center on the meaning derived from parenthood. Because the herd is virtuous, it is the elite that is dangerous, in Rorty's view. The elites' ability to cast doubt on people's fundamental beliefs gives them a unique potential to do harm.

Rorty thought that to challenge the fundamentalist masses to reconsider their beliefs would be cruel. Thus the ironists' abilities at this more trans-formative sort of contest, the sort favored by Honig, must be carefully lim-ited to particular situations.

Rorty also refigures the overman and the herd as the adult and the child—the child who must be protected against the dangers of contest and contingency. It is here where Rorty's distinctions most dramatically break down, and virtue and contest undermine rather than supplement each other or peacefully coexist. First, a love for our own children can turn us inward and undermine the public uses of parental virtue. Second, ironists can forget their place and threaten to get their hands on the kids, or at least their ideas into them. By inspiring imitation in realms where they should not, ironists threaten to "take possession of the souls of young girls," to borrow Honig's evocative description of Rorty's "gothic" fears.[5] Wherever children go—through their daily lives, off to university, into third-world sweatshops, or to the camps of the holocaust—there appears an opportunity to expand the politics of virtue based on parental senti-ments. But wherever children go, contest must also be limited. Third, and perhaps worst of all, the children can get their hands on the ironists—exposing their self-creation as a mere imitation. Though ironists must be citizens, and citizens must be motivated by hopes for children, Rorty refused to imagine the ironist parenting. Just as ideas about parenting tempted Nietzsche to indulge in the fixed, the stable, the comfortable and unexamined, parenting threatens to reveal truths about ironists—more precisely about ironists' tastes for fundamental truths—that Rorty found difficult to face. While Rorty confronted the first two sets of problems in ways we can weigh and find persuasive or unpersuasive, he avoided this third most assiduously. The result is that Rorty arrived at a parent-centered theory of politics that depends on a source of virtue that is suspect and an account of political contest wherein the competition of ideas and convic-tions is rendered largely meaningless.

Philosophical Contest and the Turn to Family

Before Rorty began limiting contest in the realm of politics, he made his name by recovering it in the realm of philosophy. Rorty's early career, culminating in his *Philosophy and the Mirror of Nature,* was marked by his efforts to disabuse his fellow philosophers of the idea that they might

avoid the uncertainties of contest and arrive at foundational truths or fulfill their quests for certainty through discoveries about the "real" nature
of the world. Rorty thought philosophers should abandon efforts "to get
behind reasons to causes, beyond argument to compulsion from the object known, to a situation in which argument would be not just silly, but
impossible, for anyone gripped by the object in the required way will be
unable to doubt or to see an alternative. To reach that point is to reach the
foundations of knowledge."[6] Thus Rorty hoped to reclaim for philosophy
what contest theorists hope to reclaim for political theory and politics:
a sense that claims are contingent, contestable, held to the standards of
persuasion rather than truth or virtue, and subject to revision and being
abandoned. Rorty did not see his reclamation of contest for philosophy
to be particularly political, however. His account of philosophy, he suggested, "is a story of academic politics—not much more, in the long run,
than a matter of what sort of professors come under what sort of depart-
mental budget."[7] Rorty acknowledged that "there *are* relations between
academic politics and real politics," but he argued that "they are not tight
enough to justify carrying the passions of the latter over into the former"
(*Consequences of Pragmatism,* 229).

In the years that followed, however, Rorty dedicated himself to exploring those relations, in part because his interpreters saw political implications in his work and sought to pull him in that direction. One of these
was Cornel West, whose ideas about politics and parenthood I turn to in
the next chapter. In an account of Rorty's early work,[8] an effort that Rorty
called "as informed and sympathetic a treatment as [my work] has ever
received,"[9] West depicted Rorty as a case of unfulfilled potential. West was
impressed that Rorty had taken on "the ambitious project of resurrecting
pragmatism in contemporary North America."[10] But West worried that in
continually arguing with philosophers about the uselessness of abstract
philosophy, Rorty had become too satisfied with tearing down previous
ideas. He hoped Rorty would take on the task that Rorty's own philosophical work seemed to identify as the only important one: offering useful
rather than "true" accounts of contemporary real-world problems and describing compelling suggestions regarding the right way to deal with them.
West believed that in arguing that we can accept, live with, and celebrate
contingency, Rorty had become complacent in his relatively arbitrary
preference for "liberal-democratic" ideals and too quick to accept the idea
that "bourgeois capitalist" politics are "irrelevant to most of the problems

of most of the population of the planet."[11] West worried that in becoming satisfied with irony, Rorty's philosophical project reflected and could contribute to "the deep sense of impotence among the middle classes in contemporary capitalist societies, the sense of there being no liberating projects in the near North Atlantic future, and hence to the prevailing cynicism, . . . narcissistic living, and self-indulgent, ironic forms of thinking."[12] West hoped instead that Rorty might follow the example of John Dewey, whom Rorty admired, by articulating the sort of political projects that answer the contingency of current arrangements with compelling accounts of how they might be improved as well as which commitments were worth preserving—and do so in a way that dealt with the profound inequalities and injustices in the North Atlantic and beyond.

West summed up his critique of Rorty in a telling way—using reproductive language. He thought, "[Rorty's] project, though pregnant with rich possibilities, remains polemical . . . and hence barren. It refuses to give birth to the offspring that it conceives."[13] It was right about the time that West offered this critique that Rorty began to articulate his ideas about the importance to the public realm of citizens' hopes for their children. West, at that time in his career, was writing about the role of hope in politics in the context of the Christian and pragmatic traditions. Following this particular exchange, West and Rorty each went on to make ideas about parenthood more central to their political thought.

But first Rorty saw fit to defend his particular version of philosophical impotence (to borrow West's description). He did so with a lament regarding the sort of family-centered sentiment that he would later give a central place in his political ideas. Rorty was still suspicious of the "passions" of politics and the potential of those passions to cross boundaries (like those between politics and academics) and corrupt reasonable discussion. In responding to West, Rorty maintained that pragmatist philosophy would struggle to find a way to be helpful in contemporary political arguments— largely because argument had devolved into sentiment, particularly sentiment of the resentful sort.

> Nowadays nobody even bothers to back up opposition to liberal
> reforms with argument. People merely say that taxes are too high,
> that their brother-in-law would have a better job had it not been
> for his company's affirmative action program, and that it is time for
> the poor and weak to start looking after themselves. In Dewey's

America, as in Emerson's, there was work for intellectuals to do in cracking the crust of convention, questioning the need for traditional institutions. But nowadays, as far as I can see, the problem is not a failure of imagination—a failure of the sort which philosophers might help with. It is more like a failure of nerve, a fairly sudden loss of generous instincts and of patriotic fellow feeling. ("The Professor and the Prophet," 76)

In the example Rorty offered, family feeling gets in the way of fellow feeling. Sympathy for a brother-in-law obscures our responsibility to fellow citizens. In the years that followed, Rorty began to face this problem in the only way he knew. Rorty liked to call the sort of work that philosophers should undertake *redescription*. Rather than trying to make their ideas conform to some "truth" about the world, Rorty's "method is to redescribe lots and lots of things in new ways, until you have created a pattern of linguistic behavior which will tempt the rising generation to adopt it" (*Contingency, Irony, and Solidarity*, 9). For the purpose of politics, Rorty chose to repeatedly redescribe one thing—family. But his descriptions of family were parental rather than fraternal—focusing on children rather than brothers-in-law—and replaced present resentments with future hopes. He conceived of the "rising generation" not merely as a privileged audience but as the central part of the description itself.

Looking at American politics and finding it infused with resentful sentiments, Rorty saw not a "failure of imagination" but "a failure of nerve"—he initially saw no need, as a philosopher, to help crack the crust of convention. But Rorty eventually worked up the nerve to wade into the political fray. It might represent a failure of imagination that in order to do so he turned to the same sort of family-centered sentiment that he associated with wrongheaded conservatism in the example of the laid-off brother-in-law. Rather than cracking "the crust of convention" and questioning "traditional institutions," Rorty relied on conventional understandings of the institution of family.

In another description of his philosophical method, Rorty said that through our redescriptions we should try "to outflank the objections by enlarging the scope of one's favorite metaphor" (*Contingency, Irony, and Solidarity*, 44). For the purpose of politics, parenthood became Rorty's favorite metaphor, and he staked his hopes for political progress on enlarging its scope. But in its expansion, Rorty's metaphor grew out of control.

Rorty extended the parental metaphor outward into the political realm, extending family feeling toward future generations and larger communities, and in doing so, he stretched the metaphor beyond its descriptive usefulness. The metaphor came to obscure more than it illuminated. And parental sentiments also turned inward, invading the private realm of contest that Rorty hoped to preserve. The experience of parenthood became a source of personal meaning that takes on the character of fundamentalism and must be protected from challenge—at first for the masses but eventually, in the end, for the ironists as well.

Family and the Politics of Hope

Honig summarizes Rorty's ideas about the difference between private life and politics this way: "Irony is recommended for private individuals.... For citizens, however, Rorty recommends romance."[14] "Romance" is a word that Rorty began applying to citizenship only after his exchange with West in the late 1980s. West had included Rorty among those whom he criticized, along with theorists like Foucault and Derrida, as politically paralyzed because of a one-sided focus on what was wrong with the world—on criticism rather than affirmation. West believed Rorty and other contemporary American pragmatists[15] "resemble their counterparts in postmodern literary criticism—postmodern American philosophers have failed to project a new worldview, a countermovement, 'a new gospel of the future.'" Regarding Rorty in particular, West saw his ideas as backward looking. He thought Rorty's "ingenious conception of philosophy as cultured conversation rests upon a nostalgic appeal to the world of men (and women) of letters of decades past." Thus, in West's view, Rorty did not offer any "visions, worldviews or ... 'counter-philosophies' to the nihilism to which [his] position seems to lead."[16]

Rorty seemed to agree, and he admired West's efforts to be forward looking. Rorty noted that "among prominent leftist intellectuals in the United States Cornel West may be unique in that he is patriotic, religious, and romantic" ("The Professor and the Prophet," 70). It was West's romanticism, his ability to hold onto "social hope," that struck Rorty most. Rorty thought this was an aspect of West's ideas that was worth defending:

Romantic hope is, for most American leftists, a sign of intellectual immaturity. For such hope is incompatible with the ice-cold man-from-Mars style of thinking and writing exemplified by Foucault, and with the scorn for social hopes of the Enlightenment which we postmoderns are supposed to have learned from Nietzsche and Heidegger. From the point of view of most of the American Left, West's *tone* is all wrong. So much the worse, in my view, for that Left. ("The Professor and the Prophet," 70)

So Rorty began to change his own tone to be more romantic. He defended a sort of patriotic romantic hope that was first and foremost *forward looking*. And while Rorty would never endorse the sort of religious belief that West has made central to his political ideas, Rorty sought to stake his forward-looking politics on something that approximates religious faith— our hopes for our progeny. As Rorty put it, people once believed

hope of heaven was required to supply moral fiber and social glue— that there was little point, for example, in having an atheist swear to tell the truth in a court of law. As it turned out, however, willingness to endure suffering for the sake of future reward was transferable from individual rewards to social ones, from one's hopes for paradise to one's hopes for one's grandchildren. (*Contingency, Irony, and Solidarity*, 85)

So while Honig figures Rorty in terms of a turn from "Romantic individualism" to "national romance,"[17] Rorty came to embrace romance by one extra turn. He figured national politics as a family romance.[18]

While Rorty had recommended private efforts to repeatedly redescribe "lots and lots of things," in his turn to politics, he began to forgo multiplicity to take on a more singular tone: our unitary (glued-together) public culture should be given a single redescription: "Liberal culture needs an improved self-description rather than a set of foundations" (*Contingency, Irony, and Solidarity*, 52). A self-description centered on family sentiments and hope for the future was the best solution for that need. Rorty thought that liberal culture "has been strengthened by this switch." While scientific discoveries and philosophical innovations posed a continuous threat to public religion, Rorty believed that "it is not clear that any shift in scientific or philosophical opinion could hurt the sort of social hope which characterizes modern liberal societies—the hope that life will eventually be freer, less cruel, more leisurely, richer in goods and experiences, not just for our descendants but for everybody's descendants" (86).

While Rorty thought the nation's self-description should be forward looking, he defended it by first looking back, toward one of his philosophical "heroes"—John Dewey. Rorty explained that in conceiving of politics in terms of a hope for the future, he was articulating a pragmatic philosophy in the tradition of Dewey.

> Dewey argues that so far the thrust of philosophy has been conservative; it has typically been on the side of the leisure class, favoring stability over change. Philosophy has been an attempt to lend the past the prestige of the eternal. "The leading theme of the classic philosophy of Europe," he says, has been to make metaphysics "a substitute for custom as the source and guarantor of higher moral and social values." *Dewey wanted to shift attention away from the eternal to the future,* and to do so by making philosophy an instrument of change rather than of conservation, thereby making it American rather than European. (*Philosophy and Social Hope,* 29)[19]

In this sort of presentation of Dewey's ideas, we can see the connections that Rorty would like to make: a concern for metaphysics and eternal truths is tied to conservatism, the past, and Europe, and a more pragmatic approach to philosophy goes along with hope for the future and America. The latter connection is a particularly important one for Rorty. He believed America is the most fruitful ground for a pragmatic approach to both philosophy and politics because "America has always been a future-oriented country, a country which delights in the fact that it invented itself in the relatively recent past" (*Philosophy and Social Hope,* 24).

While America may have "always been" future oriented, Rorty liked to pick out and praise certain Americans, like Emerson and Whitman, who have best exemplified this spirit, and to criticize others, like Henry Adams, who did not. He began to make the same distinctions regarding his contemporaries. While Rorty praised Dewey's association of metaphysical philosophy with conservatism, Rorty identified a group of intellectuals on the *left* side of the political spectrum who, he believed, had failed to exemplify a spirit of hope for the future. They were many of the same philosophers and theorists that West had lumped in with Rorty as "nihilistic." In joining West in romantic thinking, Rorty also joined this attack.

Previously, Rorty had found uses for postmodern theory in the private realms of life. "Theorists like Hegel, Nietzsche, Derrida, and Foucault seem to me invaluable in our attempt to form a private self-image."[20] When their ideas were applied to politics, they struck Rorty as less than nefarious— "merely nuisances" (*Achieving Our Country*, 97). Such theorists and their ideas, Rorty suggested, are "pretty much useless when it comes to politics" (*Contingency, Irony, and Solidarity*, 83). But in embracing a future-oriented politics of hope, Rorty began to find them much more troubling. He came to believe that due to the work of "postmodern" philosophers,

> hopelessness has become fashionable on the Left—principled, theorized, philosophical hopelessness. The Whitmanesque hope which lifted the hearts of the American Left before the 1960s is now thought to have been a symptom of a naïve 'humanism.' . . . The Foucauldian Left represents an unfortunate regression to the Marxist obsession with scientific rigor. This Left still wants to put historical events in a theoretical context. It exaggerates the importance of philosophy for politics, and wastes its energy on sophisticated theoretical analyses of the significance of current events. (*Achieving Our Country*, 37)

The essence of Rorty's criticism of these scholars on the left is that they "prefer knowledge over hope" in that they try to get behind appearances and understand the "true" nature of oppression, power, hegemony, et cetera.[21] They are stuck in the past and in the deep origins of injustice rather than looking toward the future.

Part of Rorty's problem with this sort of analysis was that he saw it as useless on the practical level. It offered a "dreadful, pompous, useless, mishmash of Marx, Adorno, Derrida, Foucault, and Lacan. It has resulted in articles that offer unmaskings of the presuppositions of earlier unmaskings of still earlier unmaskings."[22] But more important, these ideas were affecting the "rising generation" that Rorty saw as the predominant group "redescriptions" are meant to "tempt" (*Contingency, Irony, and Solidarity*, 9). Thus Rorty was particularly bothered that "belief in the utility of this genre has persuaded a whole generation of *idealistic young leftists* in the First World that they are contributing to the cause of human freedom by, for example, exposing the imperialistic presuppositions of Marvel Comics" ("Thugs and Theorists, 569).

In these debates with the "hopeless" Left, Rorty was reenacting his old struggle with analytic philosophy. In that earlier struggle, he hoped to recover a spirit of philosophical contest from the search for foundational truths. In his battle with the postmodernists, he hoped to recover a sense of political contest from a search for deeper and truer understandings of power and oppression. While young academics influenced by this hopelessness might busy themselves with trivialities like comic books, young citizens might give up on politics altogether. "A contemporary American student may well emerge from college less convinced that her country has a future than when she entered. She may also be less inclined to think that political initiatives can create such a future" (*Achieving Our Country*, 10). So in taking on the "hopeless" Left, Rorty largely gave up his distinction between academic politics and real politics. Since the future was at stake, and the next generation was at stake, it was time for the philosopher to enter politics proper and once again "enlarge the scope" of his "favorite metaphor."

One of the political problems Rorty believed most required innovative practical thinking rather than theoretical speculation was the enormous concentration of wealth amassed by a small elite since the 1960s—the most unequal distribution of wealth in the United States since the "gilded age" of the early 1900s. To understand how the Left should confront this new gilded age, Rorty looked back toward the first one and the way the intellectuals at the time had responded. Henry Adams typified the wrong sort of response. Rorty cited favorably William James's opinion:

> Adams' diagnosis of the First Gilded Age as a symptom of irreversible moral and political decline was merely perverse. James's pragmatist theory of truth was in part a reaction against the sort of detached spectatorship which Adams affected.
>
> For James, disgust with American hypocrisy and self-deception was pointless unless accompanied by an effort to give America reason to be proud of itself in the future. (*Achieving Our Country*, 9)

Rorty believed one of the reasons the new gilded age has arrived is that after the 1960s, most contemporary leftist intellectuals "began to sink into an attitude like Henry Adams'" (*Achieving Our Country*, 14). Rorty thought these intellectuals, by engaging in "cultural" politics, "are spending energy which should be directed at proposing new laws on discussing topics as remote from the country's needs as were Adams' musings on the Virgin and the Dynamo" (14–15). And because they were discussing these topics on college campuses, Rorty worried that an Adamsesque "spirit of detached spectatorship" might be passed on to students.

Rorty believed that only by acting less like Adams and more like pragmatic, hopeful, forward-looking intellectuals such as Dewey and James, would leftist intellectuals contribute to the creation of a "new culture [which] will be better because it will contain more variety in unity" (*Achieving Our Country*, 25). One person who might have agreed with Rorty wholeheartedly is Henry Adams. He often insisted that the single most important aspect of his life story was that he was a man whose education failed to make him useful for the politics of his times—that he had nothing to contribute to his government or his society. That was the central theme of his unusual autobiography, *The Education of Henry Adams*. But Adams did venture, at the end of the book, a few practical political proposals he thought would be useful—for example, "the passage of a law obliging every woman, married or not, to bear one baby— at the expense of the Treasury—before she was 30 years old, under penalty of solitary confinement for life." Adams, childless himself, suggested that such a measure, guaranteeing the future existence of the American family, was "vital . . . to the foundation of a serious society in the future."[23] Only family and a love for children, Adams thought, might allow Americans to give direction to the chaotic forces rapidly transforming society in his time.

Despite Rorty's disdain for Adams, he staked his political hopes on a similar source of meaning. Rorty thought that liberal solidarity had been strengthened by coming to center on the shared experience of hopes for our children's future. This "social glue" was so strong because the sentiment was so deeply felt. Most people's lives, Rorty believed, are "given meaning by this hope" (*Contingency, Irony, and Solidarity*, 86). It was the public responsibility of philosophers, whatever their private "ironist" beliefs, to work with this meaning and explore its possibilities. Rorty complained that "the Left has taken less and less interest in what the rest of the country is worrying about" ("Thugs and Theorists," 570). If regular people's lives are given meaning by hopes for their children, then philosophers should focus their efforts there instead of searching for the fundamental nature of power or oppression. Rorty summarized, "Philosophy should try to express our political hopes rather than ground our political practices."[24]

Enlarging the Metaphor: From Family Outward

Rorty took on the task of expressing political hopes by expanding on the family-centered sentiments that, he believed, make our hopes feel meaningful. Family became his favorite metaphor. He engaged in politics and described his vision of citizenship by seeking to enlarge its scope. In taking up political contest in this fashion, Rorty would have to circumscribe contest as well. Contest would be constrained by the particular source of hope that gave meaning to people's lives and would involve competing efforts to expand on parental virtue. In his own efforts, Rorty made the tendency to derive meaning in our lives from the experience of family life, especially parenthood, a central aspect of his descriptions and re-descriptions of various groups in various contexts, from some Americans, to all Americans, to people in the North Atlantic democracies, to people in the West, to human beings in general. Rorty saw the depth of family feeling as the best basis upon which to expand, in a meaningful rather than purely philosophical sense, the way people think of who is in their moral community. Honig suggests it is a hallmark of virtue theorists to believe that "modern disenchantment, alienation, pain, and cruelty would be diminished if only we . . . yielded to the truth of membership in a wider community of meaning and value."[25] Rorty, in moving from the contest of philosophy to the realm of politics, would put ideas about family to use to craft a wider community of meaning and value and, in doing so, come to embrace a politics of virtue.

But before Rorty could expand family-centered virtue outward to a larger community, he had to shore up its roots in our daily lives. Rorty believed that one of the main flaws of metaphysical moral philosophy, from Plato to Kant, is that it does not appreciate the way the "natural" depth of family feeling affects humans. As Rorty puts it: "The central flaw in much traditional moral philosophy has been the myth of the self as non-relational, as capable of existing independent of concern for others, as a cold psychopath needing to be constrained to take account of other people's needs" (*Philosophy and Social Hope,* 77).[26] It is our experience with our families, according to Rorty, that prevents us from actually being this amoral psychopath postulated by western philosophy. Offering a rather upbeat take on the Freudian account of the family, Rorty summarized: "The most important link between Freud and Dewey is the one that [Annette] Baier[27] emphasizes: the role of the family, and in particular of maternal love, in creating nonpsychopaths, that is, human selves who find concern for others completely natural" (78). Rorty believed that because this concern for others feels so natural within the family, morality is not something that philosophers should feel obliged to argue for or seek theoretical "grounds" for in thinking about how we should behave:

> Consider the question: Do I have a moral obligation to my mother? My wife? My children? "Morality" and "obligation" here seem inapposite. For doing what one is obliged to do contrasts with doing what comes naturally, and for most people responding to the needs of family members is the most natural thing in the world. Such responses come naturally because most of us define ourselves, at least in part, by our relations to members of our family. Our needs and theirs overlap; we are not happy if they are not. We would not wish to be well while our children go hungry; that would not be natural. (78)[28]

This "natural" solidarity between parent and child, the sense that your well-being cannot be separate from your child's, provides the basis for the sort of relationship that Rorty wanted to see between members of larger communities.

The way to accomplish this, Rorty believed, was to tell stories that might enlarge our solidarity by enlarging the familial metaphor. In order to include more people in the way we define ourselves—more people whose well-being we care about on a visceral level rather than through a sense of obligation based on the thin stuff of metaphysical speculations about morality—we must find a way to include more people "in telling ourselves stories about who we are" (*Philosophy and Social Hope*, 79). Rousseau and Nietzsche demonstrated some of the ways that the inclusion of our children in our sense of self can introduce profound insecurities rather than merely extend our circle of care. But, in this context at least, Rorty treated our feelings for our children more simply. We would not leave our children out of our story about who we take ourselves to be, Rorty believed, and that is why our care for our children is natural. If we can find a way to include more people in our stories about ourselves, then the natural morality of parental care will expand outward to larger communities. "The desire to feed [a] hungry stranger may of course *become* as tightly woven into my self-conception as the desire to feed my family" (79). This process has little to do with abstract morality in the Kantian sense, but to Rorty it represents a sort of moral progress. "Moral development in the individual, and moral progress in the human species as a whole, is a matter of re-marking human selves so as to enlarge the variety of relationships which constitute [people's] selves" (79).

Since the feelings of trust and interdependence that Rorty hoped to ex-pand on were most typical of the experience of parenting, Rorty thought parenthood should also be central to the sorts of stories we use to enlarge our moral imagination and achieve this moral progress. Because a "hope for the future" is the crucial attitude that Rorty would like to serve as the basis of our community feeling, the familial role that would best intermingle hope for the future and a relational sense of "who we are" is the role of the parent caring about the child. For example, Rorty thought that to explain to someone why he or she should care about a stranger, a person whose habits he or she finds "disgusting," it is best to eschew arguments of the moral obligations humans have to other members of their species. Rather, "a better sort of answer is the sort of long, sad, sentimental story that be-gins, 'Because this is what it is like to be in her situation . . .' or 'Because she might become your daughter-in-law' or 'Because her mother would grieve for her'" (*Truth and Progress*, 185). Applying the idea to real events of the most horrible kind, Rorty suggested that the citizens of Denmark and Italy who scrambled to help their Jewish neighbors escape from the Gestapo were possibly motivated by imagining them, if they had no more direct connection, as "a fellow parent of small children" (*Contingency, Irony, and Solidarity*, 190–91).[29]

In stating the ultimate goal of the tradition of pragmatism with which he aligned himself, Rorty gives priority to what could be called the "pro-creative moment." "What matters for pragmatists is devising ways of di-minishing human suffering and increasing human equality, increasing the ability of all human children to start life with an equal chance of happi-ness" (*Philosophy and Social Hope*, xxix). Following the logic of Rorty's "family feeling extended" model of moral progress—it is the profound feelings of hopefulness that Rorty believes a person experiences in having a child that provides the best basis for the creation of a more ideal society. And it is sympathy with other people's hopes for their children that repre-sents, for Rorty, the culmination of the sort of moral development that he would like to encourage: "The ability to shudder with shame and indigna-tion at the unnecessary death of a child—a child with whom we have no connection of family, tribe, or class—is the highest form of emotion that humanity has attained while evolving modern social and political institutions" (*Contingency, Irony, and Solidarity*, 147).

Rorty's notion of expanding feelings of obligations from the family, where they are "natural," outward to larger groups of people bears a resemblance to Julia Kristeva's notion of cosmopolitanism as developed in her *Nations without Nationalism*. Kristeva also imagines feelings of community being extended outward from the self and family toward increasingly larger groups, each group serving as a "transitional object" for the previous one—from self to family, from family to nation, from nation to Europe, and so forth. An important difference between the two is that for Rorty, family, and especially children, always remain the important transitional object. People include others in their sense of themselves by thinking of those others in the context of their family lives, especially as fellow parents of children.[30]

The Tribe and Initiation

In suggesting that the sentiments of parenthood should be central to the "better self-description" that we give to our own lives as well as to "liberal society," Rorty seemed to favor a description of parental sentiments that is rather sanguine, perhaps naïvely so. It certainly lacks the complexity and the dark undertones of Rousseau's efforts to put parental feelings to use for virtuous politics or Nietzsche's ideas about how parenthood might affect our efforts to transform ourselves. But Rorty was not a blithe optimist. He was not so upbeat about other aspects of human existence, and he occasionally acknowledged that family-centered stories would meet great obstacles in accomplishing their goal of transforming citizens' self-conceptions and politics in turn.

> To retain social hope ... [people] need to be able to tell themselves a story about how things might get better.... If social hope has become harder lately, this is ... because, since the end of World War II, the course of events has made it harder to tell a convincing story of this sort. The cynical and impregnable Soviet Empire, the continuing shortsightedness and greed of the surviving democracies, and the exploding, starving populations of the Southern Hemisphere make the problems our parents faced in

the 1930's, Fascism and unemployment, look almost manageable.
(*Contingency, Irony, and Solidarity*, 86)

But while Rorty acknowledged the political complexities that his "long, sad sentimental" family-centered stories would have to confront, including the "shortsightedness and greed" of his own contemporaries, he was less willing to confront the complexities that emerge in our own family-centered stories and the personal experience of parenthood that might tinge our hope for a better future.

There were some moments when Rorty seemed poised to undertake this sort of examination. For example, while he gave Freud's ideas a rather simplistic spin in linking them to Dewey and Baier, he was also aware that Freud had revealed that the feelings we develop in our experiences with our families are quite complex. Freud had revealed, according to Rorty, that "nobody is dull through and through, for there is no such thing as a dull unconscious" (*Contingency, Irony, and Solidarity*, 35). And Rorty recognized that Freud's insight into the unconscious and the way the unconscious develops in the context of family dramas does as much to make us unique as to give us a common experience on which to base community. According to Rorty, Freud calls us to see "every human being as consciously or unconsciously acting out an idiosyncratic fantasy" and thus to see all people as engaged in an effort to redescribe the circumstances of their lives for their own purposes (36–37).

This redescription is a form of self-transformation, and in many cases, Rorty associated openness to self-transformation with the experience of profound doubts regarding the rightness of our way of life. One way Rorty described the experience of life as an ironist is that "the ironist spends her time worrying about the possibility that she has been initiated into the wrong tribe, taught to play the wrong language game. She worries that the process of socialization which turned her into a human being by giving her a language may have given her the wrong language, and so turned her into the wrong kind of human being" (*Contingency, Irony, and Solidarity*, 75). But in the context of Rorty's ideas about family, the experience of doubt about one's ideas and identity is notably absent. Rorty sometimes acknowledged that in some ways, particularly given Freudian insights into the subconscious, the ironist's openness to the contingency of her way of life, her efforts to engage in self-criticism and self transformation, is something that occurs in everyone's life: that the "ironist" intellectual "is just a

There is a persistent theme in Rorty's work about the importance of poor, weak, and humiliated people confessing their stories of poverty, weakness, and humiliation to the rich, powerful, and dignified and couching these stories in terms of family. Whenever this theme comes up, Rorty seems to identify with the powerful group—the parental group that listens to the appeals of those who are weaker.[36]

A psychologist might suspect this had something to do with the bullies Rorty encountered in high school. Rorty offered his own explanation—a rather practical one: the rich control the world. So it is rich people's way of thinking and behaving that has to change if we are to improve the world. Rorty thought the best way to change how the wealthy think and behave is through sentimental appeals to their pity and especially to their family feeling. Rorty believed that one of the reasons people search for a metaphysical source of moral obligation (like Kant's effort to ground moral duty in the human capacity for reason) is that the idea of having to achieve progress by appealing to the sentiments of the rich strikes many people as distasteful.

> The residual popularity of Kantian ideas of "unconditional moral obligation"—obligation imposed by deep ahistorical noncontingent forces—seems to me almost entirely due to our abhorrence to the idea that the people on top hold the future in their hands, that everything depends on them, and that there is nothing more powerful to which we can appeal to against them. (*Truth and Progress*, 182)

However, while the people on top hold the future in their hands, they also craft their connection to the future, as Rorty so often notes, through parenthood. The powerful often have children. Compared to the children of the less well-off, the children of the powerful tend to do pretty well in accumulating their own power in turn.[37] It seems possible that the particular aspirations one has for one's own children might interfere with, rather than provide the basis of, one's commitment to improve the life prospects of other people's children.

Rorty himself offered several gestures in this direction. Though he prided himself on his "cold-war liberalism" and staunch anticommunism ("Thugs and Theorists," 572),[38] Rorty thought at least one aspect of Marx's insights had continued relevance: "To say that history is 'the history of class struggle' is still true, if it is interpreted to mean that in every culture, under every form of government, and in every imaginable situation . . .

the people who have already got their hands on money and power will lie, cheat and steal in order to make sure that *they and their descendants monopolize both forever*" (*Philosophy and Social Hope*, 206, emphasis added).[39] Even when he was feeling less sweepingly Marxist, Rorty recognized the tendency of the rich and powerful to seek advantages for their own children at the expense of other people's children.[40] Sometimes Rorty wrote about this dilemma in terms of a "superrich" class, liberated by globalization from traditional obligations and economic ties to poorer Americans. This group, in Rorty's analysis, seems to have had their moral development move in exactly the opposite direction from the "family-outward" development of sentiment that Rorty prefers. The superrich, instead, have morally regressed from a feeling of responsibility to America to an exclusive focus on their own descendants.

> The economic royalists whom Franklin Roosevelt denounced still had a lot invested in America's future. For today's super-rich, such an investment would be imprudent.
>
> There is too little public discussion of the changes that this globalized labor market will inevitably bring to America in the coming decades. Bill Bradley is one of the few prominent politicians to have insisted that we must prevent our country from breaking up into *hereditary economic castes.* . . . [There are plausible scenarios in which] America, the country that was to have witnessed a new birth of freedom, will gradually be divided by class differences of a sort that would have been utterly inconceivable to Jefferson or to Lincoln or to Walt Whitman. (*Philosophy and Social Hope*, 258–59, emphasis added)[41]

So for the superrich, family feeling and caring for your children does not radiate warmth and care outward toward the larger community. Rather, family feeling legitimates the consolidation of wealth and contributes to the development of "hereditary economic castes." But the superrich are different from the rest of "us," right? Not necessarily, since Rorty offered a very similar analysis of the behavior of the entire American middle (or upper-middle) class.

> It is as if, sometime around 1980, the children of the people who made it through the Great Depression and into the suburbs had

decided to pull up the drawbridge behind them. They decided that although social mobility had been appropriate for their parents, it was not to be allowed to the next generation. These suburbanites seem to see nothing wrong with *belonging to a hereditary caste.* (*Achieving Our Country,* 86)

While Rorty wrote about the hereditary castes of the superrich as a frightening possibility the future might hold, he wrote about the hereditary castes of the well-off suburbanites as something that had already come about. He worried not whether hereditary castes might form in the future, but "if the formation of hereditary castes *continues* unimpeded..." (87).[42] And he worried not if the United States would *some day* be split apart into groups defined by family but rather accepted that the split had already occurred and worried instead whether Europe would follow our lead and "create such castes not only in the United States, but in all the old democracies" (87).

Rorty did not bring this economic analysis of the consequences of family feeling and parental care, in which wealth and power are consolidated and preserved for one's children rather than other members of the community, to bear on his family-outward theory of moral development. He never considered whether family-centered economics might suggest that family-centered morality offers, as Dewey might suggest, "a consecration of the status quo." In fact, Rorty did nearly the opposite. While the family feeling of the rich makes them a threat to economic progress, Rorty nonetheless saw them as ethically superior. He suggested that the children of the powerful do not merely do better financially but are also better off in terms of their morality. Good morals, for Rorty, were largely a matter of being born at the right place and the right time. Noting how many of his privileged students seemed progressive on issues of race, for example, Rorty wondered how to teach them to think about less tolerant people. He decided the proper message is that "the bad people's problem is... that they were not as lucky in the circumstances of their upbringing as we were. Instead of treating all those people out there who are trying to find and kill Salman Rushdie as irrational, we should treat them as deprived" (*Truth and Progress,* 180). They were not lucky enough to be born in the right place and at the right time and thus were condemned to moral inferiority.

When it came to lucky birthrights, however, the economic trumped the moral in Rorty's analysis. Economic security provides the foundation upon which the superstructure of "moral progress," in the Rortian sense of expanded sympathies, can be built (*Philosophy and Social Hope*, 79). Speaking about the "deprived" and "bad" Muslims out to kill Salman Rushdie, Rorty wrote,

> Foundationalists think of these people as deprived of the truth, of moral knowledge. But it would be better—more concrete, more specific, more suggestive of possible remedies—to think of them as deprived of two more concrete things: security and sympathy. By "security" I mean the conditions of life sufficiently risk-free as to make one's difference from others inessential to one's self-respect, one's sense of self-worth. These conditions have been enjoyed by North Americans and Europeans . . . much more than they have been enjoyed by anyone else. (*Truth and Progress*, 180)

For Rorty, self-respect and sense of worth seem to be almost synonymous with material wealth, and economic insecurity is synonymous with envy and self-loathing. Material wealth is also synonymous with sympathy, since "security and sympathy go together" (*Truth and Progress*, 180). For the poor and the unlucky, "the tougher things are, the more you have to be afraid of, the more dangerous your situation, the less you can afford the time or effort to think about what things might be like for people with whom you do not immediately identify. Sentimental education works only on people who can relax long enough to listen" (180). For the poor, family-centered sentimental stories cannot work their moral magic.

So a curious dichotomy existed in Rorty's ideas about wealth and family. Describing wealth in terms of our luck at "being born" into a wealthy society bestows a certain innocence on the experience of wealth; we didn't *ask* to be born here, after all. Rorty continually figured citizenship in the contemporary West as "lucky."[43] This "accident of birth" allows the wealthy to avoid guilt and instead think about how wealth might be morally productive in providing the leisure to cultivate family feeling into a more inclusive identity—expanding our sympathies outward by hearing family-centered stories about the tragic lives of others. Yet the development of "hereditary economic castes" is regrettable, even execrable, and Rorty thus indirectly acknowledged that parental sentiments can help stiffen economic structures and prevent social mobility.

Elsewhere Rorty seemed to acknowledge that the feelings associated with parenthood might also stiffen the moral imagination. For example, Rorty suggested that the only way our society "shall do justice to gays" is when "we become as indifferent to whether our children turn out to be gay or straight as we are to whether they become doctors or lawyers . . . and yet how many parents at the present time can even imagine such indifference?" (*Truth and Progress*, 224).[44] With this example, Rorty completed a full circle from the brother-in-law scenario he had offered a decade earlier in response to West's "romantic" hopefulness. But while a brother-in-law losing his job might offer an excuse for thoughtless opposition to progressive policies like affirmative action, Rorty's example of a parent with a gay child gets at something deeper. The former suggests that familial sentiments might interfere with the public uses Rorty hoped to make out of hopes for the future. The latter suggests that parents' love for their children and hopes for their future might get wrapped up with a specific future they imagine for their children. Parental sentiments can conflict with a child's desire to set out on her own path. In other words, parenthood can conflict with Rorty's most essential *private* activity—self-creation.

Enlarging the Metaphor: From Family Inward

Rorty's efforts to think about politics, solidarity, "social glue," and public obligations in terms of extending the sentiments of parenthood outward to a larger community led to contradictions he failed to resolve. In thinking about the private realm and the activity of self-creation that Rorty most valued in that realm, the expansion of the experience of parenthood would prove problematic in ways he refused to confront. By placing family feeling and parental sentiment (counterintuitively) on the public side of his public–private divide, Rorty mostly avoided confronting the ways that parenthood and family complicate self-creation. But the metaphor would not sit still and eventually morphed again in Rorty's work—seemingly despite Rorty's own hopes and intentions—moving *inward* until parental sentiments came to occupy his private realm and invade the soul. Centering on questions of imitation, the relationship between parent and child threatened to undermine the self-creation that Rorty believed to be humanity's highest activity and the point of liberal society.

One can watch the familial metaphor enlarge in this fashion on the pages of the book in which Rorty first introduced its importance: *Contingency, Irony, and Solidarity*. It was there that Rorty began to articulate and defend a division of human activities into two basic categories that coincide with the private and the public. For Rorty, the most important private activity is an effort to achieve some measure of what he referred to alternatively as "self-realization," "self-creation," or "self-perfection." This is a version of the sort of contest he thought appropriate to philosophy, whereby individuals work to redescribe and reconceive the circumstances of their life, aware that they can never arrive at final answers, be free of doubt, or be immune from persuasion to see things another way. Rorty used the label "ironist," or sometimes "ironist intellectual," to describe the person who best embodied this mode of existence. Being an ironist, it turns out, is not unlike hunting orchids in that it involves a heroic admixture of superior evolution, eroticism, and control over who will experience pain and humiliation.

Rorty believed that all people, including ironists, have a particular set of ideas that they use to "justify their actions, their beliefs, and their lives" (*Contingency, Irony, and Solidarity,* 73). Ironists are different in that they have "radical and continuing doubts" about the ideas they use to justify their way of life (73). While "radical doubts" has a negative ring, perhaps, these doubts actually provide the ironist with an opportunity—one related to Nietzschean ideas about self-transformation. Ironists are able to engage new ideas and new values, challenge their cherished beliefs and their inherited habits of thinking, and recraft themselves into something unique and individual—to place their own impress upon the ideas they inherit and the circumstances of their lives. They are "capable of telling the story of their own production in words never used before" (28). In describing the result, Rorty was fond of borrowing Nietzschean language: the ironist intellectual who has successfully redescribed the circumstances of her life in her own terms has turned "all 'it was' into a 'thus I willed it'" (29).

The pleasures of irony and the self-creation it makes possible struck Rorty as exquisite enough that they alone could justify the arrangements of an "ideal" liberal society.

> The social glue holding together the ideal liberal society . . . consists of little more than a consensus that the point of social organization is to let everybody have a chance at self-creation to the best of his or her abilities, and that that goal requires, besides peace and wealth, the standard "bourgeois freedoms." (*Contingency, Irony, and Solidarity,* 84)

But, as noted previously, Rorty more often thought of the shared experience of our hopes for our children as the social glue that holds liberal society together. In leaving the realm of the ideal liberal society for actual liberal society, his discussion of self-creation slid into a discussion of child-creation. The reason for the difference is that in actual liberal society, not everyone is capable of facing the challenges of irony.

Rorty noted that while ironist intellectuals are able to accept and even embrace contingency, the general public is more metaphysical in the sense that they seek the comforts of certainty and truth. An ironist is able to "see one's language, one's conscience, one's morality, and one's highest hopes as contingent products, as literalizations of what once were accidentally produced metaphors" (*Contingency, Irony, and Solidarity*, 61), but the metaphysical masses are "doomed to spend [their] conscious lives trying to escape from contingency rather than, like a strong poet,[45] acknowledging and appropriating contingency" (28).[46] Rorty saw this difference in the way ironists and nonironists respond to contingency, whether they embrace or avoid contest, as more than minor. He explained that as a greater proportion of intellectuals have become ironists rather than foundationalists of the sort he began his career criticizing, "This has widened the gap between intellectuals and the public" (82).[47]

Rorty believed these nonironist masses are the reason that parental sentiments must be central to solidarity for a liberal society in which irony is not endurable for everyone. He often used the word *vocabularies* to describe the words and phrases that people "employ to justify their actions, their beliefs, and their lives" (73). The ironist constantly refigures and improves her particular vocabulary in her private existence. For the purposes of politics, she sticks to the "banal, familiar," and hopeful shared sentiments that guide political discussion. But because ironists are rare, their dichotomous experience is not typical. For others, "the vocabularies are, typically, parasitic on the hopes—in the sense that the principal function of the vocabularies is to tell stories about future outcomes which compensate for present sacrifices" (86). So hopes regarding our children, described by Rorty as a public source of shared meaning for a liberal society in which private experiences of what is meaningful are more varied and complex, turn out to dominate the private realm as well. Rather than crafting their own unique meaning in life, the private existence of most people, their deepest conception of themselves, becomes parasitic on parental public rhetoric—their lives are "given meaning by this hope" (86).

For most people, the public identity as parent (or as a quasi-parent motivated by hopes for future generations) is their private identity as well because, as nonironists, they cling to one identity wherever they go.[48]

The Ironist at School

So for the nonironist majority, parental sentiments leave their proper
place as the earnest yet "banal [and] familiar" shared sentiments that
guide political discussion and invade their private existence to become a
fundamental and unquestioned source of meaning. How do ironists avoid
becoming parasitic in this way and keep parental sentiments and hopes
for their children from becoming a fundamental source of meaning in
their lives? There is no clear answer because Rorty refused to imagine the
ironist parenting. In fact, though he wrote often about the importance of
family-centered stories, Rorty had very little to say about the actual experience of parenting for ironists or anyone else. Instead, Rorty called in two
important reinforcements when thinking about raising children: teachers
and professors. When Rorty considered how children are socialized, he
almost always wrote in terms of educators rather than in terms of parents.
He referred to a "rhetoric" in which the young are socialized and labeled it
"the public rhetoric." The ironist does have a role to play in the socialization process—the role of professor—but that role became endangered as
the family metaphor enlarged once again.

Rorty used his ideas about socialization to help explain the distinction he drew between ironist intellectuals and the more metaphysical
mass public. One reason that the general public has failed to become
ironists, Rorty explained, is that we are "in a liberal culture whose public
rhetoric—the rhetoric in which the young are socialized—is still metaphysical" (*Contingency, Irony, and Solidarity*, 87). Rorty hoped to see a
slight improvement in this state of affairs. He hoped that in an ideal liberal
society, rather than being socialized to be metaphysical (in the sense of
believing some truths to be fundamental and unchanging), the common
people may be taught to become "commonsensically nominalist and historicist." By this, Rorty meant "they would see themselves as contingent
through and through, without feeling any particular doubts about the
contingencies they happened to be" (87). The question that immediately
jumps to mind is why these nominalist-historicists might not make that
final step, becoming true ironists like Rorty and, like him, enjoy a nice

tussle with their "radical and continuing doubts." Rorty's answer to this question seemed motivated in part by an admirable concern for the young and in part by a desire to maintain the ironist's singular status. In classic Rorty form, there is a social purpose and a private one. Rorty wrote in his social purpose/admirable concern mode:

> But even if I am right in thinking that a liberal culture whose public rhetoric is nominalist and historicist is both possible and desirable, I cannot go on to claim that there could or ought to be a culture whose public rhetoric is *ironist*. I cannot imagine a culture which socialized its youth in such a way as to make them continually dubious about their own process of socialization. (87)

What accounts for this failure of imagination? The answer is that Rorty thought an ironist education might interfere with the sort of "hope for the future" that should motivate politics in liberal society. Thus the "public rhetoric" of socialization needs to inculcate a certain story about what it means to be an American, a story that will foster a "hope for the future" by creating a particular understanding of the past. Here is Rorty's summary of "the socialization that American children should receive":

> This socialization [consists] in acquiring an image of themselves as heirs to a tradition of increasing liberty and rising hope. . . . The children [should] come to think of themselves as proud and loyal citizens of a country that, slowly and painfully, threw off a foreign yoke, freed its slaves, enfranchised its women, restrained its robber barons and licensed its trade unions, liberalized its religious practices, broadened its religious and moral tolerance, and built colleges in which 50 percent of its population could enroll. . . . The inculcation of this narrative of freedom and hope [should] be the core of the socializing process. (*Philosophy and Social Hope*, 121–22)[49]

In Rorty's description, it is primarily the job of teachers, rather than parents, to pass on this rather optimistic take on American history—"the moral and political common sense of the society as it is" (*Philosophy and Social Hope*, 116). The schools carry the burden of actually undertaking socialization—they must get students to the point where they both understand and believe this story about America. So when Rorty criticized the middle class for being "greedy and heartless," it was not because greed and heartlessness are bad things for parents to model for their children. Rather, the problem is that greed has caused this middle class to "let the quality of education a child receives become proportional to the assessed value of the parents' real estate" (121). Rorty also worried about the "cynicism" of those who produce "televised fantasies," which infiltrate "into our children's vocabularies of moral deliberation" (121). Television producers are noteworthy socializers, but parents are not.

Parents lurk in the background of Rorty's story—sitting on school boards, for example—and to the extent that they play a role, it is a conservative one. The watchful eyes of school-board parents means that there is not too much that can be done for students whose personal experience makes the upbeat story of America seem less than compelling. "Sympathetic high school teachers often assist curious or troubled students by showing them where to find alternatives to this common sense," but "the Right has pretty much kept control of primary and secondary education, . . . our system of local school boards means that pre-college teachers cannot, in the classroom, move very far from the local consensus" (*Philosophy and Social Hope*, 116).

This process of inculcating the hopeful version of America's path to the present is important enough, in Rorty's view, that it needs to be "finished"; the story needs to be swallowed if students are to become competent citizens. It is only when socialization is finished that stage two, which is overseen by college professors, can begin. Rorty sometimes described the work of college professors as a process of simply complicating the narrative that was dispensed without complication in high school. Professors "do their best to nudge each successive college generation a little more to the left, to make them a little more conscious of the cruelty built into our institutions" (*Philosophy and Social Hope*, 116). At other times, he wrote about the job of college professors in terms of a more radical difference. Rorty thought too many people "ignore the fact that the word 'education' covers two entirely distinct, and equally necessary, processes—socialization and individuation" (117). According to Rorty, primary and secondary schools should accomplish the former, and colleges the latter.

This "individuation" that is accomplished in college bears a strong resemblance to the self-creation that is the expertise of ironist intellectuals. "The point of non-vocational higher education is . . . to help students realize that they can reshape themselves—that they can rework the self-image foisted on them by their past, the self-image that makes them competent citizens, into a new-self image, one that they themselves have helped to create" (*Philosophy and Social Hope*, 118). Professors do this by providing a model of Rorty's idea of private self-perfection that students might be drawn to imitate—something like Nietzsche's exemplars, who provoke us to look for the productive uniqueness within ourselves. Noting that professors are often called "loose cannons," Rorty argued:

> College students badly need to find themselves in a place in which people are not ordered to a purpose, in which loose cannons are free to roll about. The only point in having real live professors around instead of just computer terminals, videotapes, and mimeoed lecture notes is that students *need to have freedom enacted before their eyes by actual human beings.* . . . Teachers setting their own agendas—putting their individual, lovingly prepared specialties on display in the curricular cafeteria, without regard to any larger end, much less any institutional plan—is what higher education is all about.
>
> Such enactments of freedom are the principal occasions of the erotic relationships between teacher and student that Socrates and Allan Bloom celebrate. . . . Such erotic relationships are occasions of growth, and their occurrence and their development are as unpredictable as growth itself. Yet nothing important happens in nonvocational higher education without them. (125, emphasis added)[50]

In his invocations of the unpredictable and the erotic—the exposure of young people to the highly evolved and profoundly unique—Rorty was back in the heady realm of his private experience in the mountains with his beloved orchids. Indeed, his description of college education seems consonant with his ideas about the activities of self-realization appropriate to the private realm.

In *Contingency, Irony and Solidarity*, Rorty carefully defined self-creation as a private, and therefore nonpolitical, concern. But in thinking about the role of college professors, Rorty's neat private–public distinctions break down once again. He believed that college education also carries political burdens. "The socially most important provocations will be offered by [college] teachers who make vivid and concrete the failure of the country of which we remain loyal citizens to live up to its own ideals" (*Philosophy and Social Hope*, 123). So Rorty blurred the border that he had carefully drawn elsewhere by suggesting that the "sparks that leap back and forth between teacher and student," though they form a relationship "that has little to do with socialization but much to do with self-creation," are nonetheless "the principle means by which the institutions of a liberal society get changed" (126). This is because without these relationships, "students will never realize what democratic institutions are good for: namely, making possible the invention of new forms of human freedom, taking liberties never taken before" (126).[51]

The college classroom is where the ironist bridges the private and the public—the place where the ironist can turn from the solitary work of "creat[ing] a pattern of linguistic behavior" to the test of whether his or her creation might "tempt the rising generation to adopt it" (*Contingency, Irony, and Solidarity*, 9). It is, in a sense, a diffuse version of the scrutiny between a child and parent that interested both Rousseau and Nietzsche. But in moving this scrutiny to the classroom, Rorty makes it a bit safer. The student's scrutiny of the professor, as described by Rorty, is intense, perhaps, but not too intense. The context can be carefully staged. Lectures can be written beforehand, and topics can be carefully chosen to show the ironist professor at his or her best. And there is safety in numbers. Rousseau worried that the witness of a child might reveal that his way of life was actually unworthy. Rorty avoided this problem by substituting hundreds of students and the "sparks" between teacher and student for the intensity of the relationship between parent and child. With so many students seeing a professor perform his or her best stuff, a few are bound to get caught up in the topic.

Nietzsche's primary concern, on the other hand, was that in getting wrapped up in our relationship to a child, and in passing on a version of ourselves and our sense of the right way to live, we might abandon the always-unfinished task of self-creation. Rorty came to face the same difficulty. He saw the college environment—the loose cannon's space to roll around—becoming constricted. It was under pressure from two sides. On one side, the high schools were not completing their task of socialization. If the high schools do not do their job—the situation Rorty saw developing in the 1990s—then professors cannot do theirs. Because the high schools are failing to inculcate the narrative of hope, "as things unfortunately—and with luck temporarily—are, the colleges have to finish the job of socialization. Worse yet, they have to do this when the students are already too old and too restless to put up with such a process" (*Philosophy and Social Hope*, 124).

If unsuccessful high schools were squeezing Rorty from one side, a misguided group of professors was squeezing him from the other. Often it is in having to defend something that we learn to fully accept it, and Rorty seemed to accept his task of completing the future-oriented and hopeful socialization of his students in defending them against this other set of professors—the "hopeless Left" that had inherited Henry Adams's spirit of "detached spectatorship." While ironists should indulge in their "radical and continuing doubts" about their way of life, these dangerous leftists indulged in more sweeping doubts about the nation, the globe, or modernity itself. "The contemporary academic Left seems to think that the higher your level of abstraction, the more subversive of the established order you can be. The more sweeping and novel your conceptual apparatus, the more radical your critique" (*Achieving Our Country*, 93). While such efforts are useless on the practical level, Rorty believed, they are particularly dangerous because they might be seductive to the rising generation—setting off sparks of their own between professors and students who, because they have not "finished" their socialization of hope, are vulnerable. This is why Rorty worried about that student who might "emerge from college less convinced that her country has a future than when she entered." It is not merely that the student has been discouraged, but she has been overcome. "The spirit of detached spectatorship, and the inability to think of American citizenship as an opportunity for action, may already have entered such a student's soul" (10–11).

While professors are supposed to complicate the hopeful narrative of American progress, the "hopeless" Left complicates the story too much. Their doubts are too radical and perhaps too seductive. Honig seizes upon Rorty's description of the hopeless Left's vision of America as "a Gothic world in which democratic politics are a farce" (*Achieving Our Country*, 95). She notes that Rorty's portrait of the cultural Left is gothic in its own right. According to Honig, Rorty portrayed this element of the Left as "a creature so pervasive and monstrous that it takes possession of the souls of young girls."[52] Honig suggests that Rorty's "horror-gothic call to romanticize rather than gothicize the nation" sets in motion a "dynamics of demonization"[53] in which Rorty attempted to exclude certain perspectives from the contest of political ideas, "to insist on the unity of the nation or the demos." In Honig's eyes, Rorty fails to take on the challenges of contest, to submit to "one of democracy's strictest tests, the challenge to work and live and share not just with people with whom we have a great deal in common but also with those with whom we just happen to be bound up."[54]

Squeezed on two sides, Rorty and other hopeful ironists are forced to change their role—to become a stable fortress rather than a loose cannon, to be a protector rather than a complicator of the hopeful public rhetoric in which children are socialized. They become defenders of stable virtue rather than practitioners of self-transformation. Rorty's favorite metaphor, caring about children, had taken over his workplace. As was the case for Nietzsche, a concern for young people tempted Rorty to give up on the politics of contest.

The Ironist at Home

Denied the pleasures of irony at work, one wonders what ironist professors do if they have their own children at home.[55] Rorty never offered an answer. Since Rorty believed we cannot socialize children to be ironists, perhaps they fake fundamentalism, perform metaphysics rather than irony, until the schools have completed the process of socialization that every citizen requires. Perhaps Rorty wanted to think of raising children in terms of the teacher instead of the parent because he suspected that in creating children we might get implicated in the fundamentalism of the regular parents who sit on school boards enforcing the status quo and the common sense—as the college professor gets drawn into completing and defending the less interesting work of high school teachers. For an ironist to have and raise a child could require pretending to believe simple stories that you know are more complicated. It could mean pretending that values are fixed and real when you know they are contingent and contestable. Or perhaps the experience of having and raising a child threatens to reveal that every ironist harbors his or her own metaphysics and foundational values.

In Rorty's view, children *need* to inherit something foundational. But it is not quite for their own sake. It is actually the private needs *of the ironist* that are the most important reason that socialization and "public rhetoric" cannot be ironist.

> On my definition, an ironist cannot get along without the contrast between the final vocabularies she inherited and the one she's trying to create for herself. Irony is, if not intrinsically resentful,

at least reactive. Ironists have to have something to have doubts
about, something from which to be alienated. (*Contingency, Irony,
and Solidarity*, 87–88)

Something is occurring here on both the individual level and the social
level. On the individual level, a person has to be brought up with a sort of
noble lie. They have to be told that the principles that govern their community, even though they are based on accidents and historical contingencies, are without doubt the proper principles by which a person should
live. A young person is not to be encouraged to have any of those "radical and continuing doubts" that Rorty and his fellow ironist intellectuals
carry around with them. The reason is that if potential future ironists had
not been given a set of principles and taught that they were true, then the
ironist would not be sure what to doubt. One has to have been certain
about something first in order to experience *as exquisite* the tortures of
radical and continuing doubts.

On a social level, if people were socialized to be ironists, or if socialization did not at least specifically discourage it, than being an ironist might
simply feel normal. The ironist is like Nietzsche's overman in that he or she
"needs the opposition of the masses, of the leveled, a feeling of distance
from them! He stands on them. He lives off them."[56] Rorty did not want
to feel normal, and he believed that he is a member of a particular breed of
human for whom feeling normal does not work. Harold Bloom, a favorite
of Rorty's, tends to talk about this breed in terms of the extent to which
they feel "the anxiety of influence." The anxiety is a feeling of "horror of
finding oneself to be only a copy or a replica" of one's parents or other
influences (*Contingency, Irony, and Solidarity*, 24).[57]

The extreme importance Rorty places on the "radical and continuing" doubts that rack the ironist intellectual might have something to do
with Rorty's own anxiety of influence. Rorty makes an erotically charged
relationship between teacher and student central to his ideas about socialization. But since Freud, it has been commonly understood that it is
the erotically charged relationship between *parent and child* that is most
central to the development of the individual. Particularly for boys, if the
oedipal complex is negotiated in the expected way, the son is expected to
internalize the authority of his father in the form of his own superego. In
fact, in philosophy and politics, Rorty, prophet of self-creation, had a lot
in common with his parents.

Rorty made his reputation by rebelling against the orthodoxy of analytic philosophy.[58] Bernstein suggested that "there seems to be something
almost oedipal—a form of patricide—in Rorty's obsessive attacks on
the father figures of philosophy and metaphysics. It is the discourse of
a one time 'true believer' who has lost his faith."[59] But at the same time,
few philosophers are more obsessively loyal to their philosophical influences. Rorty declared his loyalty to his "hero" Dewey in nearly every one
of his writings after *Philosophy and the Mirror of Nature.* Dewey was also
a favorite of Rorty's parents, a point they got across to young Richard
by repeatedly telling him, "with great pride," the story of how "when I
[Richard] was seven I had the honor of serving little sandwiches to the
guests at a Halloween party attended . . . by John Dewey" (*Achieving Our
Country,* 61). Other parental loyalties abound in Rorty's work. He argued
that the Left should give up frivolous philosophical debates and return to
a focus on labor politics. Rorty's father wrote about union organization
for socialist newspapers (60). Rorty believed the Left should concentrate
on offering progressive policy proposals in the tradition of the New Deal.
He also pointed out that "a lot of my relatives helped write and admin-
ister New Deal legislation" (60). Rorty prided himself on having been a
staunch anticommunist and cold warrior in the tradition of Sidney Hook
and Lionel Trilling. He admitted this was "partly, perhaps, because I had
been bounced on their knees as a baby" (61).

Nietzsche, in one of his many aphorisms about the difficulty of overcoming the basic character we inherit from our parents, said that "the man
resembles the child more closely than he does the youth: what this process
probably indicates is that a temporary alienation from our basic character
occurred during our youth but has been overcome by that accumulated
strength of manhood."[60] Rorty's own life played out in much the same way.
At the age of fifteen, Rorty "escaped from the bullies" in his high school by
enrolling in the Hutchins College for teens at the University of Chicago
(*Philosophy and Social Hope,* 7). There he fell under the sway of a group of
philosophers who were less pragmatic than the sort his parents brought to
their home.

> All seemed to agree that something deeper and weightier than
> Dewey was needed. . . . This sounded pretty good to my 15-year-old
> ears. For moral and philosophical absolutes sounded a bit like my
> beloved orchids—numinous, hard to find, known only by a chosen

few. Further, since Dewey was a hero to all the people among
whom I had grown up, scorning Dewey was a convenient form of
adolescent revolt. (8–9)

In the story Rorty tells, his rebellion against the Dewey–parent complex
lasted about twenty years until, upon rereading Hegel, "I found myself
being led back to Dewey . . . suddenly things began to come together"
(12). It was this return to Dewey, and the response to Rorty's *Philosophy
and the Mirror of Nature*, in which he first declared his loyalty to Dewey,
that "[gave] me a self-confidence I previously lacked" (12). Contrary to
Bernstein, Rorty was not a "true believer" who had lost his faith but rather
a true believer who had rediscovered it. Rorty became himself by return-
ing to his parental inheritance. Rorty at least could take comfort in knowing that while he had accepted what his parents had taught him, he also
experienced and entertained radical and continuing doubts about it. But
in caring for children and the next generation, in protecting them from the
wrong influences—influences less like Rorty's parents—he was forced to
become more strident in his beliefs and insistent about his point of view.
Rorty was forced to abandon the challenges of contest for the stability of
parental virtue.

The Politics of Pity

Given the completeness of Rorty's return to his childhood values, it is
striking that he was so insistent that his own notion of the ideal way to
live, ironism, cannot be socialized and should never be a parental inheritance. He thought a "metaphysical" socialization is the only way the youth
of tomorrow will have something nonironist to feel anxiety about. Those
young people with the proper restlessness and the proper talent can rebel
toward Rorty and irony instead of rebelling (perhaps temporarily) against
it. Rorty considered himself a good democrat, and he scolded theorists
whose work did not take an interest in what regular people were worrying
about, but Rorty also seemed deeply invested in maintaining the exclusiveness of the experience of irony.

One way to understand Rorty's insistence on nonironist socialization
is to look at his ideas about the importance of avoiding cruelty. It is the
ironist's particular relationship to cruelty that offers him or her a social
role of profound magnanimity to supplement the lonelier satisfactions of

exclusiveness. Rorty was fond of Judith Shklar's notion that at the core of liberalism is the idea that "cruelty is the worst thing we do" (*Contingency, Irony, and Solidarity*, xv, 74).[61] In considering cruelty, Rorty noted that one thing "we share with all other humans is the same thing we share with all other animals—the ability to feel pain" (177). Rorty dismissed the reaction that someone like Peter Singer might have to this fact, the idea that "our moral vocabulary should be extended to cover animals as well as people" (177).[62] Rorty thought that a better approach "is to try and isolate something that distinguishes human from animal pain" (177). What he arrived at is our socialization. Rorty argued that "human beings who have been socialized—socialized in any language, any culture—share a capacity which other animals lack. They can be given a special kind of pain: they can all be humiliated by the forcible tearing down of the particular structures of language and belief in which they were socialized (or which they pride themselves on having formed for themselves)" (177).[63] Rorty, despite his return to his parental inheritance, believed he and a small group fell into the latter category of self-creators and that most other humans fall into the former.

For this reason, contests are often not fair, and humiliation is a real danger. Rorty often summarized the challenges that faced the nation, the challenges that could be met only through engaging each other on the shared grounds of our hopes for our children, simply as "selfishness and sadism" (*Achieving Our Country*, 80, 83, 98). He described social responsibility in terms of the need to "sort out one's relations to this world . . . in which ugly and ungifted children . . . are humiliated and die" (*Contingency, Irony, and Solidarity*, 168).[64] In a world imagined in this way, Rorty and other ironist intellectuals are cast in the role of hero whether they are passive or active. They are a type that lives dangerously for themselves, relentlessly tearing apart their own beliefs. In certain circumstances, among those who have been fully socialized, they will perform this freedom for an audience, usually in a college classroom, carefully provoking without humiliating. But to avoid being cruel, they must be virtuous in public and tread carefully for the sake of the precious beliefs of others, for the sake of politics and solidarity, and for the sake of future generations.

Rorty's project offered a reclamation of pity—the pity that Nietzsche worried would convince us to cling to one identity so as not to hurt those we cared about. But Rorty defended pity not against Nietzsche's theory of contest but against Kantian notions of virtue. He noted that Kant be-

lieved the best way to develop democratic institutions and political consciousness "was to emphasize not pity for pain and remorse for cruelty
but, rather, rationality and obligation—specifically, *moral* obligation. . . .
[B]y contrasting 'rational respect' with feelings of pity and benevolence,
he made the latter seem dubious, second rate motives for not being cruel"
(*Contingency, Irony, and Solidarity*, 193). Rorty sought to make pity and benevolence first rate again because pity and benevolence are what people
like him, ironist intellectuals, feel for the general public. It is what they
must feel if they are to avoid casually devastating regular people with their
ability to inject doubts into any belief. Pity is the ironist's virtue.

Kant had his reasons for thinking pity was second-rate and an unworthy sentiment on which to base a community of equals. Nietzsche,
less concerned with equality, was suspicious of pity as well. At one point,
Rorty characterizes the Nietzschean project of "becoming who you are"
as becoming "'whom one turned oneself into in the course of creating the
taste by which one ended up judging oneself.' The term 'ended up' is, however, misleading. It suggests a predestined resting place. But the process of
becoming aware of one's causes by redescribing them is bound to be still
going on at one's death" (*Contingency, Irony, and Solidarity*, 99). Nietzsche's
ideas about parenthood, as I explored in chapter 2, suggest the pull of a
resting place other than death. In embracing pity, Rorty found places to
seek respite from the challenges of contest as well. Pity for children means
teaching them the tenets of virtue and not contest. But the child lives on
in the adult, in the form of the ideas about right and wrong in which they
were socialized. So Rorty must pity adults as well and protect the adult
public sphere from the challenges of contest. Rorty's politics, so caught up
in hopes for the future, looked not only forward but down. And in looking down to the child who lives on in the soul of nonironist adults—the
oldest part of them, the part it would be most cruel to challenge—he ultimately looks back to the past, to his parents' day, to the old Left and to
simpler patriotism.

Having embraced pity and enlarged the metaphor of parental sentiment
as far as it could go, Rorty wound up with the worst parts of Nietzsche. Re-
versing the terms of Honig's appropriation, Rorty gave up on Nietzschean
contest but embraced Nietzschean elitism. Ultimately, Rorty's politics
of parenthood led him to conceive of a politics of breeding analogous to
Nietzsche's. "Producing generations of nice, tolerant, well-off, secure, other-
respecting students . . . in all parts of the world is just what is needed—

indeed *all* that is needed—to achieve an Enlightenment utopia" (*Truth and Progress,* 179), he wrote. For Rorty, the future depended on how many "youngsters like this we can raise" (179). In the face of this repro-ductive politics, in which pity passes for virtue and parental sentiments mark a dubious path from the dreary present to a future salvation, it might have behooved Rorty to look again at his own analysis of Derrida. Noting Derrida's hesitancy to ever reach a resting place, "a result, a conclusion," Rorty mentioned a passage in which Derrida equates the desire for ab-solutes with the desire for a child. As Rorty quotes Derrida, the child is "the most beautiful and most living of fantasies, as extravagant as absolute knowledge" (*Contingency, Irony, and Solidarity,* 130).[65]

Rorty wrote in *Contingency, Irony, and Solidarity* (23) that one poem helped him more than anything else to "pin down what [he] wanted to say" regarding the pleasures of self-creation and the contest made possible by the embrace of contingency: Philip Larkin's "Continuing to Live."[66] It is, however, as Rorty acknowledged, a poem about the futility of self-creation, written from the perspective of a dying man. Looking back on our lives from the "green evening when our death begins," Larkin suggested, the ef-fort we have put into creating ourselves "is hardly satisfying, / Since it ap-plied only to one man once, / And that man dying." By giving such central place to our hopes for our children, to what we pass on to them, and to how to preserve and protect it, Rorty gave in to the sentiment of Larkin's verse. Like Nietzsche, he came to believe that self-creation in the present is pointless if we cannot control its impact on the future. Parental senti-ments ultimately pushed self-creation aside, and Rorty arrived at a politics preoccupied with humiliation and pity, breeding and preservation. It is a politics bleak enough to call to mind a different verse of Larkin's, this one about family: "Man hands on misery to man. / It deepens like a coastal shelf. / Get out as early as you can, / And don't have any kids yourself."[67]

CHAPTER 4

Deadbeat Citizens:
Cornel West and the Parent as Prophet

If we can produce this magical parent power, we can go to the very heart of our darkness and make the center hold.

Sylvia Ann Hewlett and Cornel West

A S A YOUNGSTER, Cornel West beat up a pregnant woman. West had refused to salute the flag because of his anger over America's racial injustice, and when his teacher tried to force him, finally slapping him, he lost his cool. Once he calmed down, West was relieved to find out that "the baby was fine."[1] But the incident prefigured a tension that would reemerge in the mature West's political thought. Parenthood has come to play a complex role in West's efforts to balance hope for the future with an acknowledgment of America's tragic past and problematic present. In his quest to identify transcendent sources of meaning that might inspire individuals to redeem American politics from its cruel history and rescue it from new dangers, West has often turned to the sentiments associated with parenthood. West sees parenthood as a concrete experience in people's lives that can create unity across disparate groups of citizens and can help instill values that are crucial to the right sort of citizenship: love, hope, and an orientation toward the future. These qualities, West believes, must be central to American efforts to ward off the nihilism that results from the chaotic forces of the market and to stifle an impulse to authoritarianism that threatens American freedom and democracy. Thus he and his coauthor Sylvia Ann Hewlett call for "nothing less than a moral awakening around the significance of parenting . . . [which will] reinvent government and banish the apathy and cynicism that haunt our public life" (*The War against Parents,* 258). But in staking so much of his American political project on parenthood, West creates new difficulties. Nihilism can overwhelm the virtuous sentiments associated with parenthood and family. When this bastion of love and hope is threatened, West is tempted by solutions fueled by despair and threatening to democratic freedoms.

In his focus on parenthood, West undermines many of the political commitments he developed in his engagements with black Protestant theology, Marxist social analysis, and pragmatist philosophy. In particular, West's ideas about parenthood undermine a productive tension he has long developed between the contest and virtue conceptions of democratic citizenship. West the theologian suggests that citizens might learn from the Christian gospel the importance of a willingness "to contradict what is . . . to transform and to be transformed." He also accepts that the results of such a transformation "are circumscribed by human imperfection."[2] But in turning to parenthood to inform citizenship, West finds imperfections less tolerable and turns to traditional values and an intrusive state for solutions. West suggests that theology offers solutions to "the two basic challenges presently confronting Afro-Americans . . . self image and self-determination . . . the human attempt to define who and what one is . . . [and] the political struggle to gain significant control over the major institutions that regulate people's lives" (*Prophecy Deliverance!* 22). But in coming to recommend parenthood as the best source of self-definition, West finds reasons to give established institutions greater control over citizens in order to preclude poor decisions regarding the directions of our lives.

West admires Marx but worries that Marxist "romantic quests for harmony and wholeness . . . may result in aborted authoritarian arrangements."[3] Thus he seeks to highlight Marx's commitment to "the precious values of individuality and democracy that can guide and regulate such quests and movements" (*The Ethical Dimensions of Marxist Thought,* xxi). Turning to the tradition of pragmatist philosophy in the United States, West admires the attempt to find a middle ground between "rapacious individualism and . . . authoritarian communitarianism. To walk a tightrope between individualism, hedonism and narcissism . . . and . . . conceptions of community that impose values from above, thereby threatening precious liberties" (*Beyond Eurocentrism,* 32–33). But West also articulates a romantic quest for personal wholeness and political harmony centered on parenthood and suggests political measures that limit personal freedom and enlarge the scope of state power.

In his more general considerations of the challenges facing twenty-first-century American democracy, West suggests that "democratic individuality requires mature and free persons who . . . shun innocence, illusion, and purity" and argues that one of the most dangerous ideas in our democracy is that we are "the most virtuous."[4] But he also endorses a "new social movement" premised on the idea that parents have unique access to the "most sublime and selfless feelings" and "the better angels of human nature" and the "magical force" of love (*The War against Parents*, xvi–xvii, 42)—qualities that West believes entitle parents to special rights and privileges as citizens.

So, in thinking about the use of parenthood for citizenship, West manages to contradict many of the commitments he has developed through a variety of projects in an unusually wide-ranging intellectual career. Throughout that work, West, like Rorty, incorporates aspects of both the virtue and contest conceptions of democratic citizenship. As the previous chapter argued, Rorty balanced virtue and contest notions of citizenship through a problematic division of spheres in which he confined self-creation and contest to a private realm, and he suggested family feeling as the key to a virtuous orientation to politics—a division that his ideas about parenthood persistently helped to undermine. West's inclination is in many ways the opposite of Rorty's. If Rorty attempts to strike a balance between virtue and contest by pushing his ideas, seesaw style, to the far ends of the plank, West balances by straddling the middle—with, predictably, more dynamic results. West is willing to let his commitments to the values of virtue and contest come to bear on one another. He has sought to integrate these two traditions of thinking about citizenship, to preserve the strengths of both and develop them in ways that are eclectic, searching, and experimental. Throughout these efforts, West identifies resources for the sort of democratic individuality he favors by unearthing commitments to virtue and contest in black theology, Marxism, American pragmatism, and American politics more generally. In dealing with persistent problems that emerged through his work, he has become attracted to parenthood as the experience that best informs citizenship. In doing so, he re-creates versions of the pathologies of the parent as citizen identified in earlier chapters. Imagined by West as a bastion of virtue in the face of a creeping nihilism, he discovers that parenthood threatens to reveal our failures. Described by West as an experience that instills openness and engagement, parenthood ultimately pulls West toward fundamentalism and authoritarian arrangements.

In offering his wide-ranging exploration of democratic citizenship and the traditions and experiences that best inform it, West has become a controversial and often misunderstood figure. His work is often praised without real engagement and other times contemptuously dismissed.[5] But there is a good deal about West's work that justifies the middle path of serious consideration. In particular, West looks to the tradition of American Protestantism to uncover resources for progressive politics during an era when political entrepreneurs on the Right were crafting a profoundly successful conservative movement with an evangelical version of protestant Christian morality at its center.[6] West emphasizes the role that religious faith can play in creating a self-critical yet hopeful "democratic individuality" during the period when the Christian Right often brought a spirit of self-righteous fundamentalism to American politics. And in the same era that the conservative movement in the United States has relied on complex ties to white citizens' feelings about black citizens in the post–civil rights era,[7] West makes the challenges and opportunities presented by post–civil rights black citizenship central to his explorations of religious, socialist, and pragmatist thought. The result is that West is a thinker whose commitment to and exploration of American citizenship is worth attending to—and whose deviation from those commitments in the name of the political uses of parenthood is telling.

Furthermore, the work that West began in the 1980s and 1990s has taken on increased significance in the new century. West weaves together an account of the contributions that Christianity, the black experience, concern for the working class, and pragmatism might make to our notions of citizenship. In this way, West's work engages the set of concerns and influences that were central to the pre-presidential political career of Barack Obama—the values that guide Obama and make his message and his story compelling, as well as the commitments that sometimes complicated his trajectory toward the presidency. West and Obama share, among other things, an interest in the Christian pragmatist philosopher Reinhold Niebuhr, a philosopher whose attempt to articulate a version of democratic citizenship that strikes a balance between the hopeful and the tragic inspires both men.[8] Obama's speech explaining the role that his membership in the Trinity United Church of Christ played in his life—an effort to attend to the hopefulness he encountered there along with anger at racial injustice—was among the most important moments of his 2008 campaign. The speech touched on territory similar to that which West has written about since the 1980s—black anger and black hope, affirming

America's progress without trivializing what is left to be done, and love that endures despite conflict and misunderstanding.[9] Obama is like West in that he is fond of invoking parenthood as the source of the sentiments that should be most important in our politics. To the extent that West's goals are worthy ones for the political community, to the extent that the election of Obama indicates these goals are compelling to citizens, to the extent that we sympathize with West's efforts to salvage a self-directed democracy from the chaotic pull of market forces—it is useful to see what complications emerge when he attempts to put ideas and feelings about parenthood in the service of his goals.

Virtue, Contest, Romance, and Tragedy

In articulating his version of contemporary citizenship, West responds to previous accounts of modern citizenship rooted in virtue and contest. He attempts to weld these two traditions together in a version of citizenship that ties a Rousseauvian wish for perfectibility to a Nietzschean desire to affirm life in the face of unavoidable tragedy, pain, and unpredictability. In doing so, West creates what might be thought of as a productive tension in his thinking about citizenship—a tension that allows him to offer accounts of both what is useful and what is counterproductive for contemporary democratic citizenship in the variety of theories and traditions he investigates. In developing and maintaining this tension in a political outlook he often refers to as "prophetic pragmatism," West wants to create a version of citizenship that is hopeful without ignoring profound and intractable challenges, one that incorporates variety and individuality while holding to a particular vision of the good.

> This interplay between tragic thought and romantic impulse, inescapable evils and transformable evils makes prophetic pragmatism seem schizophrenic. On the one hand, it appears to affirm a Sisyphean outlook in which human resistance to evil makes no progress. On the other hand, it looks as if it approves a utopian quest for paradise. In fact, prophetic pragmatism denies Sisyphean pessimism and utopian perfectionism. Rather it promotes the human possibility of progress and the human impossibility of paradise. (*The American Evasion of Philosophy*, 229)

But while West develops and deploys this productive tension in his work, he also struggles at times to endure the pull of competing commitments and indulges in dreams of resolution. West seems to worry that the competition inherent to democratic individualism can dissolve into a standardless chaos—a "nihilism" he associates with the market—if a particular vision of virtue is not preserved. The dominance of market values "redefines the terms of what we should be striving for in life, glamorizing materialistic gain, narcissistic pleasure, and the pursuit of narrow individualistic preoccupations—especially for young people" (*Democracy Matters*, 4). At the same time, West worries about "escalating authoritarianism rooted in . . . our traditional fear of too many liberties, and our deep distrust of one another" (6). West identifies these two possibilities, nihilism and authoritarianism, as the chief threats to "snuff out the democratic impulses that are so vital for the deepening and spread of democracy in the world" (8).

At times, West makes the case that these two threats to contemporary democracy feed off each other—for example, when the market responds to authoritarian impulses.

> The market-driven media . . . abetted by profit-hungry monopolies have severely narrowed our political "dialogue." . . . We are losing the very value of dialogue—especially respectful communication— in the name of the sheer force of naked power. This is the classic triumph of authoritarianism over the kind of question, compassion, and hope requisite for any democratic experiment. (*Democracy Matters*, 7)

However, West is also aware that authoritarian impulses are just as likely to feed off the desire to overcome the nihilistic and escape from "a life of horrifying meaninglessness, hopelessness, and (most importantly) lovelessness" (*Democracy Matters*, 26). One example can be found in Rousseau, whom West appreciates because he "unleashed unprecedented human energies and powers, significantly transformed selves and societies, and directed immense human desires and hopes toward the grand moral and credible political ideals of democracy and freedom, equality and fraternity" (*The American Evasion of Philosophy*, 215). In elaborating his position as a "prophetic pragmatist," West suggests he is part of a "third wave" of romanticism—the first wave of which he traces to Rousseau. But in noting that the uncompromising beauty of Rousseau's ideals contributed to the excesses of the French Revolution, West identifies a worrisome relationship between the utopian impulses of romanticism and the pull of authoritarianism (216).

So even as West attempts to find, preserve, and articulate the sort of hopeful and utopian impulses he calls "romantic" he is careful to balance it with the importance of contest and self-criticism. This is the case with the variety of traditions that West turns to as resources for his own vision of democratic citizenship. In his early books, *Prophesy Deliverance!* and *The Ethical Dimensions of Marxist Thought,* West argues for an "alliance of prophetic Christianity and progressive Marxism," which he believes "provides a last humane hope for humankind" (*Prophesy Deliverance!* 95). West worries that Marx's stirring call to overcome alienation and create a harmonious society has encouraged the authoritarianism of those who would form governments in his name (*The Ethical Dimensions of Marxist Thought,* xx). So West offers a reexamination of Marx "step by step, text by text" to uncover "his ethical values of individuality and democracy" (xxi). Among those inspired by Marx, West supports those who are democratic and "Marxist in the American grain: experimental in method, moral in motivation, and optimistic in outlook."[10]

In bringing Christianity, especially the black Protestant tradition in America, into alliance with Marxist concerns, West hopes that he might bring along a sense of human fallibility. West believes the black church offers insight into the importance of persisting in a struggle despite the fact that "ultimate triumph eludes it and imperfect products plague it" (*Prophesy Deliverance!* 96). The black religious tradition suggests, West believes, that the best response to the inevitability of such flaws is to embrace a version of perpetual contest rather than give in to the temptation to resign from the burdens of politics or suspend politics through authoritarian arrangements. Such fallibility, according to West, "is not an excuse which justifies the existing status quo, but rather a check on utopian aspirations which often debilitate and demoralize those persons involved in negating and transforming the status quo" (96). West believes it is a special strength of the black church, thanks to its problematic relationship to the state, that the "black church holds that Christian intervention into the public arena must speak the common moral language of the society as a whole: namely, the language of rights" (*Prophetic Fragments,* 23). Thus, unlike the evangelical movement represented by the Moral Majority, movements rooted in the black church "have avoided calls for . . . an authoritarian imposition of 'Christian' values upon non-Christians in the public sphere" (23). In this way, West contrasts the Christian sentiments he finds useful for democratic citizenship—especially a deep sense of the equality of every person in the eyes of God—to forms of "Constantine Christianity" in which a faith that should be "fundamentally based on tolerance and compassion" is united with the strong arm of the state and imposes its values from above (*Democracy Matters*, 148). When West writes about Islam and black Muslim leaders, he brings similar concerns. He suggests, for example, that "to build upon the best of Malcolm X, we must preserve and expand his notion of psychic conversion that cements networks and groups in which black community, humanity, love, care and concern can take root and grow . . . [and] reject Manichean ideologies and authoritarian arrangements in the name of moral visions."[11]

In acknowledging the danger that citizens with "romantic" political hopes might be attracted to authoritarian means to accomplish them, West is careful to suggest that we not take our caution too far. Citizens and political thinkers should not let a fear of authoritarianism prevent them from articulating an account of the good and defending the political projects in which they believe. West associates this sort of paralysis most often with postmodern theorists like Foucault and Derrida. "Foucault is the exemplary anti-romantic, suspicious of any talk about wholeness, totality, telos, purpose or even future" (*The American Evasion of Philosophy*, 223). Theorists like Foucault frustrate West by refusing to attempt precisely the balance between virtue (or romance) and contest that he articulates. They "shun any theory that promotes political action with purpose; for them, any social project of transformation reeks of authoritarian aims."[12]

West turns to Nietzsche to defend his claim that the postmodernists had taken their suspicion of political projects too far. Noting the extent to which postmodern theorists are indebted to Nietzschean insights, West argues that Nietzsche believed his critiques of inherited values and ideals "lead to a paralyzing nihilism and ironic skepticism unless they are supplemented with a new worldview, a new 'countermovement' to overcome such nihilism and skepticism."[13] West argues that Nietzsche's purpose in questioning the moral values of his time was to create the space to articulate new and more humane values in their place and to create an ethic of contest and criticism in which those values might be questioned, revised, and overcome in turn.

Honig argues that Nietzsche endorses some attempts at "ordering a contingent world as part of an attempt to maintain a community and its form of life."[14] But, she notes, Nietzsche endorsed such attempts to articulate a positive vision of how to live only if they were conceived of in the context of ongoing struggle and contest. "Nietzsche prefers the sort of law that operates as a means in a struggle and not as a weapon against all struggle."[15] West takes similar lessons from Nietzsche to endorse contemporary political movements against postmodern theorists made nervous by them.[16] West believes that such movements can incorporate the "relentless criticism and healthy skepticism" that "Foucault rightly wants to safeguard" but also "take seriously moral discourse—revisable means and ends of political action, the integrity and character of those engaged and the precious ideals of participatory democracy and the flowering of the uniqueness of different human individualities" (*The American Evasion of Philosophy*, 226). West calls for postmodern theorists to avoid a descent into "nihilism" by articulating and defending a "countermovement" as part of the politics of contest. Eventually, a fear of nihilism of a different sort— an everyday lived nihilism experienced by regular people rather than academic nihilism—would convince West to privilege one worldview in particular: the worldview of the parent as citizen. And instead of embracing the continual contest of movements and countermovements, he would seek a lasting unity cemented by this worldview.

West, Rorty, Pragmatism, and Hope

West argues for a version of democratic citizenship that maintains a productive tension between the hopeful and utopian impulses of Rousseauvian romanticism and the skepticism, openness, and suspicion of fundamentalism of Nietzschean contest. He worries about the authoritarian impulses that might result from romanticism and about the nihilism that lurks on the other end of the spectrum. But it is possible to detect in his work a competing desire that such tensions be resolved—that a single solution be discovered that can redeem politics and provide a respite from the difficulties of contest. West's impulse to find a source of unity and harmony was something that Rorty noticed in the 1980s, before either West or Rorty began to write extensively about family and parenthood. It is possible to see in this exchange the shared interests that would lead each to give parenthood a prominent and problematic place in their thinking as well as the differences that would determine the divergent ways that they would put ideas about parenthood to use.

As mentioned in the previous chapter, West saw Rorty's critique of analytic philosophy as backward looking and self-satisfied—happy to tear down ideas but not eager to build alternatives in their place. This frustrated West because he believes the American tradition of pragmatism might offer valuable ideas for thinking about contemporary democratic citizenship— the sort of hopeful and future-oriented yet self-critical and antiauthoritarian citizenship that West favors. West explores this possibility more extensively in *The American Evasion of Philosophy,* his book on the pragmatist tradition. West argues that the tradition of American pragmatist philosophy offered resources "to reinvigorate our moribund academic life, our lethargic political life, our decadent cultural life, and our chaotic personal lives for the flowering of many-sided personalities and the flourishing of more democracy and freedom" (5).

What West likes most about the American pragmatist tradition is very similar to what Rorty praised in it: its thinkers attempt to articulate hopeful and progressive political projects that respond to the actual circumstances of the moment rather than "metaphysical" and "epistemological" questions. In other words, pragmatism offers a compelling argument for the politics of contest balanced by the hopeful spirit of the romantic. In doing so, West believes, the pragmatic tradition can prove itself far more useful than the sort of philosophy that seeks to be "a tribunal of reason which ground claims about Truth, Goodness and Beauty" (*The American Evasion of Philosophy,* 4). But West believes pragmatism has often failed to meet its potential and has stagnated in contemporary times. He hoped his book would "speak to the major impediments to a wider role for pragmatism in American thought" (7).[17]

Rorty found much to appreciate in the West volume that criticized him. But Rorty also identified in West's thought a "basic tension . . . between a wish to evade philosophy and a hope that something rather like philosophy will take its place."[18] Following West, Rorty referred to this "something rather like philosophy" as the "prophetic" and linked it with the sort of "social hope" that would come up so often in Rorty's own later philosophy. And though he had yet to do so himself, Rorty seemed to endorse West's efforts to articulate a "prophetic pragmatism." As Rorty put it, "[Pragmatism] is socially useful only if teamed up with prophecies— fairly concrete prophecies of a utopian social future."[19]

But while Rorty acknowledged the importance of articulating social hope, he was critical of one particular way that West went about it—the hope for a deeper theory of oppression. "I agree with West that what the American Left most needs is prophecy—some sense of a utopian American future. . . . Sometimes (as in Rousseau, Dewey, and Unger) theory has been the helpful auxiliary of romance. But just as often it has served to blind the intellectuals to the new possibilities that romantics and prophets have envisioned."[20] In particular, Rorty worried that West's search for a more complete "worldview" was hindering his appreciation of specific, partial, contingent political claims and movements. Thus Rorty did not see much promise in West's hopes to discover "a unified theory of oppression . . . [integrating] issues of race, class and gender."[21] It annoyed Rorty that West would temper his appreciation of a particular pragmatist and romantic political project—like the one articulated by Roberto Unger in his *Politics*—by calling it "Eurocentric and patriarchal" because it does not "grapple with forms of racial and gender subjugation" (*The American Evasion of Philosophy*, 223). Rorty worried that West might undermine his own appreciation of pragmatism's greatest source of political potential—the willingness to articulate claims and visions for a community without reference to universal, metaphysical, and timeless truths or conceptions of the good—through his attraction to such a unified theory of oppression. West believed that Rorty had accepted contest, but only so far as it is trivial—linguistic, conversational, personal, ironic. Rorty, on the other hand, suspected that West's embrace of contest was endangered by his longing for a deeper unification or a final answer.

Parenthood and the Attainment of Unity

Rorty was right to worry. Following this exchange, both theorists would start down the path that led each to give ideas about parenthood a prominent place in his political thought. One can sense in Rorty's description of Foucault as "ice-cold" and "man on the moon" that he did not like how West had lumped them together by linking Foucault's "paralyzing" anti-authoritarianism with Rorty's commitment to irony. In turning to family and social hope, Rorty tried to warm up his philosophy. As the previous chapter argued, Rorty began to think of parents' love for their children as the source of "social hope" that provided the best motivation for political projects. And though he had been critical of West's attraction to universals, Rorty argued that the best way to expand the circles of concern that define communities was to tell sentimental family-centered stories about the lives of the poor, the foreign, and the weak—making the case that everyone is alike in their love for children. In thinking about family, Rorty became more like the West he criticized.

But they did not become just alike. Rorty treated the sentiments of parenthood and family feeling as natural and assumed—leaving them largely unexamined and offloading the problematic question of socialization to teachers and professors. By keeping the actual experience of parenthood at a distance, Rorty found it uncomplicated to presume that an ever-expanding unity and moral universalism might be achieved through the shared experience of a child-centered hopefulness. West examines the role of parenthood in personal and political identity more closely. In bringing his existing set of concerns to bear on the role that parenthood might play in citizenship, he brings a quest for unification—theoretical and otherwise—along with him. In doing so, he undermines his commitment to a productive tension between the politics of virtue and contest that he developed in his other work.

Whereas Rorty attempted to insulate his commitment to contingency and irony from his family-centered universalism by splitting apart the public from the private realm, West is a lumper and not a splitter. Throughout his career, West's instinct has been to combine insights and combine traditions in search of a more useful theory and orientation toward politics. For example, in ending his study of pragmatism, West summarizes that "prophetic pragmatism" would borrow from "Emerson's sense of vision . . . rechannel[led] through Dewey's conception of creative democracy and Du Bois's social structural analysis" and incorporate "the tragic sense found in Hook and Trilling, the religious version of the Jamesian strenuous mood in Niebuhr, and the tortuous grappling with the vocation of the intellectual in Mills" (*The American Evasion of Philosophy*, 212). Such a project is combined with others. Thus Iris Marion Young, in describing the orientation West developed over his career, adopts the agglomerative label "genealogical materialist prophetic pragmatism" and describes its development in terms of "additions" of "ingredients" to a "theoretical mix."[22]

Young appreciates this aspect of West's work, and she is critical when she detects a shift from his "theoretical projects" and his later "popular and political" coauthored works.[23] According to Young, West forgets his recipe of theoretical commitments when he turns to consider, with Hewlett, the family. She argues that "in his eagerness to offer solutions to America's persisting sources of suffering and cynicism, West has wrongly distanced himself from the subtlety of genealogical materialist prophetic pragmatism."[24] But it was actually the turn to parenthood that struck West as a way to finally weld together issues of race, sex, and class[25]—a project he has pursued for his whole career.

However, West accomplishes this not through the sort of theoretical complexity that Young admired but by sentiment and shared transformative personal experience. West and Hewlett would like to use the experience of parenthood to transform American politics, much as Rousseau helped transform Europe. Their book *The War against Parents,* blurbed by several senators as well as the CEOs of both the NAACP and Toys "R" Us, focuses on the way having children induces a self-transformation that can change the way a person thinks about and participates in politics. It is the depth of this personal experience and its transformative potential that allows it to transcend the divisions that West hoped to overcome. "By giving moral heft to the art and practice of parenting and by crafting a political agenda capable of delivering new and substantial support to parents, we have found a repository of comfort and strength that has the potential to bridge the deep divides of race, gender and class" (*The War against Parents,* xi). The authors use themselves as an example. To an extent that is unusual in an academic work, Hewlett and West focus on the relationship between the authors—the experiences that brought them together and that qualify them to write about the topic. The book begins,

> Ours is a special partnership. A black man and a white woman come together to confront our nation's war against parents and our consequent inability to cherish our children. Such a collaboration is rare and precious. . . . And our work together is not merely some cloistered, scholarly endeavor but involves high-stakes political action. It requires nothing less than the launching of a new political movement. (xi)

What allows Hewlett and West to come together is not the effort to solve difficult problems by juxtaposing different perspectives but rather a common experience: "The fact is, our 'blackness' and 'femaleness' pale in the light of an even more fundamental identity: that of being a parent. After all, we share the bedrock stuff: we are crazy about our kids" (xii).

So Hewlett and West's political project is about the building of consensus out of democratic variety, but it does so through the exploitation of a more fundamental similarity. This is also the case for the population of parents at large. "Strange as it may seem, the identity of being a parent—unlike those based on race, gender or class—is relatively undeveloped in American society, and enormous potential lies in identifying people first and foremost as parents" (xii). Just as, despite their different backgrounds, the authors found they shared a fundamental outlook because they have "the bedrock stuff" in common, the authors believe the American population of parents has uniform opinions if a person knows where to look. Hewlett and West argue that parents in American society only *seem* to have different opinions on matters of public concern because politicians "like to use parents as political footballs in their ideological games, magnifying differences and dividing a constituency that is already weak and vulnerable" (216). The authors present the results of a poll they conducted to show that if you ask the right questions, there is "a remarkable degree of consensus among parents" and that "there is *enormous unity across race, class, and gender*" (215–16).

This unity also carries across generations, allowing Hewlett and West to sympathize with their parents' suspicions regarding liberalism, feminism, self-realization, and nonfamilial sources of emotional fulfillment. They worry, for example, that feminists spread the idea that "the enormous quantity of other-directed energy absorbed by families gets in the way of freedom of choice and ultimately self-realization . . . which is why radical feminists tend to see motherhood as a plot to derail equal rights and lure women back to subservient, submissive roles in the family" (95). And this unity across generations also extends forward toward the future, allowing Hewlett and West to believe that parents should be able to represent their children's interests by literally casting votes for them. "This makes intuitive sense: today's elections will affect today's children well into maturity, and they should have an opportunity to influence that future, if only through their parents. But the measure also has immense practical ramifications: overnight it would almost double the potential size of the parent vote" (240–41).[26] The authors see no problem with the assumption that parents can be trusted to offer an enlightened representation of their children's interests in the election booth, since "the data from our survey . . . [reveals that] parents display a vision that is extremely responsible. They have no desire to offload their kids; on the contrary, they are struggling to take back territory and function. Without necessarily knowing the theory or the jargon, they understand that the parent–child bond is precious and that it is imperiled in new and serious ways" (219).[27]

In discovering a long-elusive unity across race, class, gender, and generations through the experience of parenthood, Hewlett and West appear to have developed a unified theory of virtue—describing how the experience of parenthood instills the "most sublime and selfless feelings" and "heroic energies" and renders parents "extremely responsible" (xvi, 25, 219)—rather than the unified theory of oppression West long sought. But oppression looms nearby. The parent–child bond is precious, but it is also "imperiled." This oppression is implied by the title of the book and confirmed by its substance: *The War against Parents* focuses less on parents than on the hostile culture that opposes them. Because of this oppression, heroic energies can lag and sometimes disappear. The book's opening lines suggest "a black man and a white woman come together" not only because they love their kids but because they cannot: they are united by an "inability to cherish our children" (xii). They acknowledge that they "share a load of impotence and guilt—and mounting rage—with other parents" (xii).

The authors are eager to pass this guilt on to someone else. Their book uncovers new culprits: "One of the best kept secrets of the last thirty years is that big business, government, and the wider culture have waged a silent war against parents, undermining the work they do" (xiii). This is a very particular sort of unity then, the unity of victimization, which allows West to recapture the spirit of the Marxist philosophy he explored in *The Ethical Dimensions of Marxist Thought*. Describing Marx's ideas as "fecund criticism" and "pack[ed] with life juices so that it will not only condemn, but give birth," West quotes Marx's description of what gives the working class its unique status in history. The proletariat is

> a sphere of society having a universal character because of its universal suffering and claiming no *particular wrong* but *unqualified wrong* is perpetrated on it; a sphere that can invoke no *traditional* title but only a *human* title . . . a sphere . . . in short, that is the *complete loss* of humanity and can only redeem itself through the *total redemption of humanity*. (42)

Parents would come to play a similar role for West: united and universal because of their suffering, afflicted at the most existential levels of human existence and for those reasons uniquely suited to lead us to redemption.[28]

Suffering and Citizenship

Neither of these ways of conceiving of the role of parents in politics—a uniform and morally superior group waiting to be mobilized or a victimized group at war with a hostile culture—seems very promising for democratic citizenship as West develops it elsewhere in his work. Neither appears to fit well with West's commitments to a democratic individualism that, rather than being virtuous, incorporates "relentless self-criticism and inescapable fallibilism"[29] and that, rather than being defensive, has an "exploratory, expansive, prospective temper" (*The American Evasion of Philosophy*, 123). But in conceiving of parents this way, West is not treading on entirely new ground. West has long been interested in the sort of political perspective that results from the experience of suffering and oppression. In a manner typical of West, he considers the perspective of those who suffer in terms of both virtue and contest and works hard to strike a balance. The care he brings to interrogating the problems and potential of the appearance of citizen-sufferers in the public realm makes West's treatment of parents particularly revealing of the problems with the use of ideas about parenthood in theorizing citizenship.

The question of the perspective that results from suffering is a crucial one for West, as it would be for any author who writes about American citizenship with an emphasis on the poor and the black communities. His stridency regarding the importance of bringing this perspective into politics has made some of his critics nervous. Rorty, for example, thought that West gave the perspective of suffering pride of place in political argument. In criticizing West's search for a unified theory of suffering, Rorty argued that "the oppressed have different purposes and wants from their oppressors, but they do not have deeper insight into reality."[30] West has written some things that imply he believes otherwise, and sometimes quite directly: "Truth is all about allowing suffering to speak" (*Hope on a Tightrope*, 37–38) and "The premier prophetic language is the language of cries and tears because human hurt and misery give rise to visions of justice and deeds of compassion" (*Democracy Matters*, 214).[31] However, even when West suggests that those who are in pain have unique access to truth, he usually manages to tie this idea to his commitments to democratic contest. If West plays up the profundity of suffering, it often seems he does so to give those who suffer an entrance into the realm of politics, and not in the expectation of a certain predetermined end once they get there.[32] When a weak or victimized group becomes political, West is careful to suggest that the values of political contest be applied to them as well. There is one exception, and that is when West turns to the suffering of parents.

For West, suffering is not always associated with absolute truth but with one important perspective among many: "The quest for truth, the quest for the good, the quest for the beautiful, all require us to let suffering speak, let victims be visible, and demand that social misery be put on the agenda of those with power" (*Hope on a Tightrope*, 37). While West believes that black Americans must play an important role in improving American politics, it is "not because black people have a monopoly on virtue or are always on the side of justice" (47). West can be hard on people he believes get this wrong. As a young writer, he criticized Marcus Garvey and Martin Luther King for embracing a black self-image that is "defensive in character and romantic in content." West believes that in creating a virtuous self-image in "reaction to the doctrine of white supremacy," Garvey and King both offered "an attempt to build Afro-American pride and self-worth upon quixotic myths about the past, exaggerated expectations of the present, and chiliastic hopes for the future" (*Prophesy Deliverance!*, 75). But in turning to parenthood as a source of self-identity, the later West marvels at the "supernatural" achievements of past generations and anticipates the complete transformation of American politics both present and future (*The War against Parents*, 5). He sees the obstacles that parents encounter not as a case of politics as usual but as unfair attacks on a special class of people.

When West writes about other oppressed groups entering the political sphere, he generally does not suggest they should be immune to the difficulties of politics understood as contest. Discussing the Obama candidacy on the eve of his election, West writes, "Now here we are in 2008. America finds itself looking to its blues people again to provide vision to a nation with the blues. That is a source of hope. Yet hope is no guarantee. Real hope is grounded in a particularly messy struggle and it can be betrayed by naïve projections of a better future that ignore the necessity of doing the real work" (*Hope on a Tightrope*, 6). Putting it more succinctly, he writes, "When you're full of hope, you're in the midst of the muck (15). This "real work"—work in the midst of the muck—is the difficult work of politics. West worries, particularly in light of Obama's successes, about complacency and the "illusion" that "entrance, or opening the gates, results in significant redistribution of cultural benefits. Inclusion makes possible new dialogues, new perspectives, and critical orientations and questions. Yet only discipline, energy and talent can produce quality" (40).[33]

This hard work of politics, for those who have suffered as for anyone, also involves taking chances, placing oneself at risk, and the task of self-criticism. Discussing "black people" and their political claims, West writes, "We should never be arrogant enough to think we can create some kind of critique-free situation. Neither should we despair because we are human and therefore inadequate, thinking that we don't have the capacity to be better" (*Hope on a Tightrope*, 199). Further, he argues that the claims of black citizens are not uniform, nor should they be. "Traditionally, black people have labored under the false notion that we must be homogenous to be strong. They confused homogeneity with unity. Strong unity actually comes from affirming our diversity" (199). This sort of language is missing from West's book on parents, where he emphasizes the similarity of parents' transformative love, their shared struggles, and their uniform concerns and opinions.

The reasons for this are not obvious. While West believes parents in the contemporary United States face harsh conditions, in his previous work, he wrote about conditions that seem harsher: the terrible history of race in America, the plight of the working class, and the imperialist oppression of the "wretched of the earth."[34] It was in crafting a notion of democratic citizenship that responds to terrible circumstances that West developed that particular balance of virtuous and contest notions of citizenship that mark his work. In examining these experiences, West seeks lessons that would be useful for democratic politics—a notion of citizenship that would not deal in abstractions but be grounded in real human conditions and respond to even the most difficult problems. So, for example, West has argued that the African American experience can provide guidance to American politics after 9/11—to the way Americans respond to new feelings of vulnerability and anger. He argues that to be black in America "for 400 years is to be unsafe, unprotected, subject to random violence and hated for who you are . . . we've got some experience that might be useful" (*Hope on a Tightrope*, 18). West recalls moments in which black leaders and black citizens, Martin Luther King and Mamie Till, responded to terrible violence with calls for justice that attempted to "keep track of the humanity of the very people that dehumanized [them]" (20). This is an important part of West's notion of the role of contest in democratic citizenship.

In a democratic society, you cannot demonize because demonizing
means that you have lost contact with the humanity of your foes.
You struggle, you take a stand, you fight. But once you demonize,
then you are calling into question the possibility of dialogue or
further engagement down the road. (*Beyond Eurocentrism,* 35)

In describing the social forces that oppose parents, however, Hewlett and
West use labels like "ruthless" and "poisonous" (*The War against Parents,*
29) and favor restrictions on the dialogue that occurs in the public sphere.

For West and Hewlett, the victimization of parents is made worse by
the responsibility parents feel to prevent their children from suffering as
well. Throughout his work, West takes an interest not only in those who
suffer but also in those motivated by their sympathy for them.[35] West gives
this sort of sympathy-based citizenship a central place in his conception
of "prophetic pragmatism." "Here's the bottom line: to be inspired by
[those] . . . who undergo suffering, but who have the courage to imagine a
different future and are willing to fight for it, and to decide to fight along
with them. That is prophetic thought and prophetic action as I understand it" (*Hope on a Tightrope,* 38). It is a notion of politics that has roots
in West's Christian faith, in "the biblical injunction to look at the world
through the eyes of its victims" (*Keeping Faith,* 133). This perspective helps
foster the qualities of citizenship West most admires. The Christian faith
"that helps us to care in a palpable way about the injustices we see around
us . . . drove Martin Luther King Jr., Rabbi Abraham Joshua Heschel,
Dorothy Day, and millions of other Americans to deepen our democratic
project. . . . Prophetic love unleashes ethical energy and political engagement" (*Democracy Matters,* 215).[36]

West is tough even on those he admires when they fail to allow sympathy with suffering to motivate their politics in the right way. He criticizes
King and Garvey for lacking a genuine connection to the poor and for offering "symbols and rituals to the Afro-American masses which are useful
for enhancing the social mobility of Afro-American professional and business groups. [They] generate cathartic and amorphous feelings of Afro-
American pride, self-congratulation and heroism that contain little substance" (*Prophesy Deliverance!,* 77–78). In recent decades, West believes,
the lack of sympathy for the underclass among black leaders and the black
middle class have become even worse. He worries that post–civil rights
leaders lack anger and humility—two qualities that allow for connection

to those who suffer. Writing from this perspective in *Race Matters*, West finds reason to praise King, among others, for a humility that allowed him to forget his status and "revel in the accomplishments and potentials of others" (59). West is also impressed by King's anger. King was "almost always visibly upset about the condition of black America. . . . One even gets the impression that [his] own stability and sanity rested on how soon the black predicament could be improved. . . . This anger fueled [his] boldness and defiance" (58).

Similarly, while West believes parents suffer, it is the suffering of their children that affects them most and can threaten their sanity. While parents are described as victims in his book with Hewlett, it is the pain inflicted on children that is expressed in the starkest of terms. While parents are "trampled on, sneered at," "bashed," "besieged, belittled, and bewildered" (*The War against Parents*, 26, 112, 257), the suffering of children is described in terms that call to mind America's history of lynching: "without a skin," "burned," "stunted and seared," "bleeding," and "dangling" (29, xiii, 59). According to Hewlett and West, the desire to protect and love their children in the face of social and economic pressures that make it difficult is the most painful aspect of parents' lives. In a section of the book that bemoans the way divorce and welfare laws unnecessarily alienate men from their children, Hewlett and West sympathetically relate the story of a John P. Royster. Royster loved his son "more than life" but was eventually "cut off" from seeing him by his ex-wife. "John P. began to spiral down." Eventually, he murdered a girlfriend. (170–71). Hewlett and West also have some sympathetic words for another father whose separation from his children reenacted his own father's absence: "O.J. Simpson had a large load to deal with on the father absence front" (167).

It is strange to encounter West, who does not exempt many figures from the critical edge of his attention, engaging in such uncritical sympathy with alienated parents driven over the edge. As a younger man, West had harsh words in *Prophesy Deliverance!* for many who worried about the suffering of blacks and the poor: Martin Luther King ("romantic and defensive," p. 75), James Baldwin ("parasitic" and not political, p. 85), Walt Whitman ("too fabricated . . . fails to ring true at all," p. 34), and the entire Harlem Renaissance ("mediocre . . . basically portrayed stereotypical lifestyles with which they were scarcely acquainted," p. 77). But the flaws of parents (even deeply flawed parents like O.J. Simpson) elicit a profoundly uncritical response. If children are suffering, it is not their parents' fault.

We demonstrate that at the heart of our children's plight is a truly frightening erosion of the parental role—of the ability of moms and dads to come through for their children. This is happening not because parents are less devoted than they used to be. They do not love their children less. The truth is, the whole world is pitted against them. (*The War against Parents*, xiii)

This description of parents as uniformly virtuous, and attacked from all sides, seems like an exaggerated version of the "romantic and defensive" posture that West criticized in King and Garvey. Hewlett and West are eager to insulate parents, from the overworked to the murderous, from self-recrimination and self-hatred.

Self-hatred is a problem that West has dealt with in subtler ways elsewhere in his political thought. It is another area where West's conception of democratic citizenship parallels the defense of a politics of contest that Honig develops in her reading of Nietzsche. Honig emphasizes that Nietzsche's critique of the morality of virtue was an effort to "free ourselves from the 'will of man to find himself guilty and reprehensible to a degree that can never be atoned for'"[37] According to Honig, the Nietzschean way to escape such self-hatred is to cease to judge oneself according to ethical ideas that impose a uniform standard of virtue that is hostile to the messiness and variety of life. Instead, we should embrace the idea of self-creation in which a person develops "an individuality, by working with, reshaping, and exploring the possibilities contained in and presented by raw materials that we did not choose."[38]

West confronts the problem of self-hatred, particularly in the black community, in an analogous way. He attempts to articulate a version of self-creation that would overcome self-contempt and be useful for politics. This is a theme of West's early work on the history of black thought in the United States and its use for thinking about democratic citizenship.[39] He identifies four "traditions of response" to the dominant white culture among black intellectuals and artists and notes the counterproductive role that "self-hatred and shame" played in several of them (*Prophesy Deliverance!*, 81). Nor does West think it is useful to posit black culture as uniquely virtuous in comparison to the racism and oppression carried out by whites—the above-mentioned "defensive" reaction that creates unlivable standards and fosters self-doubts (75).[40] West preferred the "humanist tradition," exemplified by Jean Toomer among others. In distilling Toomer's message about how black Americans might overcome self-hatred, West invokes a process of open-ended self-creation.

> [Toomer's] profound message to Afro-Americans is that in modernity, where alienation is commonplace, it is important to be aware of roots, but even this provides no assurance of ability to achieve a positive self-image in the ever-changing present. The search for personal identity is never a pleasant one if only because the very need for it connotes a misplacement, dislocation and homelessness of the self. The act of self-definition forever remains open ended, with no guarantee of triumph. Indeed, the process takes precedence over the result, since any static self-identity soon disintegrates the self. (87)[41]

One can hear echoes of Nietzsche in West's description of the humanist tradition—an awareness of one's origins, an attempt to transfigure them, a recognition that the task is never over. West's descriptions of the "humanist response" also call to mind what attracted Nietzsche to parenthood as a political identity—and would pull West in that direction as well. West writes that humanism is "the expression of an oppressed human community imposing its distinctive form of order on an existential chaos, explaining its political predicament, preserving its self respect and projecting its own special hopes for the future" (85). It was the hope that one might pass on to the future the results of self-crafting, the imposition of order on one's own chaos, that drove Nietzsche's interest in parenthood. West follows a similar path. For West, as for Nietzsche, conceiving of self-definition in terms of the experience of parenthood makes it particularly hard to endure the idea that it is "forever open-ended." When parents reconsider their lives, it can lead to feelings of betrayal and invite the very self-recrimination that the recrafting of self was meant to avoid.

The Tragic, the Church, and Natal Alienation

Both Nietzsche and West acknowledge that we confront the task of self-creation under difficult circumstances. Our chaos can seem impossible to reorder, our predicaments overwhelming, and our hopes for the future difficult to maintain. This was a central aspect of Nietzsche's thinking about self-creation—epitomized by his attention to the "tragic"—and it is an important idea for West. West makes an affirmation of life in the face of the tragic a central part of—and a central problem in—his thinking about citizenship.[42] Nietzsche believed that in creating a self, we must confront and even affirm the tragic aspects of life—that we affirm life in the face of "suffering ... torment, destruction," the "absurd and ugly" and the "questionable and strange."[43] Nietzsche, of course, saw Christian faith as one of the principal ways Europeans had avoided this challenge—had sought to escape the tragic rather than accept and affirm it. But West's unique take on the Christian tradition leads him to put the religious instinct to use for the quasi-Nietzschean purpose of affirming life in the face of the tragic. "My Christian perspective—mediated by the rich traditions of the black church that produced and sustains me—embraces depths of despair, layers of dread, encounters with the sheer absurdity of the human condition" (*The Making of an American Radical Democrat,* 13). West sees this sense of the tragic as both guiding "how to live one's life day by day" (13) and as serving a larger political purpose. "The reason I am preoccupied with a sense of the tragic is that I am preoccupied with our moment in which we must look defeat, disillusionment and discouragement in the face and work through it. A sense of the tragic is an attempt to keep alive some sense of possibility, some sense of hope" (*Beyond Eurocentrism,* 32). Thus the tragic is also the point at which political and religious sensibilities overlap.

> People tend to think that religious talk is different from political talk. You can talk about the kingdom and say it's just a metaphor. But actually it's very real. You have to have deep, deep religious faith to stay in the struggle for a long time.... Faith is our primary source of empowerment. If you haven't dealt with the bondage of death and despair, then you are going to be disillusioned after the first laps. (*Hope on a Tightrope,* 79)

West thinks this tragic sense—this determination to preserve hope and get to work even when circumstances tempt us to despair—is crucial to democratic citizenship in particular. "I believe a deep sense of evil and the tragic must infuse any meaning and value of democracy."[44]

But for West, this tragic sense, and its connection to the black church, was born of the least democratic aspect of our history—the particular form of American slavery, especially the way slavery related to family. Slavery and its legacy in the black community are at the origins of West's particular understanding of the relationship between the experience of parenthood and Christian faith. West is fond of citing Orlando Patterson's description of the central aspect of life for American slaves as "natal alienation."[45] The essence of this condition was the loss of connection between an individual and his or her parents and children—a legal disconnection as well as a literal one in many cases. As West describes it: "The loss of ties at birth [to] ascending and descending generations, a loss of ties to both predecessor and progeny has... created an airborne people, a dangling people, a people who must forever attempt to acquire their self-identity and self-image in a positive way as they are bombarded with negative ones" (*Beyond Eurocentrism*, 149). According to West, the black church developed its tragic sensibility in response to this condition.

The church was a "communal response" to the "existential and political situation" created by natal alienation (*Prophetic Fragments*, 4–5). Religious practices, and the black church that eventually grew out of them, were the way the black community developed a "worldview... [with] the utterly and undeniably *tragic* character of life and history at its center" and passed it on to new generations in a way that families often could not. The role the black church plays in inheritance is so important to West that he suggests that it trumps the strictly religious function of the church. "Black people do not attend churches, for the most part, to find God, but rather to share and expand together the rich heritage they have inherited" (163). This was the case when slavery tore black children from their parents, and it continued after emancipation when the fragility of black families caused them to struggle to sustain this heritage.[46] "Historically for so many, but especially for black people, the church has been an extended family. The church gave you a sense of history, memory, and the need for struggle" (*Hope on a Tightrope*, 92).

West not only sees the black church serving the Nietzschean purpose of affirming life in the face of the tragic, he believes the church does so in Nietzschean ways. Nietzsche believed that words were inadequate—too shallow—to pass on the results of a self-transformation and a sense of life that had reached down to the level of instinct. West, in turn, believes the central message of the black church "can only be existentially appropriated (not intellectually grasped)" (*Prophesy Deliverance!*, 98). Thus West rarely dwells on the words of Christian preachers so much as on Christian rituals that reach deeper into the soul—dance and music. Thanks to "the kinetic orality and affective physicality inherited from West African cultures and religions . . . black Christianity has a strong Dionysian element" (*Prophetic Fragments*, 162).[47] When West does attend to preaching, he suggests its most important elements reach beyond the words that are spoken: "The black Christian tradition of preaching and the black musical traditions of performance . . . , though undoubtedly linked to the life of the mind, are oral, improvisational and histrionic" (*Keeping Faith*, 72–73).[48]

What this music accomplishes is to convey precisely the "humanist" lesson about the importance of crafting a hopeful and affirmative self-identity—the sort of identity West finds most useful to democratic citizenship—in the face of difficult circumstances. While he praises Toomer's "humanist" novels, West believes that

> the best example of the Afro-American humanist tradition is its music. The rich pathos of sorrow and joy which are simultaneously present in spirituals, the exuberant exhortations and divine praises of the gospels, the soaring lament and lyrical tragicomedy of the blues, and the improvisational character of jazz affirm Afro-American humanity. (*Prophesy Deliverance!*, 85–86)

In his veneration of the "tragicomic" in black music, West shares with Nietzsche an appreciation of those who can be joyful in the face of the difficulties of self-creation in cruel circumstances. West gives the same outlook a central place in his appreciation of "humanist" writers—who depict "perseverance and fortitude" but also "a joy derived from . . . Christian faith and its Dionysian rituals" (*Prophesy Deliverance!*, 88). West praises "the ability to laugh and retain a sense of life's joy—to preserve hope even while staring in the face of hate and hypocrisy—as against falling into the nihilism of paralyzing despair" (*Democracy Matters*, 16). He includes this "tragicomic hope" among the elements of his "democratic armor" (217).

When West turns to the experience of parenting, he preserves aspects of this musical and joyful sensibility in thinking about the way a sense of life that goes deeper than words is passed on. He cites Jerome Kagan's notion that "precisely how a parent feeds an infant or disciplines a teenager is less important than 'the melody those actions comprise.' The feelings that parents bring to the role—their pleasure in parenting . . . are extremely important" (*The War against Parents*, 48). West argues that what parents need most is the opportunity to spend time with their children so that these "melodies [can] work their magic" (48–49).

Failure, Crisis, and the Turn to Parenthood

West thinks magical solutions are becoming increasingly necessary. West saw the black church as a resource for democratic citizenship in the face of the tragic, in the first place as a sort of replacement for the family in the face of the horrors of "natal alienation" and then later as a partner with the fragile black family after emancipation. He would come to focus on parenthood directly when he perceived that the problems church and family were meant to confront were worsening. When the house is in danger of collapse, one seeks to shore the foundation. The developing crisis centered on children, and the seriousness of the crisis is reflected in existential and tragic matters—in life and death.

Since the mid-1980s, West has been concerned by the phenomenon of suicide among young people and specifically about the statistic that "until the early seventies black Americans had the lowest suicide rate in the United States. But now young black people lead the nation in the rate of increase in suicides" (*Race Matters*, 24). West saw this as a sign of growing nihilism among black youth—a nihilism he describes as "the lived experience of coping with a life of horrifying meaninglessness, hopelessness, and (most important) lovelessness" (22–23). West sees this growing nihilism as a sign of the failure of the black institutions—especially family and church—that were responsible for passing on the tradition of hope in the face of the tragic. While it had been "the genius of our black foremothers and forefathers . . . to create powerful buffers to ward off the nihilistic threat," the "traditions . . . of black religious and civic institutions that sustained familial and communal networks of support" were failing to do their job (23–24). That "for the first time in black history, there are no viable institutions and structures in black American life that can effectively transmit values like hope, virtue, and sacrifice—institutions that put the needs of others higher than those of oneself . . . is what makes this era so terrifying" (*Hope on a Tightrope*, 174). He explains the failure in two ways: "I believe the two significant reasons why the threat (of nihilism) is more powerful now than ever before are the saturation of market forces and market moralities in black life and the present crisis in black leadership" (*Race Matters*, 24). The particular way these factors intertwined would help determine how West turned to parenthood for a solution to the crisis.

West would go on in his book *Race Matters* to offer sharp criticism of black leaders at the time, from Jesse Jackson to new black conservatives.[49]

But elsewhere he would generalize the blame—indicting himself and his generation more generally. As he put it in one speech: "This is what frightens me more than anything else . . . the inability to transmit meaning, value, purpose, dignity, decency to children" (*Beyond Eurocentrism*, 16). West describes his reaction upon first hearing about the problem of suicide during a discussion with students at a Brooklyn high school.

> As I drove home to New Haven, I pondered this situation—in fear and trembling. I asked myself whether our cultural and religious resources were no longer adequate to sustain the younger generation; whether we Christian adults were merely enacting a holding operation which simply conceals (mainly from ourselves) the explosive nihilism harbored by our young people. (*Prophetic Fragments*, 155)

It is a description that begins to formulate a self-indictment—West as part of the generation whose cultural work had become inadequate and had been reduced to a mere holding operation. But it was not a self-indictment West would dwell on. On the same drive home, his mind turned to market forces and the question of how "power elites in mass media" were exploiting this nihilism for financial gain (155).

This maneuver—in which feelings of self-recrimination are briefly engaged and then pushed aside to focus on external hostile forces whose nefariousness explains one's failure—is recreated in West's work on parenthood. In order to face the crisis of nihilism that undermines citizenship, West turns from religious and cultural institutions to parenthood, from natal alienation to the experience of natality, from supplements to family to the family itself.

In doing so, West's self-recriminations would cut deeper, so the hostile forces would have to be inflated in turn. The result is that West arrives at the notion of a "war" against parents and comes to undermine many of his previous commitments regarding citizenship. West's war is politics by other means than democracy.

Parenthood, Virtue, and Despair

If parenthood itself would have to solve the problem of nihilism, it is because nihilism struck West as a different sort of problem. Nihilism results from the "market forces" that "infiltrate" and "saturate" people's daily lives

(*Race Matters*, 24–25). These forces suffocate the political capacities that West had long sought to identify and elucidate in the variety of American traditions he examines. Nihilism cuts people off from the past traditions that nurtured these capacities and from the hope for the future that is central to them. In their place, the market offers "the provision, expansion and intensification of *pleasure.* . . . In the American way of life pleasure means comfort, convenience, and sexual stimulation. Pleasure, so defined, has little to do with the past, and views the future as no more than a repetition of a hedonistically driven present" (26). The shallowness of these experiences brings with them a "sense of worthlessness and self-loathing" (27)—the sort of self-hatred that West had sought to banish from the experience of citizenship.

In describing what is lost in the face of this new and deeper threat, West begins to change his terms regarding just what his favored traditions offer us. The values of political contest, like self-criticism and openness to challenge, recede, and the values of political virtue, especially altruism and self-sacrifice, emerge. He worries that "the predominance of the market-inspired way of life . . . edge[s] out nonmarket values—love, care, service to others—handed down by preceding generations" (*Race Matters*, 27). The response to nihilism, then, involves a different sort of politics. "Nihilism is not overcome by arguments and analyses; it is tamed by love and care. Any disease of the soul must be conquered by a turning of one's soul. This turning is done through one's own affirmation of one's worth—an affirmation fueled by the concern of others. A love ethic must be at the center of a politics of conversion" (29). Contest must be set aside and virtue must take its place.

But the appeal to Rousseauvian virtue brings with it the risks of Rousseauvian tragedy. West suggests cryptically in *Race Matters* that the "best example of this love ethic" is "Toni Morrison's great novel *Beloved*" (29). *Beloved*[50] offers a pretty dark message when it comes to the use of parenthood for politics in desperate times. In *Democracy Matters*, where West suggests that the problem of nihilism has spread beyond the black community to become a general "waning of democratic energies" and "deep disaffection of youth" (2), he offers a reading of *Beloved*. West describes the "profoundly democratic action" enacted by the character Sethe. He quotes Sethe's reflections on how the experience of slavery made her think about her daughter. To be a slave, said Sethe, means that

> anybody white could . . . not just work, kill or maim you, but dirty you. Dirty you so bad you couldn't like yourself anymore. Dirty

you so bad you forgot who you were and couldn't think it up. And though she and others lived through and got over it, she could never let it happen to her own. The best thing she was, was her children. Whites might dirty *her* all right, but not her best thing, her beautiful, magical best thing—the part of her that was clean. (94)

Sethe cuts her daughter's throat to spare her the horrors of slavery.

West's book on parenthood as a political identity gets pretty dark as well. It offers its own stories of murder, of dead children, and its own explanations for throats cut open.[51] It is infused with a fear of the dirty things, the petty things, which might threaten what West takes to be our own magical best thing—our relationship with our children—and threaten the hopes for citizenship that he ties to this relationship.

Hewlett and West describe the experience of parenthood as precisely the sort that might overcome nihilism—one in which love inspires a conversion. But in their description, it is usually parents, not children, who are converted by love. They see having a child as the deepest and most fundamental experience imaginable. "How can any of us forget the bewildering rush of gut-wrenching, life-bending emotion we felt when we first held a newborn son or daughter?" (*The War against Parents*, xiv). This life-changing experience invests the parent with virtue. This "most elemental emotion" and "most elemental bond" summons "the better angels of human nature, drawing upon our most selfless instincts" (xii, xvii). To witness your child's "pure joy . . . cleanses the soul" (xvi). The authors themselves, having recently become a mother and grandfather while writing the book, "were once again inspired—and humbled—by the astonishing power of a small child to evoke our most sublime and selfless feelings. Parenthood does indeed present astonishing opportunities, for individuals and for nations" (xvi).

Parenthood provides an opportunity for the nation because it is precisely this conversion experience that makes parenthood useful for politics. The experience of parenting is "the wellspring of compassion, competence, and commitment in society. In fundamental and far-reaching ways parents affect the strength of our communities, the capacity of our economy, and the vitality of our democracy" (xiv). So Hewlett and West believe that it is only through an effort to "revalue and revitalize the art and practice of parenting" that we can "renew our nation" (xvi).

However, the project's dark undertones lie close to the surface. Hewlett and West suggest that on a personal level the project of articulating the political uses of parenthood "goes to the core of our beings. We feel the healing power of the work we have done together in the recesses of our souls" (xvi). What makes it necessary to heal is that while the experience of parenthood might inspire a conversion, it does not always inspire a conversion that is complete or lasting. Hewlett and West suggest that "at a fundamental level of analysis, the parent–child bond is the strongest and most primeval of all human attachments, . . . the ultimate source of connectedness in society" (41). But as their own analysis moves forward, this primeval bond, and the new virtue a person acquires with it, is depicted as surprisingly fragile and fleeting. As they explain, "In a world where a hit song by the group Megadeth tells the world that 'parents are dickheads,' it is hard to conjure up the commitment to be a good parent" (143). And Megadeth is not alone. Films that depict parents as irresponsible, including "hugely popular movies such as *Home Alone* and *Honey I Shrunk the Kids*," are "profoundly demoralizing" (127). The result is that many parents "get the message that devoting their best time to raising children is a mug's game—a lonely thankless undertaking" (30). Parents are failing in their role, and many fathers are simply walking away.[52]

The book's spectacle of parents who have been cleansed by a baby's "pure joy" and yet fail their children or leave them behind provides another dismal point of comparison to West's take on the strengths of the black community during the years of slavery. In a later book, West reminds readers:

> Black folk had to deal with social death for 244 years. When they sang, "Nobody knows the trouble I've seen. Nobody knows but Jesus," they are not talking about Disneyland or Peter-Pan-like realities of innocence and purity. They're talking about human wounds, scars, and bruises, and still somehow being able to transmit and bequeath certain senses of grace and love to their precious children, even if they couldn't keep track of them as the were sold from one part of the country to the other. (*Hope on a Tightrope*, 30)

While the black community's history is one of finding a way to transmit their best qualities to children despite their bondage, contemporary parents fail to retain the qualities of virtue they attain through parenthood—and thus fail to pass them on to the younger generation—in large part because of their freedoms. Hewlett and West discuss the way that falling incomes and a lack of resources make it difficult for parents to spend enough time with their children, but they also make it clear that the burdens of freedom as much as economic problems are the heart of the matter. The authors note that they themselves have not lacked for resources in their lives but nonetheless have struggled to come through for their children. Discussing the "surprising" aspects of their own partnership, they note, "Even more unexpected—and certainly more fraught—is what we share in our adult struggles to be a good father and a good mother. We have both discovered that adequate resources and a desperate desire to do a good job by our kids are no guarantee of success in this parent-hurting society" (*The War against Parents*, 3).

The problem is that new freedoms and new opportunities can be as challenging to democratic responsibilities as the lack of freedom. Freedoms can be put to democratic purposes but also tempt us toward shallower pursuits. Hewlett and West struggle with this. "As recent beneficiaries of liberation movements (feminist and black), we find it particularly hard to face the bare, bald truth: children deserve prime time and attention and need to sit in the center of life. This is bound to curtail some hard won freedoms. So be it" (xviii). But accepting such a compromise is easier said than done. Both Hewlett and West have learned this the hard way, and for each it is as much the experience of failing as a parent as the magical moment they became a parent that has transformed them. Hewlett believes her refusal to scale back on her academic work when she became pregnant with twins in the busy year before her tenure review contributed to their being stillborn. Her description of the experience is heartbreaking. "I screwed up my eyes and plugged my ears so that I could not see my dead and dying babies being born, but I felt them through my agony, warm and wet against my thighs" (20). The loss cut deeply. She writes, "The dark winter of 1979–1980 permanently changed my priorities and my perspective. It put me profoundly in touch with the deep tradeoffs between self-fulfillment and child well-being" (20).

West calls the struggle to be a good parent after his first divorce the source of "the greatest challenges of my life" (21). He realized after the separation that he was not successfully building a relationship with his son. West was limited to selected weekend visits along with three months of custody in the summer. But even when they were together, West had a hard time fitting his son into his lifestyle. "What would I do with my son during our precious time together? My bachelor cribs in New York, New

Haven, and Princeton did not provide a supportive context" for a child (21). West's eventual solution was a return to the past—to spend summers at his parents' home. It was a decision that put him in touch with how important his stable and loving family had been to his success in life. Still, "try as I might—and I have struggled enormously to come through for Cliff—all kinds of other factors have gotten in the way. In the end, I don't have as much attention for my loved ones as Mom and Dad had. I mean I *definitely* haven't been the father or husband my father was" (23).[53] West writes that his "primary aim in life is to be of value" to his children and that he has "no doubt . . . fallen short of [his] lofty goals." Regarding his failures as a father West speaks of "soul-wrenching" pain, "pain for my children, pain for their mothers, pain for me."[54]

Such moments of brutally honest self-assessment do not provide a resolution to the ambivalence about freedom that permeates *The War against Parents*. One of the things West believes made the black church and its traditions such a resource for democratic capacities is that even as it provided support to struggling families, it always "spoke the language of rights" (*Prophetic Fragments*, 23), but West does not appreciate the language of rights so much when he considers parenthood directly.

> While it is true that liberals have spearheaded a set of government programs that have improved the lives of poor children . . . it is also true that the extraordinary emphasis in liberal circles on the rights of individuals has frequently compromised the welfare of both parents and children. Untrammeled choice and uncluttered freedoms get in the way of the altruistic, other directed energy that is the stuff of parenting. (*The War against Parents*, 94)

The answer, then, is to trammel choice and clutter freedoms, and Hewlett and West work hard to come to grips with it. They do not always succeed. While they seem disgusted that if you "scratch the surface . . . you will find at least some folks on the left who don't particularly like marriage or children" (95), when you turn the pages of *The War against Parents*, there is ambivalence there as well. Hewlett and West continually remind parents that their efforts are "precious." But the authors also describe having a child in terms of being trapped: "a hostage to fortune, one more life that is more precious than my own. . . . It means a loss of freedom. It means dealing with an undertow of care and anxiety that permeates every hour of every day" (xvii).

Reaching back for a lifeline that will save them from the undertow, Hewlett and West romanticize an earlier era. They acknowledge the repression and cold war hysteria, the sexism, the racism, segregation and lynchings, "yet, despite all the legitimate criticism, the period from 1946 to 1963 was a glorious era for the American family" (98). It is the era that Hewlett and West remember from their own childhoods.[55] "As children we had absolute confidence that we were the guts of our parents' lives" (19). The authors say the 1950s and 1960s were "a time when it seemed a whole lot easier to be a good parent" (23). But this recollection does little to make the efforts of their parents accessible as a model. Rather than seeing in their parents exemplars that they can live up to, West and Hewlett are "amazed. . . . It's virtually unimaginable today to put together the kind of devotion and attention our parents gave to us" (19). In his autobiography, *Brother West,* West describes "the character of my own father and his unmatched example as a family man of stability and remarkable integrity" in terms of "a standard I could never approximate let alone achieve" (233).

It often seems he simply would not want to. Both Hewlett and West look at their parents' lives, and they do not really seem to want to repeat them. While today the authors feel an "undertow of care and anxiety" that threatens to drown them, Hewlett looks back on her mother's life and finds a more striking metaphor: raising children "pretty much obliterated my mum. Looking back, I am both impressed and horrified by the extent to which we children took over my mother's life" (*The War against Parents,* 24). The takeover was in some ways mutual. She felt her parents were "heavy handed and relentless" in guiding her life and insulating her from market values when she "really craved normal teenage stuff like bell-bottom jeans" (17).[56]

If the authors feel some ambivalence when they look back on their parents' lives, they also sense ambivalence in their own parents about the lives they led and the freedoms and opportunities they sacrificed to place their children at the center of their lives. Hewlett's father did not want her to live a life like her mother's—so he taught his daughters to aspire to something besides motherhood and that "marriage is no solution to your lives." He taught technical skills to miners, but he "didn't want his girls to marry a miner" and stay in the part of Wales where he raised them. From the the time she was thirteen, Hewlett's father pushed her not to live like her parents but to go to Cambridge and "transform [her] life" (17). Hewlett and West describe any new parent's realization that "I know full well that if I fail to keep my children safe, I will not find life worth living" (xvii). But Hewlett also recalls her father's belief that there is no cause "worth risking one's life for" (7).

West hints at his father's despair at working all day in an Air Force supply room only to come home and punish a rambunctious son who was "head of the local gang" and liked to "bash heads against walls, that kind of thing" (12–13). The time West beat up his pregnant teacher, his father left work early to give him a whipping. "My dad was so upset by this incident that after the beating he just went into his bedroom and shut the door. He stayed in there a long time, quiet and sad. I cried like a baby, but there was nothing I could do to ease my father's pain" (13).[57] Like Hewlett's father, West's parents were pleased to see him take advantage of newly won freedoms. His mother likes to remind him, "Cornel, you would never have gotten into Harvard had it not been for the civil rights struggle . . . You sure got the talent, the grades and the board scores—never think you didn't earn your Harvard place—but in the old days such an elite institution would not have made you welcome" (18). It was the sort of opportunity that made possible West's remarkable career, but also a source of the difficult choices he would face in his adult life. The authors conclude that looking back at the "child-centeredness" of their parents' lives, which were "stunningly straightforward, undiluted by high-flying careers or marital breakdown," is a "sobering experience" (19).

Parenthood and Failure

While Hewlett and West may be right that "we cannot clone" the likes of their parents, they have nonetheless inherited from them a complex set of feelings about the fulfillment that comes from parenthood. The authors seem not to be sure they want the child-centered (and self-obliterating) past they glorify, and they are not sure their parents wanted it either. If that possibility is hard to face, even harder is confronting just what the present generation of parents—whose new freedoms allow their ambivalence about parenting to gain its full expression—might be passing on to their children. While Hewlett's and West's parents left clues that they might have liked to live a less child-centered life, the authors fear their own generation might be making their own preferences all too clear to the children they raise. At one point, describing the way an infant's eyes follow its parent, "drinking me in, learning my lines, my sounds, my smells," the authors find it necessary to point out that "despite the intense scrutiny, this is not a judgment thing" (*The War against Parents*, xvi).

In fact, as it was for Rousseau before him, parenting for West *is* a judgment thing. The verdicts can be hard to face. When the authors asked schoolchildren to paint images of their moms and dads, they found that "some of their work is lyrical and inspiring; much more is quite brutal" (xv). The judgment that parents experience in their children's eyes can be brutal because it threatens to reveal that we have failed to make use of democratic freedoms to live up to democratic responsibilities. West's version of democratic citizenship attempts to strike a balance between the utopian and the hopeful on the one hand and the self-critical and fallible on the other. But in turning to parenthood to fend off the threat of nihilism's hopelessness, fallibility becomes hard to bear because it cuts too close to the core. Regarding fathers, West and Hewlett suggest that "they want children not simply to perpetuate their names but, more important, to feel as if they matter in the world. They seek the intangible benefits of parenting—the indescribable sense of affirmation that comes from attachment to a child" (167). But failure in a task in which the meaning of one's very existence is at stake is hard to bear. The authors note that divorced fathers are "overwhelmed by feelings of failure and self-hatred"[58] and that they "respond to this feeling by withdrawing completely." Such men "can be very destructive, both to themselves and to society" (169).

Hewlett and West consider two "movements in male spirituality and solidarity" that have developed as a response to men's feelings that they have failed as fathers: the Promise Keepers and the Nation of Islam's Million Man March. "Increasingly alienated from a secular culture that denies the legitimacy of their pain, [fathers] are newly convinced that no one is listening except God" (182). The authors find much to like in the Promise Keepers, noting its commitments to "interracial unity" and that the movement is "remarkably supportive of parental energies" (192). Participants are rallied to the cause of self-transformation through the specter of their children's judgment of them: "Does your son see you as a role model? Does your daughter want to marry a guy like you?" (190). Hewlett and West are impressed with the results. They speak about the "magical transformation" participants undergo, which can turn a "frog" into a family-centered "prince" (194). They maintain that both movements help men answer the question, "How do I transform myself into a more virtuous person?" (210). Urging readers to focus on these positive qualities rather than on criticisms of the movements, they write, "If we continue to look at the Promise Keepers and the Nation of Islam and see only patriarchy reestablished or gay-bashing celebrated, we lose out on a rare opportunity to take the agony of crippled men and turn it into something good" (211).

These movements call for a return to something like patriarchy not only in the family but in politics as well. The Promise Keepers urge their members to say to their wives, "Honey, I've made a terrible mistake. I've given you my role. I gave up leading the family, and I forced you to take my place. Now I must reclaim that role. . . . Give it back! God never meant for you to bear the load you are carrying."[59] Kelly Oliver analyzes the rhetoric of the Promise Keepers to argue that their message about a father's natural power in the family also carries a particular conception of citizenship that serves a national political agenda. Promise Keepers are urged to take personal responsibility for their families, but their first promise is to ensure accountability by keeping in close contact with other members. What matters most for the Promise Keepers is the legacy of having failed as a father, which requires a constant vigilance and a certain measure of surveillance. In doing so, the Promise Keepers are tied to a chain of command that links small group leaders to local leaders to national coordinators. The resulting structure is set in motion for conservative political causes. According to Oliver, in the Promise Keepers, "accountability means submission to the chain of command. . . . The call for personal responsibility and accountability is rhetoric used to make members obedient to orders from their higher-ups." She concludes, "In the end, the Promise Keepers . . . undermines notions of responsibility and accountability consistent with democratic values."[60] The Promise Keepers are forever tainted by their failure to have been transformed into a virtuous citizen in their initial experience of parenthood. Failed fathers, they will never be ready to be full democratic citizens.

The Promise Keepers respond to their admission of failure by accepting supervision even as they reassert control over their families—a double reclamation of patriarchal politics. This is not something West notes in praising the movement. But West's investigations of parental failure do make him suspicious of citizens' abilities to live up to democratic responsibilities. Hewlett and West seem to emphasize the inevitability of parents' failure in the face of insurmountable and hostile forces. They write that one of their goals is to help all parents to understand just how isolated and attacked they are. "Regular moms and dads have a hard time comprehending the degree to which business, government and our culture are bitterly antagonistic toward them" (*The War against Parents*, 30). Their book, in describing a "war" against parents, seeks to rectify that. The advantage of the men's movements is that they already have got the message. "These men and others in the group seemed thoroughly in touch with the all-out war our society has waged against husbands and fathers. They also shared another sentiment: the only refuge in these treacherous times is their faith—and their brothers. They have given up on politics and on our democracy" (189).

But Hewlett and West want to make parental insecurity central to our politics through a new kind of democracy. Insecurity must become a central aspect of citizenship. "When the anguish of crippled men is not addressed in the public square but is siphoned off into spiritual movements, it makes for a risky future" (183). Thus West and Hewlett's parent-centered politics stands in stark contrast to West's description of the black church where he began his thinking about citizenship. West found that the church, at its best, responded to suffering that could not be addressed in a racist political culture. That church responded with hope and creativity, asked much of an oppressed people, and spoke the democratic language of rights. But West thinks parents, on the other hand, should recognize that they are "broken" and give up on rights. "Atonement is a key concept for both the Promise Keepers and the Nation. Men are required to recognize their own brokenness and ask forgiveness. . . . This emphasis on atonement and servanthood couldn't be more different from the 'rights talk' we are so used to in contemporary democracy" (210).[61]

Indeed, there is little talk of rights, or the unpredictable, open-ended political participation they enable, in the political plan laid out in *The War against Parents*. Disappointed with the choices we make in response to our democratic freedoms, West begins to embrace the sort of "authoritarian arrangements" he has long warned against. The authors' focus on parental failure indicates that the self-transformation that occurs when a person becomes a parent is not the sort that enables a continued openness to contingency, challenges, the unexpected, or Megadeth. Rather, this self-transformation demands—if it is to be lasting and truly transformational—that a very particular version of society be valued and created, induced and enforced. Sympathizing with absentee mothers and fathers, Hewlett and West write that we "need to change a system that is capable of turning a loving and valuable parent into a despised scofflaw" (179). Changing the system will mean eliminating contingencies in favor of crafting politics toward a predetermined end. Here we see West's original idea of the parent as citizen neatly reversed. It is not the experience of parenthood that prepares us for citizenship—for the burdens of freedom and challenges of responsibility. Rather, it is government that must solve these problems for parents. "Today's adults, both men and women, will be able to deal much more wisely with the age-old and ongoing tradeoffs between freedom and responsibility, self and other, which haunt the daily life of any thoughtful parent. Business, the government and the media, *properly molded*, cannot solve all dimensions of these existential problems, but they can get us part way there" (25, emphasis added).

This raises two obvious questions: What does "proper molding" look like, and what gets us the rest of the "way there" in dealing with these existential problems? The policy proposals that West took to a White House meeting with Bill Clinton[62] are puzzling given West's previous statements regarding politics and citizenship. It is certainly odd to see West follow his many years of critical thinking about black citizenship in the post–civil rights era by suggesting that a particular segment of the population should be not only privileged with enhanced voting rights but also given reserved seats at the front of public buses. He suggests both for parents, along with state mandates for priority parking at malls and discounts to parks, monuments, museums, films, and restaurants (256).

These sorts of rewards for parents will come along with a submission to new levels of control in their personal lives. Elsewhere, West warned against the temptation to respond to "rapacious individualism" with "authoritarian communitarianism," which imposes "values from above, thereby threatening precious liberties" (*Beyond Eurocentrism*, 32–33). But in turning to parenthood as the only solution to out-of-control individualism, West makes his peace with state interventions in the name of community values. Teenage mothers get a carrot but feel the stick: "We . . . recommend that government *reinstate the right to income support* for poor parents with children under six, with the provision that *unmarried teenage mothers be required to live in a home* under strict supervision of experienced mothers." It is a recommendation designed to teach them some lessons, both about parenting skills and to "detract from the lure of unwed motherhood as a way of life" (*The War against Parents*, 235). While the young and unmarried are literally confined, marriage in general would take on a bit more of the quality of detention. Hewlett and West surmise that "government should get back into the business of fostering the value of marriage as a long-term commitment." This would mean giving marrying couples the choice of a special "covenant marriage" in which divorce is possible only under dire circumstances like physical abuse. Further, they suggest that all married couples with children, if considering a divorce, "should face a three-year waiting period, during which they would be obliged to seek marriage counseling" (242). If a divorce is obtained, parents who fail to visit their children often enough "should be fined, or otherwise put on notice that such conduct is unacceptable" (244).[63]

If Hewlett and West do not think that some of these measures would detract from the lure of married parenthood as a way of life, it is in part because they sprinkle in financial incentives. West believes the reason for our growing nihilism is the way "market forces" have come to "infiltrate" and "saturate" daily lives—the way "caring, nurturing, cherishing . . . have been pushed aside to the margins by the dominant forces in American life" (28). But he and Hewlett let market thinking infiltrate their ideas about parents as citizens as well. The book does offer many nods to "the altruistic non-market activities that comprise the essence of parenting" (29). Foster parenting is criticized because of the financial incentives involved in monthly checks from the government. "These checks are sizable . . . [but] unconditional love and long-term devotion are hard to find in the marketplace" (111–12). They worry that many cases of children removed from abusive parents are distorted by the fact that "each case of child abuse or neglect unlocks significant state and federal funds, not only for the child welfare agency directly concerned but for a satellite ring of substitute caregivers, therapists and family court lawyers" (119). Yet the authors also encourage readers to think about parenthood from the perspective of dollars and cents. One can detect some resentment when they explain that "through history and across cultures, parents have often reaped at least some material reward from raising children," but "in the modern world children are hugely expensive and yield little in the way of economic return to the parent" (35). In arguing that the government needs to invest more in supporting parents, they often emphasize the social benefits of parenting in monetary terms. "The costs [of parenting] are private; the benefits are increasingly public" (93). Parents who are "good" enough to raise a child who completes college "contribute to America's store of human capital and help this nation compete with the

Germans and Koreans," (93). Their children will also "pay our collective social security bill" (218).

While they are tough on foster parents who get checks in the mail ("they do a lousy job" [119–20]), Hewlett and West sympathize with biological parents who engage in market thinking. To ask parents "to rely on large reserves of altruistic love . . . is a tall order in a society that venerates the market. We are asking parents to ignore the dominant values of our age. If they routinely fall down on the job, who can blame them?" (36). The authors do not, and they suggest a number of proposals involving special financial supports for parents that go well beyond movie discounts and the like. For example, parents (and not others) should be exempted from payroll taxes and sales taxes on products for children, get a government allowance for each child, additional tax credits if they care for their own child at home, and Medicaid benefits if not otherwise insured (238, 250). The authors ultimately surrender their own claims to altruism as well. "Who among us has a private supply of altruistic energy that can be dipped into on a daily basis for a couple of decades? Not you, not we" (xviii).

Of course, the idea of basic social supports behind some of Hewlett and West's proposals are sensible, and the absence of altruism need not be something to worry about. Certainly altruism deserves no privileged place in contest citizenship, where claims are made, territory staked, and positions negotiated. But in attempting to use parenthood to fend off the threats of nihilism, West has left behind his commitments to contest and embraced his attraction to citizenship as virtue. From the perspective of virtue, the absence of altruism becomes harder to swallow. It is the surrender of altruism that makes it particularly hard for West to answer the second half of the question regarding the "existential problems" addressed in *The War against Parents:* If molding government gets us "part way" to solving them, what gets us the rest of the way there? The passage just quoted, after confessing that altruism truly describes "not you, not we," continues into bitter, even hopeless territory: "We deal with so many layers of betrayal that it cuts deep into the space we have for watching a newborn child dream; we thus lose out on the magic unleashed by an unfolding life" (xvii). Megadeth and *Honey I Shrunk the Kids* may reflect one layer of betrayal, but one gets the feeling it is deeper layers that truly matter. Working your way into those depths will take you all the way to the center. "If we can produce this magical parent power, we can go to the very heart of our darkness and make the center hold" (53).

Giving Up on Politics

Though framed as a rallying call to virtuous citizenship, *The War against Parents* is an explanation of failure. Honig suggests that versions of citizenship crafted in the name of virtue produce "subjects ... less likely to join together as democratic citizens than they are to be joined together as a population managed by the state."[64] Hewlett and West, having appealed to the virtues of parenthood for citizenship, plea for state intervention—for government-provided incentives, supports, stigmas, and penalties—specifically to join together parents who are tempted to wander off. Presented as a plan to renew democracy, the book suggests war measures that betray West's democratic commitments. In the place of West's call for the messy and cacophonous work of democratic conversation, he raises the specter of a "silent war against parents" to insist parents mobilize "behind a single agenda" and speak "with a single voice" (53).

In focusing on parents, West relaxes the tension between the hopeful and the tragic, between contest and virtue, which he developed in his other work. West has used this perspective to uncover what was useful for citizenship, and critique what was not, in a variety of traditions—including the black church, socialist thought, and pragmatism. In his turn to parenthood, West changes the nature of the hope he articulates. West has always written of the need to preserve hope in the face of the withering despair that life's difficulties encourage. But in his other books, hope was what allowed citizens to take upon themselves the difficult and messy work of politics—"when you're full of hope, you're in the midst of the muck," as he summarizes pithily (*Hope on a Tightrope*, 15). But the hope West associates with parenthood is meant to rise above such muddy matters—the "selfless passion most of us mothers and fathers conjure up for our children is the nearest we come to transcending earthbound limits" (*The War against Parents*, xviii).

What makes it necessary to conjure up supernatural solutions is West's view of the particular nature of the contemporary threat of nihilism and the market culture that is its partner. Politics may pull a person down into the muck, but the market is something dirtier still. Such nihilism is not merely a new enemy to be taken on in the way that racism, sexism, and class domination had been in West's other work. Nihilism "infiltrates," "saturates," and invades our souls. It convinces us to use democratic freedoms—hard won by previous generations—for shallow pursuits rather than to meet democratic responsibilities. West sees the experience of failing as parent as the ultimate measure of nihilism's progress. In his descriptions of his own "bachelor cribs" and struggles as a father, West touches on the topic of one of his favorite passages in the pragmatist corpus, from Josiah Royce's *The Spirit of Modern Philosophy*. Discussing those experiences in which a person senses that "all that was most fixed in him has become shaken," Royce wrote, "An open enemy you can face. . . . But one's own foolishness, one's ignorance, . . . the fatal misunderstandings that part friends and lovers, the chance mistakes that wreck nations: these things we lament most bitterly." These are aspects of life that one cannot "easily learn to face courageously. . . . No, these things do not make life merely painful for us; they make it hideously petty."[65] West has always believed that the painful and the tragic make politics difficult and that democratic citizens must be ready to face those difficulties. But the petty is indeed harder to "face courageously"—it eats away at one's faith in one's own courage.

It was this sense of the hideously petty that convinced Royce to turn to religion as a source of hope—one reason for his appeal to West. But the growing threat of nihilism, with its petty market values, with not just lovers parted but children abandoned, convinced West to look past Christian traditions to the family itself. Parenthood, with its "most elemental" emotions, provides West with his last, desperate hope for a "love ethic" that can "turn a soul" and summon the courage to fend off the nihilistic call toward pettier pursuits. Hewlett and West call this fight America's "domestic wars" and argue that the willingness of parents to give their lives to this war puts them "on the same ethical foundation" as the veterans who benefited from the GI Bill (*The War against Parents*, 232).

But wars can be lost, and parenthood also provides a test of our success in this domestic battle. The test is the question of what parents pass on to the children they produce. As Rousseau feared, Nietzsche hoped, and Rorty sought to deny, West believes children, with their "intense scrutiny," can see into a parent's soul. Children learn "through imitation and modeling," and if "virtues are not taught within the family, they are not taught at all" (*The War against Parents*, 172). Thus West believes he developed his own "conceptions of what it is to be human, how we should act and what we should hope for" not through his academic work or rational arguments, but because "they are embedded and enacted in a form of life . . . that mediates how I interpret my experiences, sufferings, joys and undertakings" (xxix). West inherited his form of life, which helps him live "alongside the slippery edge of life's abyss," from his family and from the black church that developed to supplement families under conditions of natal alienation. This form of life was "bequeathed" to West by the "communities that came before," and the measure of how he embodies this form of life is his ability to pass it on in turn. At times he despairs of it and is tempted to abandon the effort altogether and embrace a new tradition. After divorce, and a remarriage in Ethiopia, he admitted, "After nine generations of family roots in America I feel an urge to leave" (*Keeping Faith*, xv).

Despite such occasional despair, West believes this imitation, this passing on of one's "form of life," is one of the great rewards of parenthood as well as its toughest test. Hewlett and West think it is "craziness" to expect divorced fathers to support their children financially, out of a sense of responsibility, when they are mostly denied "its main reward—loving contact with a child" (*The War against Parents*, 179). Parents want to have the "melody" of their way of living heard, to see these "melodies . . . work their magic" and hear them echoed back. But the tune of our way of living can sound terribly dissonant when re-created and played back for us. Thus West worries that the nihilism of the younger generation reflects his own generation's failures. Youth culture and "music are, in many ways, an indictment of the old generation even as they imitate and emulate us in a raw and coarse manner" (*Democracy Matters*, 184). Continuing to rally parents to the cause in his brief book reacting to the Obama campaign, West writes, "We're not going to get out of our current societal mess unless we engage the younger generation." But he admits, "They're imitating us—our materialism, careerism, and so on" (*Hope on a Tightrope*, 104).[66] And so, turning more wistful, West seems to accept that the opportunity to deploy love against nihilism has passed. "I say to myself, *We must take some responsibility. We should have taught them better how to care for and respect themselves. We should have taught them better how to love*" (156).

West considers the idea of young people finding exemplars outside the family, pointing to the experience of Malcolm X with Elijah Muhammad, and James Baldwin and his mentor Beauford Delaney. Like Nietzsche, West thinks for such a relationship to be useful, it must be fatherly—involving love and an intimate knowledge of the exemplar's way of living. Only "concrete examples" can "[stir] our souls because we [have] real access to them" (*Hope on a Tightrope*, 100). West hopes some in his generation can find it in themselves to become such exemplars—to offer "young folk . . . access to a vast array of courageous and great examples, that will

serve as the foundation for their judgment" (146). But West's hope seems
to have little foundation, and he quickly expresses his fear that precisely
the opposite will occur and that the older generation will suppress what is
best in the younger one. "We must pray that our next generation of leaders
aren't destroyed before they have a chance to arrive. We have to remember
that if it'd been up to black leaders, Martin [Luther King] would never
have surfaced" (147).

In this book on the fragility of hope, West seems tempted again to give
in to despair—to give up on his generation. "We've allowed our children's
souls to grow emptier.... It just gets worse and worse, generation after
generation.... Older black folk have seen so many efforts come to naught
and they're just trying to survive" (95). It is a passage reminiscent of West's
description of his generation as stuck in a "holding pattern" while youngsters plunge toward nihilism and suicide. But in the more recent *Hope on
a Tightrope,* West seems to hope for a miracle that does not rely on "magical parent power"—to believe that young people might generate hope on
their own despite (rather than because of) the generation that raised them.
"But young folk still have a sense of spring. I call it *spring consciousness*—a
consciousness full of dreams and possibilities, and a willingness to sacrifice" (95).[67] Thus there has emerged a new tension in West's thought—a
tension between hope that the next generation can summon the "supernatural" capacities that West's generation lacks and the tragic thought that
they have been ruined by the people who raised them. This new tension is
a bitter distortion of the democratic dialectic of hope and tragedy, virtue
and contest, which he has carefully developed over his career.[68]

West opens *Race Matters* with a quote from James Baldwin that expresses the Westian idea that "for the sake of one's children, in order to
minimize the bill *they* must pay, one must be careful not to take refuge
in any delusion."[69] But problems arise when parenthood reveals our inadequacies, rather than summons our bravery, and becomes the source of
our political delusions. A more useful idea from Baldwin might be found
in the long quotation West offers in *Democracy Matters.* In that passage,
Baldwin discusses white Americans' resistance to the realization that black
Americans don't want to be like them, that "there is little in their public
or private life that one should desire to imitate." This is analogous to the
realization that West knows parents find hardest to face. Baldwin saw that
"a vast amount of the energy" that went into the politics of race was caught
up in this desire

not to be judged . . . not to be seen as he is, and at the same time a vast amount of white anguish is rooted in the white man's equally profound need to be seen as he is, to be released of the tyranny of his mirror. All of us know, whether or not we are able to admit it, that mirrors can only lie, that death by drowning is all that awaits one there.[70]

West goes on to summarize that "Baldwin spoke the deep truth that democratic individuality requires mature and free persons who confront reality, history, and mortality—and who shun innocence, illusion and purity" (81). But West encourages citizens to seek innocence and purity in the experience of parenting and stake their self-conception as citizens on the reflection of themselves they see in their child. It is a reflection that can be hard to face, and one that can lead to anguish and ultimately resignation in the face of the challenges of political freedom. Regarding freedom, West quotes further from Baldwin's *The Fire Next Time:*

> It is the responsibility of free men to celebrate what is constant—birth, struggle and death are constant, and so is love . . .—and to apprehend the nature of change, to be able and willing to change. I speak of change not on the surface but in the depths—change in the sense of renewal. But renewal becomes impossible if one supposes things to be constant that are not. . . . One clings then to chimeras, by which one can only be betrayed, and the entire hope—the entire possibility—of freedom disappears. And by destruction I mean precisely the abdication by Americans of any effort to really be free.[71]

In his engagement with the parent as citizen, West ignores each aspect of Baldwin's warning. In turning to the parent's experience of a particular birth, and the love, life, and struggle that birth engenders, West discovers renewal to be elusive. He fears that what change we have accomplished has been for the worse. He clings to a vision of parental virtue that turns out to be chimerical. Suspicious of new freedoms, he turns to the state for solutions. West's parent, as citizen, abdicates democratic responsibilities.

Exposing the Citizen as Parent

IT IS NOT DIFFICULT TO IMAGINE an ideal way that the politics of virtue and the politics of contest might coexist in democratic notions of citizenship. Citizens would feel responsible to develop and articulate deeply felt and earnestly believed notions of the good as well as ideas about the right direction for the political community. But citizens would also understand that their notions of the good and the right are only one perspective among many and that these ideas are subject to the requirements of democratic debate. They would be open to seeing things from other perspectives and to revising their deeply held beliefs. But in turning to the experience of parenthood to find ways that aspects of this imagined citizenship might be made real in citizens' lives, Rousseau, Nietzsche, Rorty, and West suggest the possibility of a dark reverse image of this ideal citizenship: citizenship centered on parenthood can make citizens feel deeply insecure in their ability to achieve a version of virtue but nonetheless feel compelled to cling to the notion of virtue they have developed or inherited. As the examples of Rousseau and Nietzsche suggest, this dynamic can introduce difficult obstacles to conceptions of virtue and contest. The results are particularly dismal for two contemporary efforts to incorporate aspects of both virtue and contest into theories of citizenship. Rorty's effort to put parenthood to use for a politics that balances virtue and contest led to a sort of helpless and stagnant politics in which citizens wait for family-centered stories to tweak the sentiments of the powerful. West's effort to put parenthood to use for a politics that blends virtue and contest leads him to calls for an intrusive government that reinforces virtue by law and protects citizens from the difficulties of political contest.

Does this mean that these problems are unavoidable as long as there are citizens who consider the experience of parenthood to be central to their lives? In one sense, yes. Insecurity and fundamentalism will complicate democratic citizenship under any circumstances short of ideal ones, which are by definition unattainable.[1] This is not a reason for resignation but rather a call to greater vigilance and a renewed commitment to a creative engagement with the obstacles that democratic politics will forever encounter and never fully overcome. The foregoing explorations suggest that parenthood is one experience that might help to foster this insecurity and this fundamentalism—even among brilliant theorists who intended to accomplish the opposite in appealing to the experience of parenthood. Perhaps these challenges to citizenship are inextricably linked to the experience of parenthood in liberal democracies. The best response is not to try to eliminate the challenges to citizenship posed by the experience of parenthood—the sort of response suggested by Plato in the *Republic* and by Rousseau in the *Discourse on Political Economy*. But these challenges do imply that in thinking about citizenship, and particularly in thinking about citizenship in terms of the qualities of virtue and contest, we should attend carefully to the role that parenthood plays in political theory, political rhetoric, and the public imagination.

When the experience of parenthood is figured as a resource for democratic citizenship, we should be aware of the limitations of that approach. But our vigilance regarding the political effects of parenthood should not end there. When theorists offer accounts of democratic citizenship without appealing to the experience of parenthood, this does not mean that the difficulties that parenthood introduces to citizenship have been avoided. Parenthood will remain a persistent part of political rhetoric, as well as (as Macedo and Young put it) "a central, if not *the* central, project" in many citizens' lives.[2] In thinking about democratic citizenship, then, it is not enough to merely sidestep the pathologies of the parent as citizen through benign neglect. Our understanding of politics will be more compelling if we confront the way politicians and citizens rely on ideas about parenthood in conceiving of citizenship and address the difficulties that this reliance often imparts.

Parenthood and Weak Ontology

These complications that parenthood introduces to virtue and contest conceptions of citizenship are particularly relevant because two of the central questions that political theorists have addressed in recent years are how citizens might feel their commitments deeply without lapsing into fundamentalism and how citizens should represent those commitments to others in the context of democracy. As mentioned in the introduction,

Stephen White has written about a particular style of answering these questions in political theory, which he labels "weak ontology." Theorists whom White associates with this style include Charles Taylor, Judith Butler, George Kateb, and William Connolly. What these theorists have in common, according to White, is that they affirm the political importance of "fundamental conceptualizations of the self" but insist that these deeply felt commitments "are contestable."[3] In other words, weak ontology offers accounts of how we might balance virtue and contest in the context of democratic citizenship.

As is the case for West and for West's appropriation of Nietzsche, the goal of weak ontology is to move away from the purely negative and critical, or as White puts it, "from a preoccupation with what is opposed and deconstructed to an engagement with what must be articulated, cultivated, and affirmed in its wake" (*Sustaining Affirmation*, 8). But these affirmations are measured. Rather than offer metaphysical assertions regarding timeless truths or accounts of a fixed "human nature or telos," weak ontologists offer "figurations of human being in terms of certain existential realities"—including "natality and the sources of the self" (9). An important aspect of this effort, according to White, is the idea that the citizen defines herself "against some ultimate background or 'source,' . . . which evokes something like awe, wonder, or reverence" (9).

White suggests that Rorty's ideas offer an important objection to the goals of weak ontologists. "For [Rorty], a notion like weak ontology is just a philosophically stilted way of saying 'my perspective' on certain topics . . . of which one can merely say that it is more or less useful for my 'private purposes' of 'self-creation'"(15). But as I argue in chapter 3, Rorty also considered one perspective on life to be fundamental above all others for most citizens, and the most useful one for politics: the perspective of parenthood. In the cluster of ideas and concerns that White folds together into weak ontology—natality, sources of the self, wonder—one can recognize the elements that attracted Rousseau, Nietzsche, Rorty, and West to the role that parenthood might play in the formation of the self as a citizen. In searching modern experience for aspects of life that might provide a deep, visceral sense of the life-affirming, which will orient us toward the future and touch on the mysterious and awe-inspiring, each of these theorists turned to the experience of parenthood. In each case, the effort led to profound difficulties. The "fundamental conceptions of the self" that result can become a source of profound insecurity or feel cruel to retract or revise. The conception of the self as parent might then be clung to all the tighter, transforming into the sort of fundamentalism that weak ontology is meant to avoid. Or it could become a source of resignation and despair, preventing the affirmations and articulations that weak ontology is meant to encourage. In either case, the goal of "contestability" is compromised.

These similarities in concerns about and approaches to citizenship do not mean that theorists like Taylor, Butler, Kateb, and Connolly are destined to appeal to the experience of parenthood in their thinking about citizenship. But the similarities do imply that it would be wise to think critically about the role that parenthood plays in the way both theorists and citizens have tried to work out these sorts of concerns in their political thought and in their political lives. One example in which this perspective might be useful is Connolly's appropriations of Nietzsche to reconfigure "the ideals of democracy bequeathed by Rousseau" and challenge democratic citizens to move beyond mere reflection to engage in deeper levels of "work on the self."[4] Much like the Nietzschean self-transformation explored in chapter 2, the work Connolly suggests in *Neuropolitics* is "not [merely] intellectual self-regulation, but also tactics or artistry applied by the self to corporeal layers of being not sufficiently susceptible to direct conscious control" (165). Though Connolly notes that Nietzsche ties this sort of work to "a gratitude for the abundance of life," a "visceral affirmation of life" (170) and "solidarity between succeeding generations" (156),[5] Connolly does not address the ways that Nietzsche folded ideas about parenthood into his notion of deep self-transformation. Nietzsche was concerned not merely with the task of self-transformation but just as importantly with the task of communicating the results of a transformation that had reached so deeply into the self. It is the task of *communicating* what one has accomplished that makes self-transformation potentially political, but it is not a task that Connolly focuses on in his appropriation of Nietzschean ideas. It was this need to communicate and pass on what one had accomplished that drew Nietzsche to parenthood as a way to think about this task. That is why procreation struck him as the "real achievement" of the individual.

This is not to say that Connolly should appeal to the experience of parenthood when conceptualizing this sort of work on the self simply because Nietzsche did. He need not travel down precisely the same path in exploring these ideas regarding the sort of self-transformation he finds most useful for democratic politics. But if he hopes to encourage us to engage in the sort of deep work on the self that Nietzsche pursued, and in particular if he expects that work to involve efforts to "fold a visceral affirmation of life more robustly into being" (170), he might be wise to examine the obstacles to his vision of citizenship that emerge when the experience of parenthood is given privileged place in citizens' democratic self-conceptions.

Connolly looks down a different path instead in his *Identity\Difference: Democratic Negotiations of Political Paradox*—toward Nietzsche's ideas about death rather than Nietzsche's ideas about creating new life. He examines Nietzsche's call to "die proudly when it is no longer possible to live proudly." This means a death "at the proper time, with a clear head and joyfulness, consummated in the midst of children and witnesses. . . . From love of life one ought to desire to die freely."[6] Connolly suggests that this conception of a "timely death" is a useful way to understand the democratic uses of the deep layers of Nietzsche's "attachment to life" (168), life's propensity for "flowing over," and "the wish [for] continuation" (170). So Connolly asks his readers to imagine failed suicides, life-threatening accidents, or seeing a loved one slowly pass away. For those who are not familiar with these experiences, those for whom they are not a "live issue," Connolly suggests, "there are several possibilities. Reflection on Greek tragedy may be one. . . . Drawing upon the rich experience of ordinary life already available to most individuals may be another" (169).

It would not be surprising if many individuals, in seeking experiences through which to understand the depth of our affirmation of life, might turn to the experience of parenting rather than death—to the burdens and pleasures of creating and raising those "children and witnesses" whom Nietzsche imagines at our bedside if our death is timely. Nietzsche himself turned there frequently. Yes, he wrote about a timely death, but the creation of life also preoccupied him from the first sentence of his first book. As Connolly acknowledges in *Identity\Difference*, "In another of his moods Nietzsche ridicules those who spend much of their time pondering death. Such rumination contradicts the fervency of life" (170).

Contradictions aside, Connolly suggests that the point of the path he takes with Nietzsche's thought, the path of considering life from the perspective of death, is "not to provide a single, exclusive interpretation [of Nietzsche] . . . but to place another candidate into the field of discussion" (170–71). Nietzsche's ideas about parenthood suggest a different response to the realization Connolly hopes to cull from thoughts of death:

the realization that life—in the fullness of its "memories," "joys," and "evaluations"—"wants to continue" (169). Yes, it wants to continue. So we often seek to pass it on. In doing so, parents put "another candidate into the field" in a more literal way: parenting a child and—if you can manage it—passing on to that child the accomplishments of the work you have done on yourself: your memories, joys, evaluations, and "values." That child will, in a way, be given a "single and exclusive" interpretation of the right way to live, the interpretation you craft through your own life and pass on through procreation's "real bond," to borrow Nietzsche's term.[7] Connolly, in the name of democratic citizenship, would like us to learn from Nietzsche to understand and value "the work adults do on themselves to reconfigure crude childhood codes received as laws and to reconsider the intrinsic authority in which those codes are said to be anchored" (*Neuropolitics,* 172). But the figure of the parent as citizen, in Nietzsche's thought and elsewhere, also invites us to consider things from the perspective of the intrinsic authority, the conveyor of "crude childhood codes," the one who must debate the new candidate (from a position of incumbency) regarding right and wrong, good and bad, for years and years and perhaps, if things are timely, see that candidate at his or her deathbed. Nietzsche's thought invites us to see citizenship from the perspective of the parent.

Connolly hopes that thinking about "a timely death" might help us "fend off" such antidemocratic impulses as "dogmatism in identity, innocence in action, the pursuit of transparency in knowledge, and the urge to moral simplification" (*Identity\Difference,* 171). But the foregoing investigations of political theory reveal that ideas about parenthood can contribute to all four: Rousseau's hope (and dread) that a parent's true nature might be transparent and knowable for the child, Nietzsche's dogmatism regarding the identity that one embodies in a child, Rorty's simplified moral community centered on family feeling and parental hopes for their children, and West's transformative experience of a child's innocence. Those democratic capacities that Connolly believes death promises to clarify, the creation of new life threatens to complicate.

Alternatively, parenthood can make things dangerously simple just where Connolly's account of democratic citizenship (which he often labels "pluralism") counsels openness toward complexities. No matter what pluralist or weak ontological subtleties we fold into our self-identity, they might not seem that subtle when imposed across generations or when scrutinized by the child who studies a parent for clues regarding adult answers to the question of how to live. But childish things frustrate Connolly. Responding to those who feel a need for deeper assurances than his notion of citizenship provides, Connolly summarizes in *Identity\Difference*, "Our claim in a nutshell: your consuming drive to the reassurance of identity stultifies the politics of difference in the name of morality" (194). But parenting, for those who take it on, means confronting a child's consuming drive for reassurance and the child's need for a "childhood crude" code of morality. Parenthood might convince us to turn to the "authoritarianism of... command ethics" that Connolly seeks to oppose (10). It is telling that Connolly gives in to the urge to say to those who cling too tightly to reassurance: "Grow up" (195). Connolly vents his frustration at "version[s] of democracy" that are "too insipid—and too dependent. Here everyone helps everyone else" (195). This democracy Connolly disdains sounds like politics as a nursery.[8] And though he scorns it, he also feels its pull. He admits to the immature citizens he scolds, "We see our own shadows on the mirror into which you stare." This admission—the idea that we catch a glimpse of ourselves in the mirror of immaturity—calls to mind the way Rousseau, Nietzsche, Rorty, and West were troubled by the image of themselves they might see in their child.

Connolly's weak ontology seems to call for greater attention to the role that parenthood might play, both as a common resource and a likely hindrance, in a citizenship that balances virtue and contest. This is especially the case if Connolly is hoping that the sensibility he would like to encourage for democratic citizenship might be cultivated beyond sensitive readers of Nietzsche and his ideas about death. If political theorists are simply interested in having conversations with other theorists about what they think citizenship might look like, that is well and good—though they might want to attend to how theorists who set the terms of that conversation, Rousseau and Nietzsche among them, worked ideas about parenthood into the development of those terms. But if they want to develop theories that have much to do with the way that nonpolitical theorists live their lives, then it is particularly necessary to attend to the way citizens work ideas about parenthood into their understanding of themselves as citizens. Many citizens are like Cornel West (and Rousseau, Nietzsche, and Rorty) in that when they think about "the deep stuff," they often think about parenthood.[9]

Parenthood and Contingency

Occasionally, Connolly thinks about parenthood too, and in ways that hint at why parenthood might play a central role in the everyday politics of weak ontology. At one point in *Identity\Difference*, in explaining what it is to have "a contingent identity," Connolly suggests you think "of specific 'traits' and 'dispositions' installed in a self... consisting of statements that stand somewhere between your parents' characterization of you and the characterizations through which you wish to be recognized" (174). But Connolly does not explain just why this intriguingly familial juxtaposition of perspectives—one that calls to mind a Nietzschean balance between the values we have inherited and the results of our efforts to recraft them—might be the most useful one. He goes on to say that the list of qualities you generate this way contains "socially mediated traits and dispositions" that are "contingent" in one of several ways— some more "crucial to the constitution of your identity" than others (174). This contingency that comes along with social mediation is the subject of the study *Mediated: How the Media Shapes Your World and the Way You Live in It*, by the anthropologist Thomas de Zengotita. De Zengotita argues that it is precisely the experience of our traits and dispositions as mediated and contingent that helps explain why parenthood is the most common experience that people turn to for feelings of deep commitment—and why parenthood is so often crucial to our sense of identity. According to de Zengotita, in the contemporary United States there is a pervasive sense that nearly every aspect of life is contingent, a temporary choice about who we want to be rather than an inescapable sense of who we are. De Zengotita would agree with Connolly that "the accelerated pace of contemporary life pulls people away from attunement to intrinsic purpose" (*Neuropolitics*, 18). De Zengotita believes the resulting way of life has a sense of "thinness." But he believes this thinness also contributes directly to something he calls "the cult of the child" and the fact that "no society in history has ever sanctified children the way we do" (*Mediated*, 33).

De Zengotita frames his argument as a refutation of Rorty's claim that no culture can socialize its children in a way that is ironist. "Where has Professor Rorty *been?*" he asks (*Mediated*, 36). But de Zengotita seems to prove Rorty's point despite himself, offering an interesting view of just the spectacle Rorty refused to consider: the ironist parenting. Though de Zengotita gives a somewhat ironic depiction of his own experience of parenting, he also gets across just how deeply parenting is felt. In a world of transient choices, the choice to parent, he writes, is "momentous . . . irrevocable and transformative" (37, 41). De Zengotita depicts the decisions one makes regarding children, from prenatal nutrition to bicycle helmets, as consistent with other aspects of contemporary life—involving a never-ending series of "choices." But he also makes it clear that parenthood is one realm in life where individuals have a deep sense that there is a right choice and a wrong choice, and to make the wrong choice would be corrosive to the person's sense of self. In fact, many such choices are hardly choices at all. Regarding the bike helmets that his generation did without, he notes, "Now that they are an option, it would be downright irresponsible not to strap one on [to your child's head] . . . you end up opting for these options because it's better than not opting for them" (29). These choices on behalf of children are different from any other choices in life; they are less contingent and are held to a higher standard. They are "choices that might bring benefit or harm to this precious dependent creature (so desperately precious; like nothing else could possibly be)." In lives filled with "schemes and projects, . . . no project feels more essential than the well-being of our children" (39).

But de Zengotita's "cult of the child" goes deeper than personal safety. It involves the way the experience of parenting pulls us into layers beneath the thin surface of contingency and choice, into matters central to our being. He argues that children offer parents access to the "given"—to what lies beyond the contingent. This is because, in seeking to make sense of the world, children approach the world as if there are right answers to important questions—as if the world is, to use de Zengotita's phrase, something "given" rather than something to be endlessly manipulated and reinterpreted. "What we see in children, through children, is all things given for the first time" (42). We witness and guide a child's efforts to understand the rules and codes of the world they enter and hear them interrogate adults regarding human practices as if they were important and meaningful rather than arbitrary choices. "Children are what is left to us of metaphysics" (44).

This interaction takes on a new profundity at a time "when the routines we follow are *less* entrenched than at any time in human history," when "we are so deeply and constantly, if half-consciously, aware of the arbitrariness of the ways of our lives, . . . [and] haunted by the knowledge that things could be otherwise" (43). Things cannot be otherwise for children because of the choices we have made for them.

> The child's-eye view of this mediated world is the view of one *who has no choice but to live in it*. That is, for the child, there is no difference *in kind* between our world, saturated with representations and options, and an African savannah in the Paleolithic. To a child, thrown into an individual existence, they are equally given.
>
> Through the eyes of a child, the world we know as a construct becomes a mysterious necessity once again.
>
> In this way, children connect us to the real. They are the affirmative complement of illness and death on the other horizon of our lives. (*Mediated*, 43)[10]

It is not simply in *watching* children learn about the world that adults get access to "the real" in a mediated culture. Rather, it is in being watched by children and scrutinized for answers to fundamental questions. "In the case of children, we are the instruments and vessels of their becoming. They are the beyond *in* us, the given *in* us, and so, by irresistible implication, the givenness of our lives as well. . . . That is why your child's attention—the gaze upon your face, the concentration on your words, the thoughtful response—feels like the light of heaven" (44).

But as the previous chapters have explored, the light of heaven can reveal too much. Self-scrutiny channeled through a child, like the Calvinist self-scrutiny described by Weber, can lead to profound doubts with profound consequences. De Zengotita notes that this is why "some parents shy away from their children" (44). Richard Sennett has also uncovered the darker side of seeing ourselves through our children's eyes in a world characterized by contingency. In *The Corrosion of Character,* he uses a series of profiles to examine the stresses and challenges that contemporary American careers often entail. The study is about the anxieties of contingency—of work in the new "flexible capitalism" in which workers "are asked to behave nimbly, to be open to change on short notice, to take risks continually."[11] Sennett describes citizens who feel that these sorts of careers have "set [their] emotional, inner life adrift" (21) and made their own sense of character elusive. This drift is exacerbated by the sort of frequent moves, from job to job, city to city, that contemporary careers of contingency require. The result is that "no one . . . becomes a long-term witness to another person's life." No one, that is, except one's family. And so Sennett's subjects focus their anxiety onto their kids and what children might learn from watching their parents build lives that look like a wandering pursuit of material comfort. Discussing one of his subjects, Sennett writes, "He wants to set for his son and daughters an example of resolution and purpose, 'but you can't just tell kids to be like that'; he has to set an example. . . . His deepest worry is that he cannot offer the substance of his work life as an example to his children of how they should conduct themselves ethically" (21). De Zengotita's analysis suggests that contingency, a necessary condition for the politics of contest, also pulls us toward a particular source of virtue—our sense of ourselves as parents. Sennett's study suggests that contingency also undermines parents' sense of their own virtue. Together these takes on the contingency of modern life form a bitter paradox for the parent as citizen.

Parenthood and Biopolitics

The relationship between citizens' sense of the right way to live and their experience of procreation has become an important part of some theorists' efforts to explore the modern phenomenon of biopolitics. "Biopolitics" refers to the way government has come to focus on the management of populations rather than on the control of territory. The preoccupations of the weak ontologists, and specifically Connolly's appropriation of Nietzsche, point to one reason it would be useful for contemporary theorists to examine the way parenthood complicates democratic citizenship. Connolly's critique of Giorgio Agamben's notion of biopolitics and sovereignty suggests another. In *Pluralism*, Connolly is critical of Agamben for his focus on the persistence of an ancient "logic" of sovereignty that lurks behind the power of the state—including its power to manage, guide, and snuff out human lives. Connolly argues that Agamben ignores the potentially countervailing power of *citizens*, who are also sovereign in democratic politics and might complicate, constrain, or enable state efforts to carry out biopolitical projects. "Politics and culture . . . do not possess as tight a logic as Agamben suggests . . . [because] in democratic, constitutional states sovereignty circulates uncertainly between the multitude, traditions infused into it, and constitutionally sanctioned authorities."[12] Thus Connolly suggests that we should abandon calls for intellectual "transcendence" of "ironclad paradoxes" (141) that issue from ancient logics regarding sovereignty in favor of an examination of the ways that citizens actually enact sovereignty in their lives—a "micropolitics of biopolitics" (143).

In such a rethinking of Agamben and biopolitics, the role of ideas about parenthood in popular notions of citizenship should be important. Contemporary theorists of biopolitics have been slow to grapple with the extent to which ordinary citizens make sense of their relationship to a politics that addresses itself to population and life through the way they think about the meaning of parenthood. Though Agamben sets for himself the goal of elucidating "the transformation of natural heredity into a political task," he has little to say about the anxieties that surround the efforts of modern parent-citizens to see their children inherit the inner qualities proper to citizenship and thus little to say about the political effects of those anxieties.[13] Agamben writes as if the great dilemma of modern politics is a failure to think about the relationship between "natural heredity" and politics. But as the previous chapters indicate, the problem is not so much a lack of thought on these matters as it is *our ways of thinking* about them.

There is a great deal to indicate—even in Agamben's own analysis— that the experience of parenthood is central to the way that modern citizens conceive of their role in biopolitical communities. In *Homo Sacer: Sovereign Power and Bare Life,* Agamben revisits the classic Greek distinction between reproductive life and politics—between "*zoē*, which expressed the simple fact of living common to all living beings (animals, men or gods), and *bios,* which indicated the form or way of life proper to an individual or a group" (1). Linking Arendt's concerns with the entry of "*homo laborans*—and with it biological life as such . . . [to] the very center of the political scene of modernity" (3) with Foucault's analysis of a politics that addresses itself to populations rather than territory, Agamben summarizes that "the interlacement of *zoē* and *bios* . . . seems to define the political destiny of the West" (188).

Though Agamben refers to this "entry of *zoē* in the sphere of the polis" as the "decisive event of *modernity*" (4, emphasis added), he turns to the ancients to understand its origins and significance—not to the Greeks but to Roman ideas about sovereignty. In Roman thought and law, the sovereign was defined foremost as having the capacity to decide who would carry the status of *homo sacer*—a person whom anyone could kill without fear of punishment, but who could not be sacrificed through the traditional rituals. To Agamben, this original sovereign act indicates that life has been implicated in law and in the sovereignty since the beginning.

But in designating *homo sacer,* the sovereign does not itself destroy life. Instead, the sovereign *produces* a particular kind of life—a "bare life" that "is not simply natural reproductive life, the *zoē* of the Greeks, nor *bios,* a qualified form of life. It is rather . . . a zone of indistinction and continuous transition between man and beast, nature and culture" (109).

For Agamben, this is the essence of biopolitics—a politics in which biological life and the qualified way of life of the citizen have become indistinct. So while biopolitics has typically, following the suggestions of Foucault, been considered distinctly modern, Agamben's explorations led him to place the origins of biopolitics much earlier. "The inclusion of bare life in the political realm constitutes the original—if concealed—nucleus of sovereign power. *It can even be said that the production of a biopolitical body is the original activity of sovereign power*" (6). Agamben believes the key to understanding modern politics is to attend to the ways in which this original conception of sovereign power has been preserved and reinforced by new political developments.

But the sovereign's production of a biopolitical body rarely turns Agamben's analytical gaze toward the sovereign citizen's reproduction of biopolitical bodies in their children. While Agamben uses the perspective of bare life to reexamine, explain, and tie together a wide variety of political phenomenon,[14] he is most interested in the deathly aspects of bare life's modern political significance. Just as Connolly elucidates contemporary uses of a Nietzschean affirmation of life through an exploration of death, Agamben's examination of biopolitics and the production of bare life focuses on decisions over killing. This is true when he is considering the origins of ideas about sovereignty and the political: "The first foundation of political life is a life that may be killed, which is politicized through its very capacity to be killed" (*Homo Sacer,* 89). It is just as true when Agamben considers contemporary politics. Referring to the Nazi death camps, Agamben suggests, "The camp—as the pure, absolute, and impassable biopolitical space . . .—will appear as the hidden paradigm of the political space of modernity" (123).

But biopolitics is not merely, or even foremost, about death. Biopolitics also involves the care for life and its creation. Agamben writes, "In modern biopolitics the sovereign is he who decides on the value or the nonvalue of life as such" (142). It is true that the death camps were the result of a state's decision regarding the nonvalue of particular ways of life. But not all decisions about the value of a life are negative or unequivocal, and not all decisions are made at the level of state policy. As Connolly points out, sovereignty in the modern West resides not just in states but ultimately in citizens. Thus it is also individual citizens, and not simply the governments that care for some populations and exterminate others, who must confront the question of the value or nonvalue of particular ways of life. Citizens must confront the question of whether they live in such a way as to be worthy of citizenship *(bios)* or if they live in a shallower, less self-directed, and more animal (or more childish) way *(zoē)*. As the previous chapters demonstrated, a central way that modern citizens and modern theorists of citizenship have dealt with this question is through thinking about parenthood. Parenthood—in which the creation of a new biological life carries with it the responsibility of passing on a particular version of the right way to live—can become a locus of the construction of a personal biopolitics that affects the attitudes, impulses, and anxieties that citizens bring to politics. Political societies whose "fundamental referent [is] bare life" *(Homo Sacer,* 122) are made up of citizens, many of whom actively craft the connection between *zoē* and *bios* by attempting to instill a way of life in a child. And these citizens are heirs to political theorists who have woven the same task into their conceptions of modern citizenship.

Regarding his attention to killing over procreation, one can say about Agamben's recent work what Nietzsche said about Darwinism, "with its incomprehensibly one-sided doctrine of the 'struggle for existence.' . . . The struggle for existence is only an exception, a temporary restriction of the will to life."[15] This is not to say that the political phenomenon that Agamben offers as his primary examples of the inclusion of bare life in politics (the Holocaust, ethnic cleansing in Yugoslavia) should not be central to biopolitical analysis. But if Agamben is correct that the key to overcoming a politics that produces the camps is to understand the interlacement of *zoē* and *bios* wrapped up in modern and ancient sovereignty, that "every attempt to rethink the political space of the West must begin with the clear awareness that we no longer know anything of the classical distinction between *zoē* and *bios,* between private life and political existence, between man as a simple living being at home in the house and man's political existence in the city" (187), then it is necessary to confront the ways that ideas about parenthood—about the way we create new life—have been central to the modern craftwork lacing *zoē* together with *bios* in the lives of individual sovereign citizens. It is necessary to confront the parent as citizen.

Agamben's own account of the origins of ideas about sovereignty suggests that the power to designate *homo sacer,* to decide who could be killed and how, was originally the power of the father. In this Agamben discovers a sort of ancient Roman reversal of Locke's response to Filmer. While Locke dispersed the paternal right of kings to bestow sovereignty on actual fathers, in Rome it was a father's individual rights over his children that became the basis for the legal principle of sovereignty. "[T]he first time we encounter the expression 'right over life and death' in the history of law is in the formula *vitae necisque potestas,* which designates not sovereign power but rather the unconditional authority *[potesta]* of the *pater* over his sons" (*Homo Sacer,* 87).[16] Roman ideas about paternal power and sovereign power "end by being tightly intertwined," and the father's power over the life or death of a son eventually became the sovereign's power over citizens (88). But the life, the *vita,* over which fathers and sovereigns held the final decision included both biological life *and* the qualified way of life of a citizen. "In a single term *[vita],* Latin brings together the meaning of both *zoē* and *bios*" (87). So the Roman father's power was to create through his son a new life with the qualities appropriate to a citizen or to destroy that life if the son failed to show himself worthy of citizenship. "It is as if male citizens had to pay for their participation in political life with an unconditional subjection to a power of death" (90). The Roman father possessed this power and responsibility in his dual capacity as biological father and as a sovereign citizen of the republic, just as the *vita* over which he was responsible was both a *zoē* and a *bios.*

As the double meaning of *vita* implies, it is not just death but the *creation* of life—the life appropriate to a citizen—that was at stake in the Roman intermingling of ideas about parenthood and sovereignty. Agamben sees that these stakes have been preserved, if reconfigured, in the modern West. As Locke took the paternal power of the sovereign monarch and broke it into as many pieces as there were sovereign citizens, so Agamben sees that

> modern democracy does not abolish sacred life but rather shatters it and disseminates it to every individual body, making it into what is at stake in political conflict. And the root of modern democracy's secret biopolitical calling lies here: he who will appear later . . . as the new sovereign subject (*subjiectus superaneus,* in other words what is below and, at the same time, most elevated) can only be constituted as such through the repetition of the sovereign exception and the isolation of *corpus,* bare life, in himself. (*Homo Sacer,* 124)

Locke, after splitting apart the sovereign power so intimately tied to parent-hood, in turn reconsidered the importance of parenthood to the new sov-ereign citizen—as did Rousseau, Nietzsche, Rorty, and West. Agamben, with his focus on death and the camps as the paradigm of modern politics, loses the thread of parenthood's role in the modern mingling of the ideas of *zoē* and *bios*. It is often through the experience of parenthood—by con-stituting *another* subject to be raised into a sovereign citizen—that mod-ern citizens attempt to negotiate the ambiguity inherent to the life of the "sovereign subject."

The role that parenthood plays in the citizen's experience of modern biopolitics—largely unexamined by Agamben—takes on a vital impor-tance if we are to pursue the goals and avoid the dangers that theorists of biopolitics have identified. If we are, as Agamben hopes, to "rethink the political space of the West," then a "clear awareness that we no longer know anything of the classical distinction between *zoē* and *bios*" must also confront the ways that the parent-citizen—whether virtuous or agonistic, whether in theorists' books or people's lives—works continually to break down that distinction (*Homo Sacer*, 187). The intractability of the problem of "the entry of *zoē* into the sphere of the *polis*—the politicization of bare life as such" is not, as Agamben suggests, that "politics has failed to reckon with this foundational event of modernity" (4). The problem, rather, is *the ways* that citizens and theorists of citizenship *have reckoned* and continue to reckon with it. As the previous chapters demonstrate, they have often dealt with it by examining the experience of parenthood as a resource for citizenship. The foregoing readings of modern political theory suggest that it is not a lack of thought that introduces bare life into modern politics but *ways of thinking* (and feeling and living). Whether citizenship is conceived of as virtuous and perfectible or contingent and agonal, it is the particular ways that citizens craft the connection between *zoē* and *bios* that pulls our politics in directions that worry theorists like Agamben and should worry us all—toward a politics that in addressing itself to life makes it "possible both to protect life and to authorize a holocaust" (3).

Parenthood and American Micropolitical Biopolitics

Just how might the role that parenthood plays in our conception of our-selves as citizens—our thinking about passing on a particular *bios* or *way of life* to our child—influence the directions of contemporary politics and the decisions of the state? One way to think about this is to follow the lead of Connolly. In his corrective to Agamben's tyranny of ancient logic, Connolly offers several examples of how the "micropolitics of sovereignty" might constrain and guide the decisions of the state. One example is a counterfactual: he suggests that the 2000 *Bush v. Gore* decision to stop Florida election officials from hand-counting ballots might have gone differently had citizens projected a different sort of interest in the controversy. There was no sense, according to Connolly, that citizens would react strongly to a halt of the recount—no "anticipation of . . . militance" that might have influenced the justices of the Supreme Court either consciously or unconsciously.[17] His other example is more Agambenesque in that it regards the Native American genocide. Connolly examines how American citizens' prevailing "ethos of sovereignty" undermined the Supreme Court's nineteenth-century affirmations of the autonomous rights of the Cherokee people in the southeastern United States. It was the popular sense that only Christians had genuine rights in the American republic, "a sovereign ethos of Christian superiority" (*Pluralism*, 142), as Connolly puts it, which allowed both citizen vigilantes and President Andrew Jackson to violate the decisions of the Court, terrorize the Cherokee people, and precipitate their tragic march westward.

How might parenthood play a role in the creation of the sort of "sovereign ethos" that Connolly describes as the stuff of biopolitical micropolitics? The case of the Cherokee offers some intriguing possibilities. While Jackson figured himself as a "father" to the Native American "children" he forced into a genocidal relocation, American citizens also thought of the Native American threat to Christians most prominently in terms of parenthood.[18] As Michael Rogin explained, the danger that Native Americans were thought to pose to whites was imagined in terms of violence aimed most intensively at mothers and children. American citizens were enraged by the specter of a threat that would snatch "the infant from the nipple of its mother and bash its head against a tree." They were infuriated by images of "the cradle stained with the blood of innocence" and "little, prattling infants butchered, mangled, murdered" at the hands of natives.[19]

Leaving Connolly's examples behind, several other events from more recent American politics illustrate the micropolitics of parenthood. When the U.S. Supreme Court committed the government to integrating schools, many white parents in the South reacted by putting their children into all-white parochial schools. The enrollment of these schools expanded dramatically in the 1960s and 1970s.[20] This move to place children in white-only Christian schools was not "a sovereign ethos of Christian superiority," since most southern blacks were Christians as well. Rather, it was a parental ethos based on the worry that the white southern way of life—the way of life southern parents strove to instill in their children—would be threatened if their children spent their school day with black children. When the Carter administration attempted to repeal the tax exemptions that lent de facto federal support to these white-only religious schools, southern whites responded by organizing politically in the church-based organizations that became the basis for the Moral Majority and subsequently the Christian Coalition.[21] This political mobilization and the interest groups that grew out of this movement exercised a profound influence on American politics—on cultural issues, foreign policy, opposition to taxes and social spending—for the next thirty years.

Writing about the broader American middle class during this same period, Barbara Ehrenreich explains trends in American politics in terms of parents' worries that their children will fail to imitate them in developing the inner qualities needed to accomplish the long ascent into the ranks of the professional class. These middle-class anxieties about their children are rooted in profound doubts about their own worthiness. The resulting politics of anxiety, focused on the fragility of social reproduction for the professional middle class, becomes the lynchpin in Ehrenreich's analysis of the rightward drift of American politics since the relatively liberal consensus of the 1960s, and in particular the Right's incredibly effective focus on the diffuse issue of "permissiveness."

According to Ehrenreich, what makes the professional middle class uniquely vulnerable to anxieties of this sort is that they owe their lofty (but not quite dominant) status, simply to

> knowledge and skill, or at least the credentials imputing skill and knowledge. And unlike real capital, these cannot be . . . preserved beyond the lifetime of an individual, or, of course, bequeathed. . . .
> In this class, no one escapes the requirements of self-discipline and self-directed labor; they are visited, in each generation, upon the young as they were upon the parents. If this is an elite, then, it is an insecure and deeply anxious one.[22]

These anxieties come to focus on children due to the relative difficulty of passing professional middle-class status on to one's offspring. The "steep barriers" (college, graduate school, lengthy apprenticeships) the professional middle class had created to protect their professional domain "not only stand in the way of 'outsiders' . . . they also stand in the way of the children of the middle class" (*Fear of Falling*, 82).

But parents' deepest and most politically significant anxieties are about their children as a reflection of themselves. Ehrenreich's analysis hinges on a shared suspicion among the members of the professional middle class that the process of inheritance, the politics of imitation, works all too well. The professionals of the 1950s and 1960s, who had been raised in the harder times of the previous decades, worried that they had grown soft during the relative affluence and acquisitiveness of the postwar years. This suspicion, this seed of self-doubt, remained just that until it faced the crucial test of the sort of children the professional middle class produced. If a child grew up to have values different from what you hoped, if he or she lacked discipline, dedication, and responsibility, that constituted proof that the parents had been soft all along and not worthy of their own status.

This is why, according the Ehrenreich, the professional class reacted with such vehemence to the student protests of the late 1960s. The protests were evidence that their children, on some deep level imitating the adults who raised them, had become unruly and irresponsible. The reaction among the professional middle class was that "it was not the young who had failed . . . but the adults—parents, professors, and professionals generally—who represent authority . . . middle class adults had simply grown too lax, too soft, or—in the word that came to dominate the middle class reassessment—too *permissive*" (*Fear of Falling*, 59). While the rhetoric of the time largely focused on the problems with permissive child rearing strategies—influenced by Dr. Spock's ideas—the professional middle class was more profoundly worried that they had become, in an era of affluence and unprecedented personal spending, permissive with themselves.

This self-doubt would have profound political consequences. Because it is difficult to actually disengage from the consumer culture that planted this seed of insecurity about one's own virtue, the middle class dealt with this anxiety through a series of political deflections. In particular, they responded to political messages from the Right centered on the issue of permissiveness in social policy toward the (racialized) poor and cultural threats to "traditional values" like abortion, homosexuality, promiscuity, drugs, godlessness, and feminism (*Fear of Falling*, 168). These are precisely the issues, along with national security more recently,[23] that have animated the rightward shift in U.S. politics from the 1970s to its culmination in the reelection of Bush.

Connolly suggests that we should attend to the "micropolitics of sovereignty" most carefully during any "sharp turn in [political] time, when a sovereign decision is needed and established precedents are insufficient" (*Pluralism*, 144). If the struggle over war and civil rights in the 1970s offered one such turn in political time, post-9/11 politics offered another. Facing a difficult reelection in the midst of a foundering war based on faulty intelligence, evidence of U.S. involvement in torture, and misgivings about warrentless domestic spying, the 2004 Bush campaign learned how to speak about terrorism in terms that appealed to parental sentiments. Bush advisors expressed confidence that "security moms" and concerned parents in general would react to news of a terrorist attack on a primary school in Russia by voting for a president they trusted to keep their children safe from another attack.[24] This confidence was rewarded by the effectiveness of "Ashley's Story," the commercial that ran most frequently on American televisions over the course of the election.[25] The most expensive commercial buy in American political history[26] was for a spot that focused on a photograph of President Bush spontaneously embracing the preteen Ashley Faulkner, whose mother was killed when the World Trade Center collapsed. Casting Bush as a surrogate parent, the commercial lingers on the president's face, clearly filled with empathy for the girl's suffering. Ashley herself reflects in voice-over, describing Bush as the perfect parent. "He's the most powerful man in the world, and all he wants to do is make sure I'm safe, that I'm okay." Meanwhile, the American style of linking good citizenship to parental sentiments was deployed to make sense of our foreign policy. Peter Pace, the Chairman of the Joint Chiefs of Staff, suggested that the key to ending the war in Iraq is to "get the Iraqis to love their children more than they hate their neighbors."[27]

Ashley's story helped earn Bush four more years in the White House, and when it was finally time for him to leave, he made his peace with that transition through a similar appeal to parental sentiment. Barack Obama, the man that Bush reassured the American people would "first and foremost" be "a good dad,"[28] wasted little time in confirming Bush's impression. Obama did so first, if not foremost, in the realm of reactionary symbolic politics by choosing a prominent homophobe and opponent of gay marriage to deliver the invocation at his inauguration.[29] But while Rick Warren, the minister who presided over Obama's swearing in, cites the

Bible to support his views, Obama justifies his own opposition to gay marriage not in terms of religion but in terms of a sovereign ethos based on
parenthood: "I believe that American society can choose to carve out a
special place for the union of a man and a woman as the unit of child-
rearing most common to every culture."[30]

Before he was elected, Obama wrote about his personal experience as
a father as the source of his deepest insecurities. "Of all the areas of my
life, it is in my capacities as a husband and father that I entertain the most
doubt" (*The Audacity of Hope*, 408). Obama wondered especially if his
political ambitions were hurting his ability to be a good father. But after
his election, in taking on the burdens of leading a nation in crisis and at
war, his tone shifted in regard to parenthood. In an "open letter" to his
daughters, he refigured parenthood from a source of personal insecurity
into a transformative experience that infused him with virtue and guides
his political actions:

> When I was a young man, I thought life was all about me—about
> how I'd make my way in the world, become successful, and get
> the things I want. But then the two of you came into my world . . .
> suddenly, all my big plans for myself didn't seem so important any-
> more. I soon found that the greatest joy in my life was the joy I saw
> in yours. And I realized that my own life wouldn't count for much
> unless I was able to ensure that you had every opportunity for hap-
> piness and fulfillment in yours. In the end, girls, that's why I ran
> for President: because of what I want for you and for every child in
> this nation.[31]

It may seem like a strange way to begin a presidency: to turn to the source
of your deepest insecurities and rely on it as the foundation of your political virtue. But, as the preceding studies of political theory suggest, it is
a time-tested technique. Unfortunately, the results of those tests are not
encouraging.

Obama will try the test on others as well. He has suggested policies
that should ensure that he is not the only citizen whose personal plans will
be transfigured by the onset of parental responsibilities. He has endorsed
an approach to fighting poverty in which the state encourages a similar
change for poor parents in urban areas—a plan in which poor citizens are
engaged by the state, "first and foremost," as parents. During his campaign,

Obama promised, "The first part of my plan to combat urban poverty will be to replicate the Harlem Children's Zone in twenty cities across the country."[32] These programs will focus on the life prospects of poor children starting at birth or even earlier thanks to its prenatal initiatives. But these programs reach children by attempting to change their parents.

The approach is the brainchild of Geoffrey Canada, an activist who grew frustrated with the failures of social programs designed to help poor adults find ways out of poverty.[33] Canada became convinced that it was not productive to attempt to create opportunities for job training or higher education for adults and young adults who had grown up poor. Their experience as children in impoverished communities had left them irreparably "short on marketable cognitive skills," and little could be done to change that once they had reached young adulthood.[34] Canada decided that it was necessary to give up on the current generation of adults and young adults and their hopes to become "fully functioning participants in mainstream American middle class life."[35] Instead, Canada believes, social services should focus on only one aspect of the lives of adult citizens living in poverty—their role as parents. It is through changing the way people in poverty parent that the programs comprising the Harlem Children's Zone hope to "save" the *next* generation rather than parents themselves. Instead of going to college, for example, these impoverished parents are encouraged to attend "baby college" where they learn about the importance of reading to children, speaking to them, and avoiding corporal punishment.[36]

The approach, as Canada puts it, is to "save the kids, rather than the parents. Our choice is to focus on [the child]."[37] Canada recognizes that this choice is a difficult realization for the parents who enter the program. He states in his interview with Paul Tough: "Its hard when you are just nineteen or twenty to accept the idea that you're not the one that is going to make it out of poverty, that instead your job is to make sure your kid makes it out." But parenthood provides a path to salvation for these parents, even a path to a sort of equal status with other citizens. Canada explains to parents,

> I know you don't have anything. I know you don't have any money.
> I know you're worried about where the rent is going to come from.
> I know you're worried about how you're going to be able to provide for your child; can you keep a roof over his head? But read to that child tonight . . . just read to that child today, just give them an

opportunity. You are doing as much for your child as that person in that nice big house that you're envying is doing for their child. *As parents you're exactly the same.*[38]

This is the path to equality that the federal government, under Obama, will support if he can convince Congress to do so: equality *as parents*.[39] Though they will remain mired in poverty, these parents will be equal to other citizens in their ability to pass on a way of life to their child. But the way of life they pass on will not be the way of life they inherited or one that they create for themselves. Instead, it will be the state's chosen way of life—the way of life that counts as successful "in the measures that count in contemporary American society."[40] It is a way of life designed by government specialists and carefully taught to poor parents.

While the goals of this sort of antipoverty program might be admirable, from the perspective of democratic citizenship the approach is disturbing. The government will reach into the lives of the most vulnerable citizens and attempt to remake them by reconfiguring their identity as parents. Impoverished parents are encouraged to attend tear-filled group sessions that resemble twelve-step recovery groups, where they discuss what was most painful about the way they were raised by their parents, confess their own ambivalence about their children, and pledge to "break the cycle."[41] These parents are remade as caretakers by a caretaking state. They are encouraged to feel ashamed of the way of life they have inherited and to remake themselves into purveyors of the way of life approved by the government. The approach resembles a sort of mild Maoism in the name of a parenthood-centered cultural revolution among the poor. And the poor undertake this self-transformation not for themselves and their own opportunities but for the sake of the future "success" of their children and the nation. The Nobel prize–winning economist James Heckman, whose research underlies the approach taken by Obama's antipoverty initiative, notes that when he makes the case for this sort of expensive government intervention on "productivity grounds," he finds it more "politically persuasive."[42]

In the national program envisioned by Obama, social workers and psychologists are not merely made available to poor parents but practically imposed upon them. Canada believes that if the majority of parents in a community do not change their approach to raising children, then the children who are in the program can be "contaminated" by neighborhood kids with the wrong values. Therefore, the state will not play a passive role and help only those parents who take it upon themselves to undertake this transformation for the sake of their children. Instead, the state must become more aggressive. Obama notes approvingly the way that social workers in Harlem spread out into the community to tempt parents with incentives and cajole them into participating. Daniel Patrick Moynihan, in his notorious 1965 Department of Labor report "The Negro Family: The Case for National Action," suggested young black men be enlisted into the army.[43] Obama will send an army to them. As he put it in his speech outlining his approach, "You don't just sign up for this program; you're actively recruited for it, because the idea is that if everyone is involved, and no one slips through the cracks, then you really can change an entire community."[44]

"No one slips through the cracks." Though the idea may seem palatable because it is couched in terms of a family-centered antipoverty program, these can be chilling words when spoken by a political leader eager to transform a society. They are words that should give us pause. It is a vision of politics worthy of Rousseau's *Social Contract,* in which all citizens have their sense of self transfigured by their membership in the state and in which those who do not will be "forced to be free."[45] At the end of his *Discourse on the Origins of Inequality,* having traced the dissolution of man from independent noble savages to isolated modern slaves, Rousseau remarked that we had arrived at "the extreme point that closes the circle and touches the point from where we started."[46] In an analogous way, Obama's initiative closes a circle in which West's concern with the dissolution of the twenty-first-century family meets Rousseau's vision in which the state imposes a particular notion of virtue when the experience of parenthood proves incapable of instilling it.

Psychologically, emotionally, even physically, parenting is one of the messiest things we humans do. This does not mean that politics should or could be made cleaner by excluding ideas about parenthood. There is a good deal that is messy in politics, and theorists of contest citizenship from Nietzsche to Connolly remind us that politics is most compelling when this messiness is accepted and engaged. The problems that haunt parenthood—insecurity, presumption, selfishness, rage, fundamentalism, betrayal—plague democratic politics as well. This means that it is not fruitful to take an experience that is messy, fix it with a particular meaning, and ask it to accomplish a particular task for political purposes. For many individuals, political claims, political capacities, and political commitments will be rooted in the experience of having children. The experience of having children and the lessons one takes from it may indeed be unique. But they should not be considered unique for the purpose of politics. For the purpose of politics, they should be recognized as first and foremost *political*—subject to uncertainty, to contestation, to reconsideration, and to being abandoned.

Notes

Introduction

1. Robert Filmer, *Patriarcha and Other Writings*, ed. J. P. Sommerville (Cambridge: Cambridge University Press, 1991).

2. John Locke, *Two Treatises of Government* (Cambridge: Cambridge University Press 1988), 194, 306–7.

3. Locke is actually quite insistent that the contributions of mothers to the raising of a child into an autonomous adult be acknowledged, but in this particular quotation, he was discussing fathers and sons.

4. This formulation of citizenship has had a profound effect on ideas about the citizenship of nonparents. For example, Lee Edelman's *No Future: Queer Theory and the Death Drive* (Durham, N.C.: Duke University Press, 2004) explores the role that the childless, and especially the childless who are gay, play in the American political imagination.

5. Heidi Collins, "Transcript: Bush Recalls Regrettable, Proud Moments" (interview with George Bush), *CNN.com*, November 11, 2008, http://www.cnn.com/2008/POLITICS/11/11/bush.transcript/index.html.

6. It is a rhetorical strategy shared by Bush's predecessor in office. In one 1997 advertisement, Clinton reminded the public: "Every day, I try my best to meet the challenges that come with doing the toughest job in the world. If I fail, the consequences could be serious. The job isn't being President—it's being a parent." James Bennet, "Clinton, in Ads, Lifts Image of Parent," *New York Times*, March 4, 1997, A18. Edelman, in *No Future*, offers an intriguing analysis of this ad and the place of children in American political culture (1–2).

7. Lauren Berlant, *The Queen of America Goes to Washington City* (Durham, N.C.: Duke University Press, 1997), 1. Several examinations of the child-centeredness of contemporary American political culture exist. They include Berlant's *The Queen of America*; George Lakoff's *Moral Politics: How Liberals and Conservatives Think*, 2nd ed. (Chicago: University of Chicago Press, 2002), which argues that two competing visions of family are the cognitive source at the root of conservative and liberal views on most political issues; Nina Eliasoph's *Avoiding Politics: How Americans Produce Apathy in Everyday Life* (Cambridge: Cambridge University Press, 1998), which explores how political activists use child-centered

language to avoid not just the appearance of but the uncomfortable feeling that comes from being "too political"; and Michael Shapiro's *For Moral Ambiguity: National Culture and the Politics of the Family* (Minneapolis: University of Minnesota Press, 2001), which explores the way the rhetoric of "family values" moralizes American politics in a way that destroys contingency and openness. When political figures write books, they most often write about parenthood and the task of passing along the values proper to American citizenship. This is true whether the politicians are Democrats (like Hillary Clinton, author of *It Takes a Village, and Other Lessons Children Teach Us* [New York: Simon and Schuster, 1996] or Barack Obama, author of *Dreams from My Father: A Story of Race and Inheritance* [New York: Three Rivers Press, 2004) or Republicans (like Rick Santorum, author of *It Takes a Family: Conservatism and the Common Good* [Wilmington, Del.: ISI Books, 2005] or John McCain, author of *Faith of My Fathers* [New York: Random House, 1999])). Lakoff argues that the principle source of conservative and liberal ideology in the United States is competing "unconscious worldviews" based upon conceptions of the proper way to raise a child.

8. Edelman, *No Future*, 2.

9. Robert Wright's response to the Bush reelection in 2004, in which he argued that Democrats should find a way to speak to Americans as parents more directly, is typical in this regard: "Though [values] issues are symptoms of moral anxiety in Middle America, I think the anxiety's ultimate source is more diffuse, and includes concerns that even many liberals share. Especially if they're parents. I've never met an American parent—left, right, center—who seemed enthusiastic about the culture in which children now grow up. Unless you put your kids in an isolation tank, their electronic and social environments will conspire to channel them toward MTV-land: a realm in which sex, money, alcohol, and rock-solid abs jockey for pre-eminence in the hierarchy of human needs. And along the way these kids will encounter lots of glorified violence—more of a concern on the left than the right, maybe, but something very few parents applaud." Robert Wright, "Moralize, Liberally," from discussion thread Why Americans Hate Democrats— A Dialogue, *Slate*, November 4, 2004, http://www.slate.com/id/2109164.

10. Barack Obama, *The Audacity of Hope* (New York: Vintage Books, 2006), 74–75. Obama extends the same line of thinking backward as well as forward. Speaking about the role that empathy plays "at the heart of my moral code," he notes, "like most of my values, I learned about empathy from my mother" (80).

11. Like Cornel West, as I explore in chapter 4, Obama believes these child-centered values are "surprisingly constant across classes, and races, and faiths, and generations" (83–84).

12. Barack Obama, "We Need Fathers to Step Up," *Parade Magazine*, June 21, 2009.

13. Biden became a single father when his wife was killed between his first

election to the Senate and his assumption of the office. In the 2008 campaign, McCain repeatedly referred to Sarah Palin as a "hockey mom," and she went on to make the birth of her son who has Down syndrome a centerpiece of her stump speech (Patrick Healy, "A Riveting Speaker, Waving the Flag," *New York Times,* October 13, 2008).

14. Leah McElrath Renna, "Joe's Tears: The Political Power of Paternal Love," *Huffington Post,* October 2, 2008. The previous vice president from the Democratic Party, Al Gore, also made the near death of his son the centerpiece of many of his speeches while campaigning. The importance of parenthood as a political identity in American politics has led a number of commentators, including Joel Kotkin and William Frey in *The New Republic,* Steve Sailor in *The American Conservative,* and David Brooks in the *New York Times,* to argue that the key to understanding the split between "red and blue" regions of the country is to look at fertility rates. As Sailor puts it, reaffirming the centrality of parenthood to a human life even as he notes its importance to vote choice, "Indeed, voters are picking their parties based on differing approaches to the most fundamentally important human activity: having babies" ("Baby Gap: How Birthrates Color the Electoral Map," *The American Conservative,* December 20, 2004, http://www.amconmag.com/article/2004/dec/20/0004). Kotkin and Frey argue that "Democrats [should] return to a worldview centered around the baby-making electorate" ("The Parent Trap," *New Republic,* December 2, 2004). Perhaps what is most interesting here is that whether the authors are triumphant about the Republicans' fertility-based momentum or are seeking a way for the Democrats to reverse the trend, both sides accept one fundamental truth: that the most important and deeply felt predisposition in the American electorate is people's belief in the role having and raising children plays in making life meaningful.

15. Monica Davey, "Palin Daughter's Pregnancy Interrupts G.O.P. Convention Script," *New York Times,* September 2, 2008.

16. Jodi Kantor and Rachel L. Swarns, "A New Twist in the Debate on Mothers," *New York Times,* September 2, 2008.

17. Kristin Lukor, *Abortion and the Politics of Motherhood* (Berkeley: University of California Press, 1984), 190–199. Lukor describes the ways in which conservatives view an unplanned pregnancy as a "surprise" that puts us in touch with the unpredictability of life, our inability to plan for all contingencies, and the necessity to transform our ideas about our priorities and the direction of our lives.

18. Dan Savage, "Status Is . . . for Gay Men; The Baby," *New York Times Magazine,* November 15, 1998, 95. Cited in Edelman, *No Future,* 75.

19. David Brooks, "The Power of Posterity," *New York Times,* July 28, 2009.

20. Edelman, *No Future,* 75. In this quote, Edelman is reacting to Savage's formulation of parent-based gay citizenship.

21. Bonnie Honig suggests that caring often demands a transformation of the

cared for into a reflection of our own self image. Critiquing the role of ideas about care in the work of Carol Gilligan and Stephen White, she argues, "doesn't care turn the other into the receptive object of our need to act out of a sense of responsibility, a mirror of our desire? Doesn't care thereby close spaces of dissonance and resistance?" *Political Theory and the Displacement of Politics* (Ithaca: Cornell University Press, 1993), 263.

22. John Locke, *Some Thoughts Concerning Education* (Indianapolis: Hackett, 1996), 44–45, 50.

23. Obama, "We Need Fathers to Step Up." In this Obama echoes contemporary American political thought, beyond the examples of Rorty and West, which I explore in detail later. John Rawls, for example, suggests that parent-citizens of the right sort become "worthy objects of [the child's] admiration . . . [and] arouse in him a sense of his own value and the desire to become the sort of person they are" (John Rawls, *A Theory of Justice* [Cambridge, Mass.: Harvard University Press, 1971], 465–66). Susan Moller Okin, noting the masculine bias in Rawl's formulation, rightly faults him for ignoring the political effects of justice within the family. In doing so, however, she implicitly agrees that the qualities of citizenship practiced by the parents will be reproduced in their children. Okin, *Justice, Gender and the Family* (New York: Basic Books, 1989).

24. Theodor Adorno, *Minima Moralia* (New York: Verso, 1978), 154. Adorno offers this analysis as a correction to Nietzsche specifically, whom he scolds for worshiping at the mantle of genuineness when a true understanding of the experience of infancy should dismiss all thoughts of the genuine. As the following chapters show, Nietzsche seized upon procreation precisely because it offered a way for a parent to pass on something completely unique, genuine, and personal—so that the effort to craft it would not be wasted.

25. Judith Butler, *Gender Trouble* (New York: Routledge, 1990), 175.

26. When political theorists do make use of ideas about imitation from the perspective of the one who imitates, the results can be problematic. Hanna Pitkin, for example, explores the role of imitation in Machiavelli's thought. Machiavelli urges those who would be founders of something new to imitate the examples of great founders in the past. Pitkin notes that "the imitation of character as a means to autonomy is inherently paradoxical." *Fortune Is a Woman: Gender and Politics in the Thought of Niccolo Machiavelli* (Chicago: University of Chicago Press, 1999), 272.

27. John Stuart Mill, *On Liberty and Other Writings* (Cambridge: Cambridge University Press, 1989), 64–66.

28. Ralph Waldo Emerson, *The Conduct of Life* (Whitefish, Mont.: Kessinger, 2004), 23.

29. Max Weber, "Politics as a Vocation," in *From Max Weber: Essays in Sociology*, ed. Hans H. Gerth and C. Wright Mills (New York: Columbia Press, 1980), 127.

30. Honig uses the term *virtù* rather than *contest*. I discuss her take on the politics of virtue and contest later. *Political Theory*, 206.

31. When concerns that mingle leadership and imitation emerge in politics, they often bring with them the language and the psychological baggage of the roles of child and parent. On the metaphorical level, this is evident in the frequent invocation of the "Founding Fathers" of a given political community, but it manifests itself in more complex and emotionally intense ways. Michael Rogin's *Fathers and Children: Andrew Jackson and the Subjection of the American Indian* (New Brunswick, N.J.: Transaction Publishers, 2000) describes the ways that presidents from Jefferson to Jackson figured themselves as fathers to Native Americans. The central question of this era in American politics, Rogin summarized, is "What meaning can be given to a policy of death and dispossession, centrally important to the development of America, over which considerable guilt is felt and which is justified by the paternal benevolence of a father for his children?" These presidents demanded that their "children" imitate the paternal culture—especially through owning and cultivating individual plots of land. These "fathers" unleashed exterminatory violence upon their children when they refused to abandon childhood for the path to maturity and culture—killing the "children" who refused to imitate them. The quotation is from Rogin's *Ronald Reagan, the Movie: And Other Episodes in Political Demonology* (Berkeley: University of California Press, 1988), 138.

32. The phenomenon of increased scrutiny and beating of children in Protestant Europe is described by Neil Postman in *The Disappearance of Childhood* (New York: Vintage Books, 1994) and by Lawrence Stone in *The Family, Sex, and Marriage in England 1500–1800* (New York: Harper and Row, 1977).

33. Jean-Jacques Rousseau, *Julie, or The New Heloise* (Hanover, N.H.: Dartmouth College by University Press of New England, 1997), 167.

34. As I explore in the chapters that follow, both virtue and contest theories of politics present modern citizens with difficult tasks. The politics of virtue are difficult because the standard of virtue is so exacting, and under the tyranny of such standards, self-doubt can be relentless. The politics of contest set high standards as well. The articulation of political claims and accounts of the good, even when recognized as contingent and contestable, demand much of citizens. To open ourselves to the possibility that our notions of the good are subject to being contested, revised, or abandoned demands even more.

35. Charles Taylor, *Sources of the Self* (Cambridge, Mass.: Harvard University Press, 1989), 292.

36. Charles Taylor, *Modern Social Imaginaries* (Durham, N.C.: Duke University Press, 2004), 105–6.

37. Jürgen Habermas, *The Structural Transformation of the Public Sphere: An Inquiry into a Category of Bourgeois Society* (Cambridge, Mass.: MIT Press, 1989), 43.

38. Taylor, *Sources of the Self*, 293.

39. Postman, *The Disappearance of Childhood,* chapters 2 and 3.

40. This is indicated by the fact that two of the theorists I deal with extensively did not engage in any parenting. Rousseau abandoned five children at birth (though he did at one point purchase a young girl, put her up in an apartment, and teach her to play the piano—see chapter 1), and Nietzsche never had any. Both Rorty and West had children. Rorty does not discuss the experience in his work, whereas West writes about it quite movingly.

41. William E. Connolly, *Why I Am Not a Secularist* (Minneapolis: University of Minnesota Press, 1999), 15.

42. Some theorists have also suggested that parenthood can benefit citizenship by providing an example of the sort of care that citizens might show for each other. I discuss this perspective later.

43. Paul Kahn, *Putting Liberalism in Its Place* (Princeton, N.J.: Princeton University Press, 2005), 201–2.

44. Bonnie Honig, in *Political Theory,* has conceptualized these two theories of politics as the "virtue" and, following Machiavelli, *"virtù."* This book forgoes Honig's alliteration, even as it reproduces the categories, and I instead refer to the virtue and contest theories of citizenship. Honig, except in a few instances, does not explore the role that ideas about parenthood play in the theories that she examines. I discuss her take on these two modes of citizenship later.

45. In the first case, West was writing about C. Wright Mills's analysis of Dewey; in the latter, his own critique of Jeffery Stout's *Ethics after Babel: The Languages of Morals and Their Discontents* (Boston: Beacon Press, 1988). Cornel West, *The American Evasion of Philosophy: A Genealogy of Pragmatism* (Madison: University of Wisconsin Press, 1989), 127; and *Beyond Eurocentrism and Multiculturalism,* vol. 1, *Prophetic Thought in Postmodern Times, Notes on Race and Power in America* (Monroe, Maine: Common Courage Press, 1993), 176.

46. In her own study of the politics of virtue and contest, Honig follows a similar method. As she puts it, "The problematic [of the displacement of politics by virtue theorists] is too broad of a point of departure for each chapter, and so I approach each thinker initially by way of a concept or concern suggested by his or her own work." Regarding virtue theorists, Honig "[calls] attention to the moments in their own accounts that belie [their] assumptions" (*Political Theory,* 5–6). Honig uses this method to great effect regarding the virtue theorists she engages. I apply this method to both theorists of virtue and theorists of contest as well as to theorists who have sought ways to balance these concerns.

47. White labels this approach "weak ontology." *Sustaining Affirmation: The Strengths of Weak Ontology in Political Theory* (Princeton, N.J.: Princeton University Press, 2000), 8. White does not write extensively about Rorty or West except to suggest that Rorty offers a challenge to the viewpoints of "weak ontologists." My chapter on Rorty shows that he has much in common with the tradition that

White describes. In the Conclusion, I discuss weak ontology and William Connolly, whom White discusses as a weak ontologist, in more detail. Other theorists, especially Connolly, label this sort of approach "pluralism."

48. Connolly, *Why I Am Not a Secularist,* 8.

49. Honig, *Political Theory,* 201.

50. Honig does not examine the role that ideas about parenthood play in the politics of virtue and contest. But she offers the most explicit account of these categories of political thinking as well as innumerable insights into the motivations, strengths, and weaknesses involved in these modes of theorizing. Thus I occasionally relate the arguments that follow to Honig's ideas, particularly those regarding Nietzsche, who serves as one of her exemplary theorists of contest.

51. This is suggested by Taylor, among others, in his account of how conversations about the meaning and power of the family dramas depicted in Rousseau's writings helped give birth to the modern democratic public sphere. Taylor, *Modern Social Imaginaries,* 105–6.

52. I engage several of these interpretations in the course of my reading of Rousseau.

53. For example, Nicole Fermon in *Domesticating Passions: Rousseau, Woman, and Nation* (Hanover, N.H.: Wesleyan University Press, 1997) and Tony Tanner, "Julie and 'La Maison Paternelle': Another Look at Rousseau's *La Nouvelle Heloise,*" in *The Family in Political Thought,* ed. Jean Bethke Elshtain (Amherst: University of Massachusetts Press, 1982).

54. Taylor, *Modern Social Imaginaries,* 181. He suggests the path begun by Rousseau passed through "the Jacobins, Marx and communism." The path begun by Nietzsche he presumably believes led to Nazism, though he does not say so directly.

55. In chapters 2, 3, and 4 and the Conclusion, I address several of the contemporary theorists of democracy who turn to Nietzsche's ideas for these purposes.

56. Honig, *Political Theory,* 8.

57. As I explain, this is a source of some of the weaknesses I identify in Rorty's approach. Honig suggests that "the best perspective . . . is generated not by virtue or *virtù* but by the struggle between them" (*Political Theory,* 205).

58. Rorty stands out among this group in his attention to gender manifest in his concerted effort to remain gender neutral in all his formulations regarding citizenship.

59. Iris Marion Young, "Mothers, Citizenship, and Independence: A Critique of Pure Family Values," *Ethics* 105, no. 3 (1995): 545.

60. Examples of scholarship that has made use of this idea in the service of insightful readings of political theory are too numerous to list comprehensively, and to lump them together in a footnote is to trivialize the important differences in approach and the subtlety of analysis scholars have brought to different political

thinkers and particular foci of concern. Nonetheless, Jean Bethke Elshtain's *Public Man, Private Woman* (Princeton, N.J.: Princeton University Press, 1981) and Mary O'Brien's *The Politics of Reproduction* (New York: Routledge and Kegan Paul, 1981) are foundational studies in this regard. Hirschmann makes this point regarding Rousseau in particular in her recent *Gender Class and Freedom in Modern Political Theory* (Princeton, N.J.: Princeton University Press, 2008): "Rousseau is the most obvious here, for he structures a vision of the family that completely segregates women from politics, cities, and indeed the public sphere altogether, to produce women who are modest, chaste, and subservient to men" (23). But she also notes that "despite his apparent basing of men's freedom on women's restriction, his theory could be reconstructed to accommodate women without sacrificing theoretical consistency" (166). I argue in chapter 1 that things are not as obvious as Hirschmann implies. Other studies that have explored this gendered aspect of political theory include Carole Pateman, *The Sexual Contract* (Stanford, Calif.: Stanford University Press, 1988); Wendy Brown, *Manhood and Politics: A Feminist Reading in Political Theory* (Totowa, N.J.: Rowman and Littlefield, 1988); Pitkin, *Fortune Is a Woman*; Linda M. G. Zerilli, *Signifying Woman: Culture and Chaos in Rousseau, Burke and Mill* (Ithaca, N.Y.: Cornell University Press, 1994); Christine Di Stefano, *Configurations of Masculinity: A Feminist Perspective on Modern Political Theory* (Ithaca, N.Y.: Cornell University Press, 1991). In the chapters that follow, particularly regarding Rousseau and Nietzsche, I will have more to say about this literature.

61. Jacqueline Stevens, *Reproducing the State* (Princeton, N.J.: Princeton University Press, 1999), 15–16.

62. Simone De Beauvoir, *The Second Sex* (New York: Vintage Books, 1989). "First violated, the female is then alienated—she becomes, in part, another than herself" (22). Unable to claim the "transcendence of . . . the man of action," through reproduction she becomes "life's passive instrument" (495).

63. This notion of parenthood as a model of the sort of caring relationship appropriate to democratic citizenship is the subject of a number of studies, including Sara Ruddick in *Maternal Thinking* (New York: Ballantine, 1989) and Jean Bethke Elshtain in "Antigone's Daughters," in *Feminism and Politics*, ed. Anne Phillips (Oxford: Oxford University Press, 1998). Mary Dietz offers an effective critique of Elshtain and Ruddick's position in "Citizenship with a Feminist Face: The Problem with Maternal Thinking." *Political Theory* 13, no. 1 (1985): 19–38. Dietz suggests Arendtian respect as a better model for citizenship than parental care. However, as I touch upon later, Arendt offers a version of the contest theory of citizenship that utilizes some parental thinking.

64. Joan Tronto, *Moral Boundaries: A Political Argument for an Ethic of Care* (New York: Routledge, 1993).

65. Stevens, *Reproducing the State*, 268.

66. In this sense, parenthood combines several senses of the idea of citizenship. Linda Bosniak, for example, identifies, among other categories, citizenship as a sense of belonging and identity and citizenship as practice (*The Citizen and the Alien: Dilemmas of Contemporary Membership* [Princeton, N.J.: Princeton University Press, 1996]). The parent as citizen, as revealed in the chapters that follow, mixes these two perspectives in a complex way in which one's identity as a citizen is put at risk by the measure of the worthiness of our practices.

67. Young, "Mothers, Citizenship, and Independence," 548.

68. The results of recent referendums on gay marriage suggest that Americans are not yet prepared to take Young's advice to accept gay and lesbian parenting among the plurality of family forms that might effectively prepare children for citizenship. Leo Bersani assigns the special place of homophobia in contemporary American politics to a fear of a particular type of self-realization: "To let gays be open about their gayness, to give them equal rights, to allow them to say who they are and what they want, is to risk being recruited" (*Homos* [Cambridge, Mass.: Harvard University Press, 2005], 27). But the activists who have successfully campaigned against gay marriage have focused on the recruitment not of adults but of children. In California and Maine, the campaigns against gay marriage focused on the possibility that children would be taught that a gay marriage was an acceptable lifestyle, indirectly by the law's example and directly in schools. Thus opponents of gay marriage seemed to tap into a fear on the part of heterosexual parents that their children might not choose to imitate their parents' way of life if given the choice. (See Abby Goodnough, "Focus of Gay-Marriage Fight Is Maine," *New York Times*, October 27, 2009.)

69. Unless otherwise noted, emphasis is in the original. Regarding "grimness," Edelman is quoting Adorno.

70. Stephen Macedo and Iris Marion Young, *Child, Family, and State* (New York: New York University Press, 2003), 1.

71. Taylor, *Sources of the Self*, 15–16, 25.

72. Thomas Dumm, *Loneliness as a Way of Life* (Cambridge, Mass.: Harvard University Press, 2008), 10, 9. Lear's lament (III.iv.20–22), cited by Dumm, 3.

73. Michael Walzer, *Politics and Passion: Toward a More Egalitarian Liberalism* (New Haven, Conn.: Yale University Press, 2006), 3.

74. Honig, *Political Theory*, 130.

75. Bonnie Honig, *Democracy and the Foreigner* (Princeton, N.J.: Princeton University Press, 2001), 17. Honig asks this question in a book on the role of foreigners in democratic theory. It is indicative of the problems of the parent as citizen that the chapter in which she asks it focuses on Rousseau's and Freud's use of foreign founders as replacements for parents, whose role in our political imagination can be to highlight our continued inadequacies as citizens. I discuss this aspect of Rousseau in chapter 1.

76. Hannah Arendt, *Between Past and Future* (New York: Penguin Press, 1961), 189.

77. Dumm, *Loneliness as a Way of Life*, 96, 101.

1. Monsters in the Garden

1. Jean-Jacques Rousseau, *Confessions* (New York: Penguin, 1953), 19.

2. William E. Connolly, *Political Theory and Modernity* (Ithaca, N.Y.: Cornell University Press, 1993), 42. See also Tracy B. Strong, *Jean-Jacques Rousseau, The Politics of the Ordinary*, 149–50 (Thousand Oaks, Calif.: Sage, 1994); Allan Bloom, Introduction to *Emile* (New York: Basic Books, 1979), 16; and Maurice Cranston, *Jean-Jacques* (London: Allen Lane, 1983), 234.

3. Rousseau, *Julie*, 619.

4. Maurice Cranston, *The Solitary Self, Jean-Jacques Rousseau in Exile and Adversity* (Chicago: University of Chicago Press, 1993), 195.

5. Ibid. The emphasis on stability in Rousseau's vision can be overdone. Rousseau was an impassioned critic of the serial adultery practiced by the upper classes in his time, and in this sense his vision favored a relative stability in domestic relationships. But Rousseau described the romantic love he favored as a thoroughly unsettling experience in which the lover was constantly unsure of who was in control. Thus at the end of *Emile*, the governor risks embarrassing everyone to carefully instruct his pupil and his bride regarding Sophie's right to refuse her sexual favors—the better to keep Emile in thrall. Elizabeth Rose Wingrove's *Rousseau's Republican Romance* (Princeton, N.J.: Princeton University Press, 2000) traces the importance of this sort of suspended uncertainty throughout Rousseau's political thought.

6. Cited in Cranston, *The Solitary Self*, 195.

7. Cited in Robert Darnton, "Readers Respond to Rousseau," in *The Great Cat Massacre and Other Episodes in French Cultural History* (New York: Basic Books, 1984), 247.

8. Ibid., 248.

9. Shklar, Judith. *Men and Citizens* (London: Cambridge University Press, 1969), 24. Rousseau's novel has come to be known by both titles, *Julie* and *La Nouvelle Héloïse*. Christopher Kelly, in editing Rousseau's collected works in English translation, suggests using both. The two are often combined as well: *Julie, or The New Eloise*. Regarding Rousseau's role in changing the popular conception of family, see also Postman, *The Disappearance of Childhood*, 56–62; and Priscilla Robertson's "Home as a Nest: Middle Class Childhood in Nineteenth-Century Europe," in ed. Lloyd de Mause, *The History of Childhood* (New York: Psychohistory Press, 1974), 410–11.

10. Taylor, *Sources of the Self*, 294–95.

11. The truth is that it is hard to find an interesting study of Rousseau that does not pay close attention to Rousseau's treatment of gender. This must be in part because, as Paul Thomas has suggested, "Rousseau wants his readers to notice it." ("Jean-Jacques Rousseau, Sexist?" *Feminist Studies* 17, no. 2 [1991]: 195–217). Some examples of insightful studies that focus on gender and sexuality in Rousseau's ideas include include Wingrove, *Rousseau's Republican Romance*; Joel Schwartz, *The Sexual Politics of Jean-Jacques Rousseau* (Chicago: University of Chicago Press, 1984); Tony Tanner, *Adultery in the Novel* (Baltimore: Johns Hopkins University Press, 1979); Nancy Hirschmann, *Gender, Class, and Freedom in Modern Political Theory* (Princeton, N.J.: Princeton University Press, 2008); and Nicole Fermon, *Domesticating Passions*, as well as many volumes on gender in political theory, including those of Elshtain, Pateman, and Zerilli mentioned in the introduction, and Susan Okin's classic, *Women in Western Political Thought* (Princeton, N.J.: Princeton University Press, 1979).

12. *Moving* and *visceral* can certainly refer to pain as much as pleasure. Along these lines, it might be interesting to note (I have not seen it elsewhere noted) the possible significance for this aspect of Rousseau's thought that it was the fear of a beating at the hands of his master that sent Rousseau away from the walls of Geneva at the age of sixteen, denying him the chance for a simple and obscure life as "a good Christian, a good citizen, a good father, a good friend, a good workman, and good man in every way" (*Confessions*, 51).

13. Jean-Jacques Rousseau, *First Discourse* (also known as *Discourse on the Sciences and the Arts*), in *The First and Second Discourses*, ed. Roger Masters (New York: St. Martin's Press, 1964), 36.

14. Rousseau, *Confessions*, 381.

15. Hirschmann, *Gender, Class, and Freedom*, 145.

16. Jean-Jacques Rousseau, *Discourse on the Origin of Inequality*, in *The Basic Political Writings*, ed. Donald A. Cress (Indianapolis: Hackett Publishing, 1987), 77.

17. Jean-Jacques Rousseau, *Emile, or On Education* (New York: Basic Books, 1979), 45.

18. Jean-Jacques Rousseau, "Botanical Writings," in *Collected Writings*, vol. 8, ed. Roger Masters and Christopher Kelly (Hanover, N.H.: Dartmouth College by University Press of New England, 2000), 156.

19. Eileen Hunt Botting also notes the tension between Rousseau's earnest efforts to make use of family for political purposes and the difficulty of what he proposed. She offers an insightful reading of Rousseau that focuses less directly than my own reading on the significance and challenges of *parenthood* (and more on questions of egalitarianism in the relationship between husband and wife). Botting emphasizes the tensions or paradoxes that Rousseau's ideas about family introduce into his thought. "Through an examination of the tension between theory and practice in his account of the proper relationship between family and

the state, Rousseau emerges not as a self-defeating utopian thinker, but rather as a political theorist who combined philosophical idealism with historical realism, and expounded upon his familial-political ideal, despite the practical obstacles he saw to its full realization, through near simultaneous composition and publication of the momentous and controversial works *Julie, Emile,* and the *Social Contract*." *Family Feuds: Wollstonecraft, Burke, and Rousseau on the Transformation of the Family* (Albany: State University of New York Press, 2006), 17.

20. This statement, from a letter Rousseau wrote to his friend Toussaint-Pierre Lenieps, is cited in Cranston's *The Noble Savage: Jean-Jacques Rousseau, 1754–1762* (Chicago: University of Chicago Press, 1991), 246.

21. The abolition of the practice of swaddling, the movement for mothers to breast-feed their own children, and a newfound attention to education and active parenting were all among *Emile*'s popular legacies (Robertson, "Home as a Nest").

22. Jean-Jacques Rousseau, *Discourse on Political Economy,* in *The Social Contract and Other Later Political Writings,* ed. Victor Gourevitch (Cambridge: Cambridge University Press, 1997), 149.

23. Rousseau describes this self-regard as "a primitive, innate passion, which is anterior to every other, and of which all others are in a sense only modifications" (*Emile,* 213). This self-love is also one of the original qualities Rousseau attributed to primitive man in his *Second Discourse* (*Discourse on the Origin of Inequality,* 15). As others have noted, amour propre often plays the villain for Rousseau, but is not universally derided by him. Christopher Kelly explores how amour propre is actually a key element of virtue for Rousseau. *Rousseau as Author: Consecrating One's Life to the Truth* (Chicago: University of Chicago Press, 2003), 15.

24. As Schwartz notes in *The Sexual Politics of Jean-Jacques Rousseau,* Rousseau seemed ambivalent about the issue of whether sexual desire constitutes a true and natural need (13–16). Rousseau weighed in on this issue in *Emile* in typically ambiguous fashion. He insisted, "It is not true that it is a true need." But his elucidation of this point obscures rather than clarifies his stance: "As for me . . . I am persuaded that a solitary man raised in the desert, without books, without instruction, and without women, would die there a virgin at whatever age he reached" (333). Well, of course. Who would not die a virgin alone in the desert? Rousseau moves on from the issue by pointing out that we are not discussing savages, but men in society who cannot be kept ignorant of these matters.

25. James Martel, *Love Is a Sweet Chain: Desire, Autonomy, and Friendship in Liberal Political Theory* (New York: Routledge, 2001), 81.

26. Rousseau cites favorably the example of a father who feared that his son's temperament would soon deliver him to chasing women. Dragging the dissolute young man to the syphilitic ward to be revolted by the suffering one finds there, the father taunts his son, "Go on miserable profligate, follow the vile inclination which drags you along. Soon you will be only too happy to be admitted to this

room where, a victim of the most infamous pains, you will force your father to thank God for your death" (*Emile*, 231). But farther on, Rousseau acknowledges that this sort of tactic is not ideal, as passion will not be long denied. "I readily admit that if you were to clash head on with his nascent desires and foolishly were to treat as crimes the new needs he is feeling, you would not be listened to for long" (317).

27. Rousseau, "Letter to Franquières," in Gourevitch, ed., *The Social Contract*, 281–82.

28. Christopher Kelly, "Rousseau on Passion and the Empty Phantom of Virtue" (paper presented at the annual meeting of the American Political Science Association, San Francisco, 2000), 8. Kelly is quoting from Rousseau's "Letter to Franquières," *Collected Writings*, vol. 8, 267.

29. Emile does not *feel* constraint, but in fact he is nearly constantly under the control of the governor, who arranges just about every event in Emile's life, though they seem to Emile to be matters of chance.

30. The topic of Rousseau's remarkable ideas about the importance of ambiguity of consent in successful sexual relations, and the use of resistance by women to unite amour propre with love in men, has been explored in great detail and with great insight in a number of studies—most notably those of Schwartz and Wingrove.

31. Even Sophie's belief in God is grounded entirely in her role in the cycle of life. Rousseau outlines the beginning of a catechism for girls, an effort that, if it were completed, "would perhaps be the most useful book ever written." After some initial back and forth, Rousseau's example of how the catechism should begin reads: "Nurse: *Who was alive before you?* Little Girl: *My father and my mother.* Nurse: *Who was alive before them?* Little Girl: *Their father and their mother.* Nurse: *Who will be alive after you?* Little Girl: *My children.* Nurse: *Who will be alive after them?* Little Girl: *Their children, etc.*" (*Emile*, 380).

32. As mentioned previously, the governor makes sure that Emile sees his fellow men in misery. It is only thus that the sentiment of pity, which Rousseau had identified as natural among primitive men in his *Second Discourse*, is able to take root in the souls of men in corrupt times.

33. Wingrove offers an interesting reading of this "doubled and discarded" Sophie. She argues that this Sophie and the other have much in common and that Telemachus looms over the relationship with Emile (*Rousseau's Republican Romance*, 82–83).

34. First, he must become more detached from his passion, even his passion for virtuous parenthood. He must learn "how to rule [his passion] like a man" (*Emile*, 445). Emile is still a slave to his desire, and he cannot bear the thought of life without his beloved. But "all that we love will escape us sooner or later. . . . There will always be privations, losses, and alarms. You will not enjoy what is left

to you. The fear of losing everything will prevent you from possessing anything" (444). In particular, it is his passion, which has served him so well since its emergence, that will eventually let him down. "You have enjoyed more from hope than you will ever enjoy in reality. Imagination adorns what one desires, but abandons it when it is in one's possession" (447). Martel suggests that Sophie can potentially dominate Emile because of the ardency of his passion. Only "if Emile can completely dominate Sophie then perhaps . . . she might then finally become incorporated into his enlarged sense of self, into the common me" (Martel, *Love Is a Sweet Chain*, 97–98). But in fact, as I will explain, this ardency will fade of its own right, and it is as father more than as husband that Jean-Jacques expects Emile to build upon his self in common with another.

35. In the *Letter to D'Alembert* (*Politics and the Arts*, ed. Allan Bloom [Ithaca, N.Y.: Cornell University Press], 1960), Rousseau argues that the "disorder of women" is the most dangerous of temptations for a people because it strikes the young, so that "reason is perverted at its birth, and man, still untamed, becomes undisciplinable before having borne the yoke of the laws" (109).

36. Hirschmann suggests regarding this trip, "It is only after Emile has secured the love of a virtuous woman that it is safe to teach Emile the potentially corrupting subject of politics." Hirschmann is right, I believe, but the direction that relationship will go, toward virtuous parenthood, is the more pressing matter.

37. She must do so by showing resistance to Emile's advances even after they are married. But he cannot feel she does so from whim but rather from modesty. Wingrove offers a brilliant analysis of this aspect of the book and the role of "consensual non-consensuality" in Rousseau's political thought (*Rousseau's Republican Romance*).

38. Throughout the novel, when the characters mention the children in their letters, they write things like "I need not describe . . ." and "You can guess whether. . . ." The notable exception is Henrietta, the child of Julie's beloved cousin Claire. The attention Rousseau pays to fatherless Henrietta highlights how little we hear of Julie and Wolmar's children.

39. Martel, *Love Is a Sweet Chain*, 84. In this sense, Martel claims Rousseau for the contest rather than the virtue tradition in political theory.

40. There is another example of an aversion to nonreproductive sexuality that is too perversely emblematic of Rousseau to exclude: prepubescent. When Rousseau was in Italy and frustrated by the expense of prostitutes, he, along with a friend, purchased a "little girl of eleven or twelve" to share. They put her up in an apartment. But Rousseau insisted he did not think of touching her until she had reached puberty. Instead, during his visits he taught her to play the piano. He did not stay in Italy long enough to see her mature, but he believed his growing paternal affection for her would have made him a "guardian of her innocence" until that day arrived (*Confessions*, 303).

41. As I argued in the previous section, Rousseau created the tragic story of the "alternative" Sophie who never finds her Emile to argue that a love of virtue must find an actual partner to exercise itself upon. But what if Emile and Sophie, having found each other could not or chose not to procreate?

42. This last comment means considerably less once we see how carefully Rousseau crafts sexual tension between Julie and her father. This aspect of the novel is explored in Tony Tanner's *Adultery in the Novel* and Nicole Fermon's *Domesticating Passions*.

43. Sophie was instructed by Jean-Jacques to cultivate a discontinuity between her eyes and mouth. Emile must hear her protests in the name of modesty but see her desire in her eyes. Wingrove offers a perceptive analysis of this aspect of desire in Rousseau's thought *(Rousseau's Republican Romance)*.

44. Tanner, *Adultery in the Novel*, 113.

45. Rousseau's *Confessions*, where I am about to turn, depicts dramatic scenes that are also carefully constructed by Rousseau, even if they are "true" stories. Wingrove *(Rousseau's Republican Romance)* suggests careful attention to the opening pages of the *Confessions* where Rousseau draws attention to the activities of writing and reading.

46. Nor, for that matter did his other long affair, with the maternal figure Mme de Warens. See *Confessions*, 210, and especially 385–86, where Rousseau compares the two women in this regard.

47. I borrow the phrase from Hannah Arendt, who had a remarkably similar view of love and childbirth. She wrote in *The Human Condition* (Chicago: Chicago University Press, 1958), "Love, by reason of its passion, destroys the in-between which relates us to and separates us from others. As long as its spell lasts the only in-between which can insert itself between two lovers is the child, love's own product. The child, this in-between to which the lovers now are related and which they hold in common, is representative of the world in that it also separates them; it is an indication that they will insert a new world into the existing world. Through the child, it is as though the lovers return to the world from which their love had expelled them. But this new worldliness, the possible result and the only possibly happy ending of a love affair, is in a sense, the end of love, which must either overcome the partners anew or be transformed into another mode of belonging together" (242).

48. *Confessions*, 322, 332–33. Rousseau offered an extended defense of the collective raising of children by the state in his *Discourse on Political Economy*, which I discuss later.

49. Cranston estimates that in 1741, five years before the birth of Rousseau's first child, 68 percent of the foundlings in Paris orphanages died in infancy *(Jean-Jacques*, 245). To be fair, one should note that a relatively high percentage of infants died in eighteenth-century Paris, whether in a foundling home or not.

50. Late in life, Rousseau finally married Thérèse, and they eventually returned to Paris.

51. Rousseau's choice of language is especially poignant when we remember the words his father would use when he would embrace the son whose birth took away his wife ("fill the void she left in my heart").

52. It could be objected that Rousseau lived in France during most of the years when it was possible that he and Thérèse might start a family. Of course, Rousseau never thought of France as anything approaching a virtuous republic. He never thought of republican citizenship as an option for the subjects of a country whose morals, manners, music, theater, philosophy, and even language, he had labored to demonstrate, were debased. But Rousseau was preoccupied with the idea of moving to Geneva during those years, as I describe later.

53. One of the sad ironies of that first abandonment was that Rousseau was forced to enlist the very person who was most unsettling to his relationship with Thérèse—her mother, Mme Levasseur—in order to overcome Thérèse's resistance. "The only scruples that I had to overcome were Thérèse's and I had the greatest difficulty in the world persuading her to accept this sole means of saving her honour. But her mother had another fear, that of a fresh embarrassment in the form of a brat, and she came to my aid; Thérèse gave in" (*Confessions*, 322).

54. Rousseau was in the habit, at the time, of supping with a rather bawdy group, and he claimed he had merely "caught the habit" of thinking their way. He adopted the "principles" but not the "morals" of a line of thought in which "the man who best helped to stock the Foundling Hospital was always the most applauded" (*Confessions*, 322). Obviously, this talk of adopting principles but not morals is a somewhat confusing elision on Rousseau's part, but he is clearly implying that he made the decision almost automatically, without ever allowing his morals and his sentiments to become involved. But as Rousseau later came to realize, "There are hardly any of our automatic impulses that we could not find in our heart, if we only knew how to look for them." *The Reveries of the Solitary Walker*, 93. I have changed the translation slightly.

55. Rousseau's most eloquent description of this moment probably appears in a letter he wrote to M de Malesherbes. "I felt my mind dazzled by a thousand lights; crowds of lively ideas presented themselves at the same time with a strength and a confusion that threw me into an inexpressible perturbation.... If I had ever been able to write a quarter of what I saw and felt under that tree, how clearly I would have made all the contradictions of the social system seen, with what strength I would have exposed all the abuses of our institutions, with what simplicity I would have demonstrated that man is naturally good and that it is from these institutions alone that men become wicked" (*Collected Writings*, vol. 5, ed. Roger Masters and Christopher Kelly [Hanover, N.H.: Dartmouth College by University Press of New England, 1995], 575).

56. Her third at least. Rousseau does not describe any miscarriages in the *Confessions*, but there is much about Thérèse that he does not describe.

57. Cranston, *Jean-Jacques*, 239.

58. In a similar vein, Julie reminds the avuncular figure of Milord Edward, "Do you not sense that only a father can have the right to counsel the children of others?" (*Julie*, 171).

59. *Emile*, 472, for example.

60. This example suggests that parenthood, as Rousseau imagines it, entails reproduction of gender as part of the production of citizenship. Sophie's cant-filled education differs significantly from Emile's in a way that makes a girl's imitation of a virtuous mother something imposed through dictate rather than a more visceral response to the parent's example—a reversal of notions of the reproduction of gender offered by a psychoanalytic thinker like Chodorow.

61. Cranston, *The Noble Savage*.

62. It was when Voltaire decided to take up residence in Geneva that Rousseau finally abandoned his hopes.

63. Rousseau warns fathers and governors: "You will not be the master of the child if you cannot control everyone around him" (*Emile*, 59). Jean-Jacques exerts this control not through his position but because people who meet him get caught up in his project with Emile. They want to be like the governor.

64. Shklar, *Men and Citizens*, 235.

65. Jean-Jacques Rousseau, *Emile and Sophie, or the Solitary Beings,* trans. Alice Harvey, in *Finding a New Feminism*, ed. Pamela Grande Jensen (New York: Rowman and Littlefield, 1996), 205. Thanks to Christopher Kelly for helping me locate this hard-to-find translation.

66. It is not clear from the text whether she has had an affair or been the victim of rape. Wingrove offers a convincing interpretation that Emile believes Sophie was raped (*Rousseau's Republican Romance*).

67. Jean-Jacques Rousseau, *The Social Contract* (New York: Penguin Classics, 1968), 41.

68. Honig, *Democracy and the Foreigner*, 27–28. Honig notes the reasons that a foreigner might be preferable to a father as the founder of good laws.

69. Connelly 1993, 59, 65–66.

70. Hirschmann, 157. The vision is remarkably similar to Tocqueville's take on the political effects of the settled family life he observed in America. But Rousseau is writing about the French, after all, where Tocqueville believed domestic disturbance fueled revolutionary ferment. Laura Janara's *Democracy Growing Up: Authority, Autonomy, and Passion in Tocqueville's Democracy in America* (Albany: State University of New York Press, 2002) offers an insightful reading of the role of family and family imagery in Tocqueville's analysis.

71. This is Rousseau's final thought before the one-paragraph conclusion in which he explains that he will not discuss the state's foreign relations.

72. Wingrove uses this aspect of Rousseau's thought to offer an intriguing interpretation of Sophie's decision to reveal to Emile that her unborn child is not his (*Rousseau's Republican Romance*, 96).

73. Hirschmann, 157.

74. Shklar, *Men and Citizens*, 156.

75. Rousseau makes it clear that Wolmar knows Julie and St. Preux were once in love. But he does not appear to know how far the relationship had progressed.

76. Kelly, *Rousseau as Author.*

2. The Tragedy of Birth

1. The evening was June 5, 1869. Ronald Hayman, *Nietzsche, a Critical Life* (New York: Oxford University Press, 1980), 110–11.

2. Friedrich Nietzsche, *The Birth of Tragedy* (New York: Vintage Books, 1967), 33. This sentence is the beginning of the text of *The Birth of Tragedy* itself. It follows the "Preface to Richard Wagner."

3. Friedrich Nietzsche, "Schopenhauer as Educator," in *The Untimely Meditations* (Cambridge: Cambridge University Press, 1983), 160, 176.

4. Honig, *Political Theory,* 262. The immanent critique of Nietzsche's ideas offered in this chapter, for this reason, takes a slightly different form compared to that of the avowed democrats explored in the other chapters. This chapter identifies those places where Nietzsche is tempted by his use of parenthood to take solace from the challenges of contest. But this chapter's reading of Nietzsche uses a focus on parenthood to raise questions about the deployment of Nietzsche's ideas in contemporary democratic theory.

5. Tracy Strong (*Friedrich Nietzsche and the Politics of Transfiguration* [Berkeley: University of California Press, 1988]), William E. Connolly (*Neuropolitics: Thinking, Culture, Speed* [Minneapolis: University of Minnesota Press, 2002]), and James Conant ("Nietzsche's Perfectionism: A Reading of 'Schopenhauer as Educator,'" in *Nietzsche's Postmoralism: Essays on Nietzsche's Prelude to Philosophy's Future,* ed. Richard Schacht [Cambridge: Cambridge University Press, 2005]) each have offered thoughtful accounts of how we might put the ideas of someone so hostile to democracy to use for democratic purposes, and they lean on this aspect of Nietzsche's thought in the service of compelling accounts of democratic citizenship. In this chapter, I argue that Nietzsche's thought offers an opportunity to better understand the reasons that the experience of parenthood is so alluring to political thinkers, including those interested in challenging our most dearly held values, and also why ideas that rely on parenthood can be perilous. In neglecting this aspect of Nietzsche's thought, even as they seek to make

use of the ideas that pulled Nietzsche toward thinking about the political uses of parenthood, contemporary theorists miss an opportunity to better understand the challenges of modern citizenship in a political environment in which "family" is sacrosanct. In the Conclusion, I explore this idea more thoroughly. Connolly offers a list of contemporary democratic theorists who make compelling use of Nietzsche: "Jane Bennett, Judith Butler, Wendy Brown, Daniel Conway, Thomas Dumm, Moira Gatens, Michel Foucault, Gilles Deleuze, Lawrence Hatab, George Kateb, Brian Massumi, Melissa Orlie, Michael Shapiro, Paul Patton, Keith Ansell-Pearson, and Bernard Williams" (*Neuropolitics*, 153).

6. Connolly, *Neuropolitics*, 165.

7. Honig, *Political Theory*, 66.

8. Ibid., 72–73.

9. These include Sarah Kofman, "Baubo: Theological Perversion and Fetishism," in *Feminine Interpretations of Friedrich Nietzsche*, ed. Kelly Oliver and Marilyn Pearsall (University Park: Pennsylvania State University Press, 1998), 21–49; Jean Graybeal, "*Ecce Homo*: Abjection and the Feminine" in Kelly and Pearsall, *Feminist Interpretations*, 152–69; Clayton Koelb, "Castration Envy: Nietzsche and the Figure of Woman," in *Nietzsche and the Feminine*, ed. Peter J. Burgard (Charlottesville: University of Press Virginia, 1994) 71–81; Lynne Tirrell, "Sexual Dualism and Women's Self Creation: On the Advantages and Disadvantages of Reading Nietzsche for Feminists," in Burgard, *Nietzsche and the Feminine*, 158–82; Jacques Derrida, *Spurs, Nietzsche's Styles*, trans. Barbara Harlow (Chicago: University of Chicago Press, 1981); Luce Irigaray, *Marine Lover of Friedrich Nietzsche* (New York: Columbia University Press, 1991); and Caroline Joan S. Picart, *Resentment and the "Feminine" in Nietzsche's Politico-Aesthetics* (University Park: Pennsylvania State University Press, 1999). Many different useful and interesting analyses have been made within this consensus. I make the case in this chapter, however, that this consensus has failed to capture an important aspect of Nietzsche's ideas about procreation, parenthood, and politics.

10. Fredrick Appel, *Nietzsche contra Democracy* (Ithaca, N.Y.: Cornell University Press, 1999), 106, 109.

11. Friedrich Nietzsche, *Twilight of the Idols*, in *The Portable Nietzsche*, ed. and trans. Walter Kaufmann (New York: Penguin Books, 1954), 533.

12. Friedrich Nietzsche, *Daybreak* (Cambridge: Cambridge University Press, 1997), 3. He also derided Rousseau as a "miscarriage," as "idealist and rabble in one person" (*Twilight of the Idols*, 553), as "grunting and greed[y]" with the instinct for revenge (514). Nietzsche saw in the person of Rousseau all of Europe's prerevolutionary "semi-insanity, histrionicism, bestial cruelty, voluptuousness, and especially sentimentality and self-intoxication . . . become flesh and spirit" (*Human, All Too Human* [Cambridge: Cambridge University Press, 1986], 367).

13. Friedrich Nietzsche, *Ecce Homo* (New York: Vintage Books, 1968), 232.

14. Nietzsche, *Twilight of the Idols,* 552. Nietzsche tended to address the issue of the decline of religious meaning in much starker terms than Rousseau. The terms that Rousseau used to discuss the decline of religious meaning, particularly in *Emile* and *The Social Contract,* were stark enough to get him expelled from France in 1762.

15. Friedrich Nietzsche, *The Gay Science* (New York: Vintage Books, 1974), 279.

16. Honig, for example, suggests that Nietzsche's ideas provide a useful alternative to Kant's notion of "an inborn duty of influencing posterity in such a way that it will make constant progress." Honig suggests Nietzsche's thought "challenges man . . . to find within himself the capacity to reclaim (in transvalued form) the present moment" (*Political Theory,* 40–41).

17. For attacks on progress narratives, see *The Gay Science* (338); *The Antichrist,* in Nietzsche and Kaufmann, *The Portable Nietzsche,* 571; and *The Will to Power* (New York: Vintage Books, 1968), 215. Another typical example can be found in *Human, All Too Human:* "When the entire history of culture opens up before our gaze as a confusion of evil and noble, true and false conceptions, . . . we are then able to grasp what comfort there lies in the idea of an evolving god: The transformations and destinies of mankind are, according to this idea, the ever increasing self-revelation of this god. . . . The deification of becoming is a metaphysical outlook—as though from a lighthouse down on to the sea of history—in which a generation of scholars too much given to historicizing found their consolation" (114).

18. Nietzsche condemned this as a "metaphysical outlook" that gives abstractions too much power over the way humans conceive of their lives. This force might be an "evolving god" with a grand plan for humanity, or it might be an ideal toward which human society is inexorably developing—lending history (as well as the present as a privileged moment in that history) a reason or purpose.

19. Nietzsche offered as an example of the latter the French revolutionaries inspired by Rousseau (*Human, All Too Human,* 169).

20. It is the accessibility Nietzsche had in mind for the exemplar—the idea that the exemplar is not a distant vision of perfection but someone we can feel close to—that convinces James Conant that this essay is among the most useful for those who would understand the uses of Nietzsche for democratic theory (Conant 2005). Conant's essay on Schopenhauer offers a vigorous defense of Nietzsche against charges by Rawls and others that Nietzsche's political thought is profoundly elitist. Conant points out that Nietzsche himself saw this essay as among the most important of his writings. Conant quotes one letter in which Nietzsche told George Brandes: "My little essay 'Schopenhauer as Educator' serves me as a touchstone: he to whom it does not speak *personally* will probably not be able to make anything of me in any other regard either" (Conant 2005, 244).

21. Specifically, *procreative* metaphors rather than the pregnancy metaphors that would become so common in the works to follow. There are no pregnancy metaphors in "Schopenhauer as Educator."

22. Earlier in the essay, Nietzsche warned the reader against losing focus on his individual self and getting caught up in the "eternal becoming . . . a lying puppet-play in beholding which man forgets himself, the actual distraction which disperses the individual to the four winds" ("Schopenhauer as Educator," 155).

23. See also p. 181, where Schopenhauer is compared favorably to Kant as "not merely a great thinker but also a real human being."

24. Nietzsche's own father died in 1849, when Nietzsche was four years old.

25. There are striking parallels between this aspect of Nietzsche's thought and Rousseau's use of parenthood and family to find a way that a person can expand his or her individuality, indulge in a little amour propre, and avoid the loneliness of complete self-sufficiency without becoming lost in the tyranny of status and opinion.

26. In the case of Schopenhauer, Nietzsche seems to have believed it was entirely his father who provided for the philosopher's incredible potential. He thought Schopenhauer's mother, if anything, worked in the opposite direction: "The perversity of the age came fearfully close to him, for example, in the person of his vain and culturally pretentious mother." It was the character of Schopenhauer's father that "saved him from his mother" ("Schopenhauer as Educator," 180). But Nietzsche did not see all mothers as a negative force to be overcome thanks to a good father's influence. For example, Nietzsche's frequent and extravagant praise of Napoleon—"the *noble ideal as such* made flesh . . . this synthesis of the *inhuman* and *superhuman*" (*The Genealogy of Morals* [New York: Vintage Books, 1968], 54)—was accompanied by great admiration for Napoleon's mother. He called her the "most recent" example of "the world's most powerful and influential women . . . [who] owe their power and ascendancy over men precisely to the force of their will" (*Beyond Good and Evil* [New York: Penguin Books, 1990], 169).

27. Nietzsche's ideas about the importance of his inheritance from his own father (and his mother) are considerably more complex than his ideas about Schopenhauer. The passage from *Ecce Homo* that most calls to mind the Schopenhauer essay includes an important and intriguing caveat: "I consider it a great privilege to have had such a father: it even seems to me that this explains whatever else I have of privileges—*not* including life, the great Yes to life. Above all, that it requires no resolve on my part, but merely biding my time, to enter quite involuntarily into a world of lofty and delicate things: I am at home there, my inmost passion becomes free only there" (226).

28. Strong, *Friedrich Nietzsche and the Politics of Transfiguration*, 274.

29. In the original German: "Die Erziehung ist eine Fortsetzung der Zeugung und oft eine Art nachträglicher Beschönigung derselben."

30. One of the things Nietzsche appreciated about Schopenhauer is that his philosophy had found a way to mitigate some of these problems. This is apparent in a longer quotation from a passage cited earlier: "Schopenhauer never wants to cut a figure: for he writes for himself and no one wants to be deceived, least of all a

philosopher who has made it a rule for himself: deceive no one, not even yourself! Not even with the pleasant sociable deception which almost every conversation entails and which writers imitate almost unconsciously; even less with the conscious deception of the orator and by the artificial means of rhetoric. Schopenhauer, on the contrary, speaks with himself" ("Schopenhauer as Educator," 134).

31. In "Schopenhauer as Educator," Nietzsche expresses a similar idea in saying what he appreciated about Schopenhauer. In this case, his frustration is not with words but with the inadequacies of conversation and Schopenhauer's ability to avoid them in his writing. He writes, "Not even with the pleasant sociable deception which almost every conversation entails and which writers imitate almost unconsciously; even less with the conscious deception of the orator and by the artificial means of rhetoric. Schopenhauer, on the contrary, speaks with himself" (134).

32. Despite his description of Schopenhauer as a "born philosopher," Nietzsche thought that "the act of being born plays no part in the procedure and progress of heredity" (*Beyond Good and Evil*, 35). Greg Moore's *Nietzsche, Biology, and Metaphor* (Cambridge: Cambridge University Press, 2002) makes the case that the biological thinking that was important to a great deal of late-nineteenth-century European thought was also important to Nietzsche's ideas. Moore points out that Nietzsche's biological thinking had more in common with Lamarck, who thought an organism could adapt to external circumstances and pass this adaptation along to its offspring, than he did with Darwin, who thought the external environment decided which random mutations survive and which die out. However, Moore does not find that Nietzsche's ideas are Lamarckian in a straightforward way. He offers a comprehensive list of ways in which Nietzsche's ideas differed from Lamarck's as well as of the similarities (34). Overall, Moore believes that Nietzsche's ideas, while still deeply influenced by the biological thinking common to his era, rejected basic premises common to both Darwin and Lamarck. Nietzsche rejected "the misplaced faith in adaptation as the principle mechanism by which life advances.... Life is not something that adapts or is adapted to. The essence of life lies rather in its activity. The organism modifies its environment to suit its needs" (197). In terms of the sort of self-transformation that Nietzsche discussed in the Schopenhauer essay and elsewhere, Moore's take seems to confirm Nietzsche's concern that the hard work of self-transformation *has an effect* beyond the self and an effect beyond the proverbial cannon's effect on a flock of sparrows. As I argue in this chapter, it is this desire for an effect on the larger culture, and an effect sufficiently concentrated to be true to the substance of one's accomplishments in self-transformation, that pushed Nietzsche in the direction of thinking about parenthood.

33. In these quotations, however, Nietzsche did not specifically identify parents as the adults with whom a child is likely to have the most intense relationship.

Other aphorisms make it clear that Nietzsche did see parents to be the main actors. See, for example, *Daybreak* (157), where those who develop a "good nature" for fear of attack from their enemies "bequeathed this whole delicate and well-tested mechanism to their children and grand-children."

34. Friedrich Nietzsche, *Thus Spoke Zarathustra*, in Nietzsche and Kaufmann, *The Portable Nietzsche*, 212. This description applied to individuals and to cultures as amalgams of individuals as well: "Some ages seem to lack altogether some talent or some virtue, as certain individuals do, too. But just wait for their children and grandchildren, if you have time to wait that long: they bring to light what was hidden in their grandfathers and what their grandfathers themselves did not suspect. Often the son already betrays his father—and the father understands himself better after he has a son" (*The Gay Science*, 83).

35. Nietzsche noted "the man resembles the child more closely than he does the youth . . . a temporary alienation from our basic character that occurred during our youth but has been overcome by the accumulated strength of manhood" (*Human, All Too Human*, 194). Nietzsche was expressing similar ideas as early as a school essay he wrote at the age of 17: "Tearing down seems easier than it is: we are so determined down to the heart's core by the impressions of our childhood, the influence of our parents, and our upbringing, that those deeply rooted prejudices are not so readily eradicated by rational arguments or mere force of will. The power of custom, the need for something loftier, . . . the doubt as to whether or not a mirage has led humanity astray for two millenia, the feeling of one's own impropriety and boldness: all these things do battle with one another, and the battle is not decided until painful experiences and mournful events finally guide us back again to the old faith of our childhood" (quoted in David Farrell Krell and Donald L. Bates, *The Good European: Nietzsche's Work Sites in Word and Image* [Chicago: University of Chicago Press, 1997]).

36. A similar point is made in *Thus Spoke Zarathustra*: "But in the man there is more of the child than in the youth" (185).

37. Friedrich Nietzsche, "On the Uses and Disadvantages of History for Life," in *The Untimely Meditations*. Tracy Strong gives this aspect of Nietzsche's thought a central place in *Friedrich Nietzsche and the Politics of Transfiguration*. Strong believes that the sort of self-transformation that Nietzsche described in this quotation from *The Untimely Meditations* (a quotation that Strong cites several times) is so central to Nietzsche's political thought that Nietzsche's doctrine of "the eternal return of the same" is best understood in terms of the effort to achieve this sort of transformation. Strong interprets the eternal return as Nietzsche "saying that the effect of constantly repeating an action (of its being 'in eternal return') can produce a change in the individual which is [not] only 'psychological,' not just 'second nature' or habit, but rather eventually becomes one's real nature, and in doing so expels the 'nature' that was present before" (274).

38. For similar ideas worked out at greater length, see *The Gay Science*, 84–85.

39. Friedrich Nietzsche, *Beyond Good and Evil*, 162–63. Nietzsche used similar language in the essay on Schopenhauer. There he said that "your true educators and formative teachers reveal to you that the true, original meaning and basic stuff of your nature is something completely incapable of being educated or formed and is in any case something difficult of access, bound and paralyzed. Your educators can be only your liberators" ("Schopenhauer as Educator," 129).

40. Honig, *Political Theory*, 73.

41. Ibid., 74–75. The quotation of Nietzsche is from *The Antichrist*, aphorism 4.

42. Examples of this middle ground between isolation and living completely outside oneself include the golden age that was the happiest epoch in Rousseau's *Discourse on the Origin of Inequality*, Emile and Sophie living among their neighbors as an example of virtue in *Emile*, and Julie's virtuous household in the second half of the novel *Julie*. Each one, of course, comes apart for the reasons I explored in chapter 1. In the case of the social contract, one does give oneself over to the community completely. Rousseau thought the social contract was only applicable to small polities and under conditions of widespread preexisting virtue.

43. Nietzsche believed it was important to consider what sort of shared cultural meanings make it more or less likely that great individuals will emerge. "The basic phenomenon: countless individuals sacrificed for the sake of a few, to make them possible.—One must not let oneself be deceived; it is just the same with peoples and races: they constitute the 'body' for the production of isolated valuable individuals, who carry on the great process" (*The Will to Power*, 360). And also, "A people is a detour of nature to get to six or seven great men. Yes: and then to get round them" (*Beyond Good and Evil*, 99).

44. Nietzsche himself did not feel immune to the temptation to lose his own way. The dangers could be both personal and political. "If a suffering friend said to me, 'Look, I am about to die; please promise to die with me,' I should promise it; and the sight of a small mountain tribe fighting for its liberty would persuade me to offer it my hand and my life." (*The Gay Science*, 270). He wrote in a letter to Jacob Burckhardt, "My entire philosophy teeters after an hour of sympathetic conversation with a stranger" (cited in Krell and Bates, *The Good European*, 197).

45. Nietzsche believed the cultivation of small communities of shared understanding might help people deal with the crucial question of meaning. "It is a measure of the degree of strength of will to what extent one can do without meaning in things, to what extent one can endure to live in a meaningless world because one organizes a small portion of it oneself" (*The Will to Power*, 318). This issue of finding a middle ground between solipsism and metaphysics through the cultivation of a small community was perhaps the central preoccupation of the volume *The Wanderer and His Shadow*, which ends with a conversation in which the latter tells the former that "of all you have said nothing has pleased me *more* than a

promise you have made: you want again to be a good neighbor to the things closest to you" (*Human, All Too Human*, 394). Earlier in that volume, on one of the rare occasions that Nietzsche chose to praise Socrates, it was because the Greek loved to argue that the true locus of all reflection and concern should be "that which I encounter of good and ill in my own house" (304).

46. At least one could not in Nietzsche's time. Thomas de Zengotita wonders how Nietzsche would have reacted to the moral implications of the technology of cloning. He thought Nietzsche "would plunge straight to the metaphysical heart of the matter, to the delicious and terrible dilemmas that cluster around the possibility of self-replication." *Mediated: How the Media Shapes Your World and the Way You Live in It* (New York: Bloomsbury, 2005), 265.

47. At times Nietzsche seemed to revel in this curious aspect of his thought. He referred to his "knowledge" about the true nature of women as "part of [his] Dionysian dowry," and wondered playfully "who knows? Perhaps I am the first psychologist of the eternally feminine" (*Ecce Homo*, 266).

48. In Nietzsche's thought, parenting is consistently figured in terms of something that a man and a woman take on. This is not to say that in Nietzsche's time, as in our own, a great deal of parenting was not done by individuals alone, or by same-sex couples, or by any of the heterogeneous groups of adults that might constitute a family. But he does not discuss family and parenthood in this way.

49. Nietzsche sometimes held that the source of this aspect of women's nature was a deeply ingrained respect for authority and custom. "However much women may honour their husbands, they nonetheless honour the recognized authorities and conceptions of society even more" (*Human, All Too Human*, 159).

50. To the extent Nietzsche did allow for women's influence in the process, he confined it to the more verbal, less instinct-driven quality of "intellect." In regard to women's intellect, Nietzsche said, "She bestows it on her children as her fundamental quality, and the father adds the darker background of the will. . . . Men possess deeper, more powerful drives; it is these that carry their reason, which is in itself something passive, so far" (Ibid., 153).

51. He thought this shame resulted from girls having been taught that sensuality is "their 'evil'; and mere knowledge is considered evil. And then to be hurled, as by a gruesome lightning bolt, into reality and knowledge, by marriage—precisely by the man they love and esteem most! To catch love and shame in contradiction and to be forced to experience at the same time delight, surrender, duty, pity, terror, and who knows what else, in the face of the unexpected neighborliness of god and beast! Thus a psychic knot has been tied that may have no equal" (*The Gay Science*, 71).

52. Nietzsche expressed similar ideas in *Ecce Homo* in the same passage, cited in note 47, in which he refers to himself as the first psychologist of the eternally feminine (266–67). See also *The Will to Power*, note 1050, where in 1888, the last

productive year of his life, Nietzsche reiterated the idea contained in the first sentence of *The Birth of Tragedy*. There he states that "the further development of man is [necessarily tied to the antagonism] between the sexes" (539).

53. The quotation is from an early and brief essay of Nietzsche's regarding "The Greek Woman" in *The Complete Works of Friedrich Nietzsche*, vol. 2, ed. Oscar Levy (New York: Macmillan, 1911), 19.

54. Ibid.

55. In his less allegorical books, Nietzsche occasionally seemed intrigued by the possibility of a "higher" form of marriage that would transcend the limitations of the typical marriages of his time, which he found to be generally so dismal. Nietzsche had ruled out the possibility of marriages that were begun on the idea of a partnership of equals, but a marriage based in love might, perhaps over time, develop a few steps toward this ideal. Nietzsche believed that "here and there on earth we may encounter a kind of continuation of love in which this possessive craving of two people for each other gives way to a new desire and lust for possession—a shared higher interest for an ideal above them." But Nietzsche did not seem to have much hope that this exception could ever become a rule. "But who knows such love? Who has experienced it? Its right name is called friendship (*The Gay Science*, 14).

56. The phrase is from *Ecce Homo*, 266.

57. This contradiction recreates in a different way the dilemma that faced Rousseau regarding where the perfect governor, father, or legislator might come from. Their emergence is miraculous, as is the transfiguration of the woman in love in Nietzsche's thought.

58. Similar formulations of the Dionysian can be found in *Twilight of the Idols* (tragedy as a "saying Yes to life even in its strangest and hardest problems" [562]) and *Ecce Homo* ("a Yes-saying without reservation, even to suffering, even to guilt, even to everything that is questionable and strange in existence" [272]).

59. Honig, *Political Theory*, 40–41.

60. Derrida called Nietzsche's "philosophers of the future . . . something like the Messiah." Jacques Derrida, *The Politics of Friendship* (New York: Verso, 2005), 37.

61. In moments such as this, Nietzsche seems to indulge in the sort of comfort in "speculative history" that Honig faults in Kant's notion of virtue. Honig writes, "Speculative history consoles man with the promise that one day he and others of his species will once again be at home in the world not as a natural creature but as moral, rational man" (*Political Theory*, 23). Such a description also matches Rousseau's project in *The Social Contract*, where the freedom of the natural savage is re-created under conditions of rational civil society.

62. Derrida, *The Politics of Friendship*, 35.

63. Ibid., 37.

64. Few scholars who have written about Nietzsche pay close attention to this aspect of his thought. One exception is Tracy Strong, who includes a section in *Friedrich Nietzsche and the Politics of Transfiguration* titled "The Question of Breeding." It is of interest both for what Strong says in it and for what is left out. Strong begins the section on breeding by saying that his interpretation of Nietzsche "forces us to go further, into territory which recent work on Nietzsche has generally avoided. Nietzsche is not (just) talking about a manner of thinking; since he thinks that men have been changed in their nature by slave morality, they will also have to be changed if they are to become overmen. It is the most 'natural' thing in the world to be slavely moral; indeed, there appears to be nothing else. It will have to appear equally 'natural' to be an overman. Hence, I am forced to take very seriously all those bothersome statements which most modern scholars of Nietzsche have simply left out of their analysis in a well-meant reaction to the distortions of the Nazis. The talk about 'breeding' and 'race' *is* important in Nietzsche's thought, and it simply won't do to pile up the quotations which say nice things about the Jews and nasty ones about the Germans. Nietzsche *is* talking about *developing* men who are not subject to the 'human all too human'" (274). Strong is completely right on this point. Where I quibble with Strong is on follow-through. The remainder of Strong's short section on breeding consists of Strong stating his disagreements with central points in Heidegger's and Deleuze's interpretations of the will to power and the eternal return. Kaufmann's chapter on "The Master Race" is very focused on refuting the misuse of Nietzsche by the Nazis and other eugenicists. Appel notes that scholars "have tended to follow Kaufmann either in dismissing outright or underplaying" Nietzsche's interest in breeding (*Nietzsche contra Democracy*, 106). Appel's *Nietzsche contra Democracy* considers more carefully the role of breeding in Nietzsche's politics.

65. A similar idea is expressed in *The Will to Power* (477), where Nietzsche imagined the creation of "not merely a master race whose sole task is to rule, but a race with its own sphere of life, with an excess of strength for beauty, bravery, culture, manners to the highest peak of the spirit; an affirming race that may grant itself every great luxury."

66. That aphorism, intended for *Twilight of the Idols*, eventually returned to the confinement of his notebooks. But Nietzsche published similar ideas. In *Human, All Too Human*, Nietzsche suggested "a practical philosophy for the female sex"— that "if we prevented the discontented, atrabilious, and sullen from propagating themselves we could magically transform the earth into a garden of happiness" (278). Elsewhere, Nietzsche softened intimations of political and social control in his discussions of breeding, searching instead for a more ideational power—a doctrine that would select out the strong in spirit from the rest. "A doctrine is needed powerful enough to work as a breeding agent: strengthening the strong, paralyzing and destructive for the world-weary" (*The Will to Power*, 458). Nietzsche flirted

with the possibility that his idea of the eternal return was the doctrine to accomplish this: "Fundamental innovations: ... in place of 'metaphysics' and religion, the theory of eternal recurrence (this as a means of breeding and selection)" (255).

67. I discuss the significance of this idea to Giorgio Agamben's notion of *Homo Sacer* in the Conclusion. Nietzsche's notion of the domination inherent to parenting might be productively contrasted to his appreciation of the Homeric idea of contest, in which domination was seen as destructive of contest. For this reason, any individual who became so strong or compelling as to dominate was banished from the community.

68. Sheridan Hough (*Nietzsche's Noontide Friend: The Self as Metaphoric Double* [Philadelphia: Pennsylvania University Press, 1997]) quotes this passage along with a passage from part three of *Thus Spoke Zarathustra*, which makes a similar point: "I flew an arrow ... out into the distant future, which no dream has yet seen ... where I found again my old devil and arch-enemy, the Spirit of Gravity, and all that he created: compulsion, dogma, need, and consequence and purpose and will and good and evil: for must there not exist that which is danced upon, danced across: Must there not be moles and heavy dwarfs—for the sake of the nimble, the nimblest?" (112).

69. Nietzsche's description of the Hindu practice of breeding seems to confirm this perspective. "What I want to make clear by all the means in my power: that there is no worse confusion than the confusion of breeding with taming" (*The Will to Power*, 215). Taming involved "caging" and making "sick" the strong and frightening, all in the name of "improving" them and making them more moral (*Twilight of the Idols*, 502). Nietzsche associated taming with priests and the Christian morality (502). The historical morality he most closely associated with breeding was the Indian law of Manu—with its serious and respectful treatment of "procreation ... women [and] marriage" (503; *The Antichrist*, 642). He considered the Indian morality embodied in the Manu to be "the most magnificent example" of "*breeding* a particular race and kind" (*Twilight of the Idols*, 503). Compared to the Christian, the man of Indian morality was "a hundred times milder and more reasonable;" he lived in a "healthier, higher, and *wider* world" (503). But the Manu did not foster a world that was free of the sickness that Nietzsche associated with ressentiment. In *The Genealogy of Morals*, Nietzsche told the story of how the reactive man inflicted the disease of bad conscience on himself and then cleverly convinced the more dangerous and noble man to submit to the slave morality that the bad conscience had helped to create. In the case of the Manu, it is the strong, the breeders, who actively seek to create disease. It is the strong who react to the danger posed by another class. "Yet this organization too found it necessary to be *terrible*—this time not in the struggle with beasts, but with their counter-concept, the unbred man, the mish-mash man, the chandala. And again, it had not other means for keeping him from being dangerous, for making him weak, than to make

him *sick*—it was the fight with the 'great number.' Perhaps there is nothing that contradicts our feeling more than *these* protective measures of Indian morality" (*Twilight of the Idols*, 503). Most prominent among these "protective measures" was a frightful exercise of control over the circumstances and conditions of reproduction among the chandala. There was "a prohibition that Sudra women may not assist chandala women in childbirth, and a prohibition that the latter may not *assist each other* in this condition . . . and thereupon again 'the law of the knife,' ordaining circumcision for male children and the removal of the internal labia for female children. Manu holds: 'The chandalas are the fruit of adultery, incest, and crime' (these, the *necessary* consequences of the concept of breeding)" (504). Thus Nietzsche ultimately concludes that "the morality of breeding and the morality of taming are, in the means that they use, entirely worthy of each other: we may proclaim it as the supreme principle that, to make morality, one must have the unconditional will to its opposite" (505). Thus Nietzsche's imagined projects of breeding must actually breed more ressentiment—a much darker vision of eternal recurrence than the one we are used to.

70. This aspect of Nietzsche's thought has been noted by other scholars, most usefully to me for this project by Hough (*Nietzsche's Noontide Friend*, xvii), who focuses on Nietzsche's pairing of the wanderer and his shadow, and by Tracy Strong and Verity Smith in their paper "Trapped in a Family Portrait? Gender and Family in Nietzsche's Reconfiguring of Authority" (paper presented at the annual meeting of the Western Political Science Association, Long Beach, Calif., 2001). Thanks to Tracy Strong for furnishing me with a copy of this paper.

71. It was a point Nietzsche made often in regard to races rather than individuals. Among strong races, he wrote, there is "wastefulness—(strength is no longer hoarded, spiritual disturbance arises through excessive tension); their existence is costly. . . . The strong are subsequently weaker, more devoid of will, more absurd than the weak average. They are races that squander" (*The Will to Power*, 463).

72. There is a section in *The Genealogy of Morals* in which Nietzsche made the point that philosophers always "abhor marriage" and would see a son as "a fetter" and "a little demon." This is a very hard passage to interpret, however, since Nietzsche was being critical of what is ascetic in the ascetic philosopher. Yet he also says that every "free spirit" would experience a thoughtful moment of the same kind (i.e., against marriage and children). The ascetic philosopher discussed in *The Genealogy of Morals* is a different sort, I argue, than the "new philosophers" Nietzsche discusses in *Beyond Good and Evil* and in his notebooks. It seems to me that those who engage in "affairs of the highest philosophical kind," as mentioned in *Human, All Too Human*, are not who Nietzsche meant by the ascetic philosopher in *The Genealogy of Morals*. So it seems there is something about marriage and children that makes it a problem even for philosophers and other humans of the highest type who overcome the ascetic.

73. This is an aspect of Nietzsche's thought that, as we see in the next two chapters, Rorty elides and West engages, each in a way that recreates aspects of the Nietzschean politics of parenthood.

74. Nietzsche does go on in that aphorism to explain why perhaps we should suffer less when we betray our own convictions.

75. Elsewhere, in language that echoes the higher marriages he described in Zarathustra, the marriages that hoped to give birth to the overman, Nietzsche wrote, "What once united us, the bond of *one* hope—who still can read the signs love once inscribed therein, now faint and faded? It is like a parchment—discoloured, scorched—from which the hand *shrinks back*" (*Beyond Good and Evil*, 223).

76. Tracy Strong describes the incident in his "Oedipus as Hero: Family and Family Metaphors in Nietzsche," in *The Family in Political Thought*, ed. Jean Bethke Elshtain (Amherst: University of Massachusetts Press), 1982.

77. Letter to Overbeck, February 10, 1883, SB vol. 6, 1883. Cited by Strong and Smith, "Trapped in a Family Portrait?" (2).

78. Strong, "Oedipus as Hero," 191.

79. Ibid., 192–93, 195.

80. Ibid., 195–96.

81. Ibid., 196.

82. Dionysus was also born from his father (Zeus, who carried him sewn up in his thigh) instead of his mother. And like a good Greek son, he carried the character of his father—though his mother was a mortal, he was a god.

83. Emerson, *The Conduct of Life*, 4.

84. Honig, *Political Theory*, 8.

85. Ibid., 8–9. Honig refers to this reinterpretation as "my radicalization of Nietzsche's overman and herd and my focus on the struggle between them in a single self."

86. Derrida, addressing not parenthood but Nietzsche's invocation of "philosophers of the future," suggests that Nietzsche creates "a double responsibility that doubles up again endlessly. . . . I/we must answer for the present *we* for and before the *we* of the future" (Derrida, *The Politics of Friendship*, 37). He explores the difficulties that this entails. "One who calls and questions oneself is not even sure that the new philosophers will be part of the free spirits that we are. . . . Perhaps those who I am calling will be unrecognizable enemies" (42). To make ourselves the enemy of the one that we have called forth, however, might be more difficult still. It is this difficulty that Nietzsche's use of parenthood ultimately required him to confront and from which he often seemed to shrink back.

3. Troubled Inheritance

1. Richard Rorty, *Philosophy and Social Hope* (New York: Penguin Books, 1999), 5.

2. Richard Rorty, *Achieving Our Country* (Cambridge, Mass.: Harvard University Press, 1998), 96.

3. In her discussion of Arendt, Honig makes it clear that she thinks the unpredictability and challenges of politics should be brought to bear on such "private" matters as class and gender (*Political Theory*, 76–125).

4. Richard Rorty, "Remarks on Deconstruction and Pragmatism," in *Deconstruction and Pragmatism*, ed. Simon Critchley (London: Routledge, 1996), 17.

5. Honig, *Democracy and the Foreigner*, 116.

6. Richard Rorty, *Philosophy and the Mirror of Nature* (Princeton, N.J.: Princeton University Press, 1980), 159.

7. Richard Rorty, *Consequences of Pragmatism: Essays, 1972–1980.* (Minneapolis: University of Minnesota Press, 1982), 228.

8. West's *The American Evasion of Philosophy* was published the same year as Rorty's *Contingency, Irony, and Solidarity* (Cambridge: Cambridge University Press, 1989) and surveys much of Rorty's published work up to, but not including, that point.

9. Richard Rorty, "The Professor and the Prophet," *Transition*, no. 52 (1991), 75. West summarized Rorty's ideas regarding philosophy in a way that began to apply his ideas to the realm of political contest. For example, West conflates disagreements about actual social practice with intellectual debates in saying that for Rorty, "in cases of conflict and disagreement, we should either support our prevailing practices, reform them, or put forward realizable alternatives to them, without appealing to ahistorical philosophical discourse as the privileged mode of resolving intellectual disagreements." *The American Evasion*, 200–201.

10. West, *The American Evasion*, 199.

11. Ibid., 205. West is quoting Rorty's *Consequences of Pragmatism*, 210.

12. Ibid., 207.

13. Ibid.

14. Honig, *Democracy and the Foreigner*, 166.

15. In particular, Thomas Kuhn, W. V. O. Quine, Wilfrid Sellars, and Nelson Goodman.

16. Cornel West, "Nietzsche's Prefiguration of Postmodern American Philosophy," in *The Cornel West Reader* (New York: Basic Civitas Books, 1999), 209–10.

17. Honig, *Democracy and the Foreigner*, 171.

18. This is a maneuver that would appeal to West as well, as I explore in chapter 4.

19. Rorty's quotations of John Dewey are from *Reconstruction in Philosophy* (Boston: Beacon Press, 1957) and from "Philosophy and Democracy," *University of California Chronicle* 21 (1919): 39–54. The idea of replacing looking for the eternal with looking to the future is one of Rorty's favorite ways to summarize what he is trying to accomplish (*Philosophy and Social Hope*, 29; *Truth and Progress* [Cambridge: Cambridge University Press, 1998], 174). Emphasis added.

20. West describes the relationship between the early Rorty and the European postmodernists this way: "Rorty . . . ingeniously echoes the strident antihumanist critiques—such as those of Martin Heidegger, Jacques Derrida, and Michel Foucault—of a moribund humanism. Yet his brand of neopragmatism domesticates these critiques in a smooth, seductive and witty Attic prose and, more important, dilutes them by refusing to push his own project toward cultural and political criticisms of the civilization he cherishes" (West, *The American Evasion,* 206).

21. See "A Cultural Left" in *Achieving Our Country* and "The Humanistic Intellectual: Eleven Theses" in *Philosophy and Social Hope.* Rorty is willing to give credit to these same leftist intellectuals for contributing to many noteworthy accomplishments, in particular for getting the United States to realize that Vietnam was a disaster and for helping people in the United States become more tolerant of and sensitive to minorities, women, and gays (*Achieving Our Country,* 68, 80–82). Rorty's and West's condemnations of continental philosophers like Foucault and Derrida are often, but not always, broadly drawn, and in many cases, their generalizations fail to do justice to the theorists they attack.

22. Richard Rorty, "Thugs and Theorists, A Reply to Bernstein," *Political Theory* 15, no. 4 (November 1987), 570.

23. Henry Adams, *The Education of Henry Adams* (Boston: Houghton Mifflin, 1973), 447.

24. Richard Rorty, "From Logic to Language to Play," *Proceedings and Addresses of the American Philosophical Association* 59 (1986), 752.

25. Honig, *Political Theory,* 3.

26. Rorty actually ascribes this view to Dewey and Annette Baier, but he is clearly presenting it as a view he agrees with.

27. Rorty is referring to Baier's *Postures of the Mind: Essays on Mind and Morals* (Minneapolis: University of Minnesota Press, 1985).

28. Obviously, Rorty's view of the feelings that occur within families is wildly simplistic and optimistic. Freud believed that there are conflicting feelings of love and hostility involved in growing up in a family. It is the effort to negotiate these conflicting feelings, rather than a sort of feel-good experience of love, that causes a person to develop a superego that determines what he or she considers moral behavior.

29. Arendt offers a very different account of the reasons for these brave responses in her *Eichmann in Jerusalem: A Report on the Banality of Evil* (New York: Penguin, 1992). Arendt saw important differences between the situation in Denmark, where political leaders openly defied the Nazi occupiers, and Italy, where resistance to the European holocaust was carried out through subterfuge.

30. Julia Kristeva, *Nations without Nationalism* (New York: Columbia University Press, 1993), 40–41. Honig sees something similar happening in Michael Sandel's notion of liberal community. She notes, for example, that Sandel argues for

the inclusion of gays in the moral community because they are *basically similar* to other Americans. In particular, gay citizens, in their desire to marry and have children, affirm the "sanctity" of "procreation and marriage" (*Political Theory*, 188).

31. Edelman uses a similar metaphor regarding what he sees as a problematically child-obsessed American political culture in general. He suggests that we "withdraw our allegiance, however compulsory, from a reality based on the Ponzi scheme of reproductive futurism" (Edelman, *No Future*, 4).

32. Nancy Scheper-Hughes has offered several studies to suggest that such hopes are indeed contingent on circumstances and are not universal. In one study, she examines the practice in some rural Irish families of singling out one child to be discouraged from developing feelings of competence in life. That child, lacking confidence to strike out on his or her own, will stay at home to care for the parents when they are elderly. In another, she examines the practice of letting particularly weak infants pass away among the shantytown poor of Brazil. Because life is difficult, not every child will want to undertake it. *Saints, Scholars and Schizophrenics: Mental Illness in Rural Ireland* (Berkeley: University of California Press, 2000); and *Death without Weeping: The Violence of Everyday Life in Brazil* (Berkeley: University of California Press, 1993). Parents, of course, do countless things that limit possibilities for their children's future. Rorty spent little time considering them.

33. Berlant, *The Queen of America*, 5.

34. Honig, *Democracy and the Foreigner*, 66.

35. Simon Stow notes the way that Rorty undermines his own efforts to suggest literature can help instill an openness appropriate to democratic citizenship by insisting on particular interpretations of literary works and dismissing alternative interpretations. Rorty does something analogous in his single-minded take on the political effects of the experience of parenting. Stow, *Republic of Readers? The Literary Turn in Political Thought and Analysis* (Albany: State University of New York Press, 2007).

36. One exception to Rorty's continual identification with the rich, the powerful, and—to use one of his favorite terms—the lucky occurs when he briefly identifies with metaphysical moralists to say, "We *resent* the idea that we shall have to wait for the strong to turn their piggy little eyes to the suffering of the weak, slowly open their dried little hearts. We desperately hope there is something stronger and more powerful that will *hurt* the strong if they do *not* do these things—if not a vengeful god, then a vengeful aroused proletariat or, at the very least, the offended majesty of Kant's tribunal of pure practical reason" (*Truth and Progress*, 182). The ever shifting, expanding, and contracting "we" in Rorty's work is explored in Michael Billig's "Nationalism and Richard Rorty: The Text as a Flag for Pax Americana" (*New Left Review*, no. 202 [November–December 1993]: 69–83), as well as Richard J. Bernstein's "One Step Forward, Two Steps Backward: Richard Rorty on Liberal Democracy and Philosophy" (*Political Theory* 15, no. 4 [1987]: 538–63).

37. Jacqueline Stevens, in *Reproducing the State,* offers a convincing argument that political arrangements, from ancient times to present, often have as their dominant purpose the preservation of property and status from parents to children. This is also a central theme in the work of Pierre Bourdieu.

38. Rorty was willing to endorse the insights of the Communist Manifesto as "still an admirable statement of the great lesson we learned from watching industrial capitalism in action" (*Philosophy and Social Hope,* 205).

39. Where I have inserted an ellipsis, Rorty listed a number of examples of historical places and periods when the people who had their hands on money and power acted to preserve it for themselves and their children. Among these examples are America under Reagan.

40. Keith Topper offers a critique of Rorty that makes a similar point in a different way. Topper is dubious about Rorty's notion that private and public can be considered separately, and in particular, that the public realm should be insulated from the complexities of private existence. Topper suggests that the work of Pierre Bourdieu, in which he demonstrated that university professors assess students on the basis of stylistic indicators of class background one picks up from one's parents, rather than on the quality of their work, demonstrates complex relations between the public and private realms that Rorty ignores. I address Rorty's take on the public role of professors later. Topper, "Richard Rorty, Liberalism and the Politics of Redescription," *American Political Science Review* 89, no. 4 (1995): 954–65.

41. It is hard to believe that Jefferson, slave-owner and the president whose executive order expanded slavery into the Louisiana territories, could not have conceived of a society in which different castes, defined by genetic criteria, have radically different life chances. Rorty discusses the same danger of America being divided into hereditary castes in *Achieving Our Country,* 98.

42. Emphasis added. Habermas noted as well that the modern conjugal family, though it conceived of itself in terms of a "community of love," was also a mechanism for the consolidation of wealth and the passing on of strict standards of behavior. "The conjugal family's self-image of its intimate sphere collided even within the consciousness of the bourgeoisie itself with the real function of the bourgeois family. . . . As a genealogical link it guaranteed a continuity of personnel that consisted materially in the accumulation of capital and was anchored in the absence of legal restrictions regarding the inheritance of property. As an agency of society it served especially the task of that difficult mediation through which, in spite of the illusion of freedom, strict conformity with societally necessary requirements was brought about" (Habermas, *The Structural Transformation,* 47). Stevens also explores this aspect of the modern family and the way the laws of the state have traditionally assisted in this familial accumulation of capital (*Reproducing the State,* 32, 264).

43. See *Philosophy and Social Hope,* 15, 162, and 203; *Truth and Progress,* 180.

44. Rorty credits the idea that parent's hopes for their children are the ultimate barometer of the acceptance of gays to Eve Sedgwick.

45. "Strong poet" is a term of Harold Bloom's, occasionally used by Rorty, that is basically interchangeable with "ironist intellectual."

46. Rorty credits Nietzsche with having developed this idea but then appropriates it as his own.

47. Many scholars have noted the elitism and self-satisfaction built into Rorty's ideas. See, for example, Sheldon Wolin, "Democracy in the Discourse of Postmodernism," *Social Research* 57 (Spring 1990): 5–30; Terry Eagleton, *The Illusions of Postmodernism* (Oxford: Blackwell, 1996); and Roy Bhaskar, *Philosophy and the Idea of Freedom* (Oxford: Oxford University Press, 1992). Billig, in "Nationalism and Richard Rorty," explores how the self-satisfaction inherent to Rorty's ideas, in mingling with his patriotism, helps provide a justification for American dominance of global culture. To Rorty's credit, perhaps in reaction to critiques like Wolin's, he seemed much less eager to expound on the differences between ironist intellectuals and the mass public in his writings after *Contingency, Irony, and Solidarity.*

48. The challenges of irony are such that Rorty could not imagine them as tolerable for the general public even in his ideal liberal society. In the Introduction to *Contingency, Irony, and Solidarity,* Rorty wrote, "One of my aims in this book is to suggest the possibility of a liberal utopia: one in which ironism, in the relevant sense, is universal" (xv). When it comes to the actual description of such a society, however, it turns out that the words "in the relevant sense" mask an invidious distinction. According to Rorty, in the ideal liberal society, "the intellectuals would still be ironists, although the nonintellectuals would not. The latter would, however, be commonsensically nominalist and historicist. So they would see themselves as contingent through and through, without feeling any particular doubts about the contingencies they happen to be" (87). In other words, in this ideal society, the public might be expected to be a little less shrill and self-righteous, but self-creation, or at least an appreciation of their self-creation as self-creation, would still be well beyond their means.

49. Rorty actually ascribes this presentation of the proper way to socialize children to what Dewey would think if he were alive—it is clear, however, that Rorty is citing this imaginary undead Dewey approvingly.

50. Rorty goes on to say that most of these erotic relationships are with "dead teachers who wrote the books the students are assigned" but admits "some will be with the live teachers that are giving the lectures" (*Philosophy and Social Hope,* 126).

51. I leave it to readers to read what they will into Rorty's praise for "taking liberties" in the context of a discussion of the "sparks" that form between a professor and a student.

52. Honig, *Democracy and the Foreigner,* 116.

53. Ibid., 117.

54. Ibid.

55. Rorty had three children of his own. He wrote nothing about them in his published work. Rorty liked to tell the story that when he was diagnosed with pancreatic cancer, the disease that also killed Derrida, his daughter remarked it must be caused by "reading too much Heidegger."

56. Nietzsche, *The Will to Power,* 464. Wolin also compares this aspect of Rorty to Nietzsche. Wolin ("Democracy in the Discourse of Postmodernism," 7).

57. Rorty is quoting from Harold Bloom, *The Anxiety of Influence* (Oxford: Oxford University Press, 1973), 80. But Rorty makes the phrase his own and uses it repeatedly (*Contingency, Irony, and Solidarity,* 24, 25, 28, 29, and 43).

58. Richard Bernstein provides a nice summary of the ways in which Rorty's *Philosophy and the Mirror of Nature* created a stir by rebelling against the foundational assumptions of analytic philosophy at the time. See "Rorty's Liberal Utopia," *Social Research* 57, no 1 (1990): 31–72.

59. Bernstein, "One Step Forward," 557.

60. Nietzsche, *Human, All Too Human,* 194.

61. Judith Shklar develops this idea in her *Ordinary Vices* (Cambridge, Mass.: Harvard University Press, 1985).

62. In dismissing such an approach, Rorty was perhaps ignoring his own advice to think of "the history of human social practices [as] continuous with the history of biological evolution" (*Truth and Progress,* 206).

63. Rorty bases this idea on a reading of Orwell, whose notion of cruelty he contrasts with Nabokov's.

64. This particular description of the world ends a chapter in which Rorty analyzes the work of Nabokov. Attempting to salvage a moral sense in Nabokov's work that the author himself repeatedly denied, Rorty notes that "the death of a child is Nabakov's standard example of ultimate pain" (*Contingency, Irony, and Solidarity,* 163).

65. The quotation is from Jacques Derrida, *The Postcard: From Socrates to Freud and Beyond* (Chicago: University of Chicago Press, 1987), 39.

66. Philip Larkin, "Continuing to Live," in *Collected Poems* (New York: Faber and Faber, 2003).

67. The poem is "This Be the Verse," in Philip Larkin, *High Windows* (New York: Farrar, Straus and Giroux, 1974).

4. Deadbeat Citizens

1. West was nine years old. He uses the phrase "beat up" in his first published description of the incident with Mrs. Yee (Sylvia Ann Hewlett and Cornel West,

The War against Parents: What We Can Do for America's Beleaguered Moms and Dads [Boston: Houghton Mifflin Harcourt, 1999], 13). Years later, he redescribed the incident as his having "socked her in the arm. *Hard* in the arm"—after which he "jumped the principal" to avoid a paddling (Cornel West and David Ritz, *Brother West: Living and Loving Out Loud* [New York: Smiley Books, 2009], 12).

2. Cornel West, *Prophesy Deliverance! An Afro-American Revolutionary Christianity* (Louisville, Ky.: Westminster John Knox Press, 2002), 17.

3. Cornel West, *The Ethical Dimensions of Marxist Thought* (New York: Monthly Review Press, 1991), xx.

4. Cornel West, *Democracy Matters: Winning the Fight Against Imperialism* (New York: Penguin, 2005), 82, 155.

5. Sometimes both approaches are offered in a single article. In her critical take on one of the books that I deal with extensively in this chapter, West's co-authored book *The War against Parents,* Iris M. Young veers from fulsome praise of West's earlier work to contemptuous dismissal of his ideas about parenthood, which she calls, at one point, "embarrassing" ("Cornel West on Gender and Family," in *Cornel West: A Critical Reader,* ed. George Yancy [Hoboken: Wiley-Blackwell, 2001]). In this chapter, I explore the connection between the sort of "subtle" analysis of race and gender that Young appreciates in West's other works and his ideas about parenthood rather than attribute to West a sort of unfortunate forgetfulness regarding his previous ideas. In the wake of a falling out with Larry Summers, the president of Harvard University where West was a professor, the media reported on a good deal of skepticism about West's work—particularly regarding his efforts to play the role of a "public intellectual" in a particular way: he sometimes writes short books using everyday vernacular rather than academic language and without copious citations; he gives many public lectures; he appears in films; he writes and performs his own music. These criticisms ignore the main thrust of West's scholarship from the beginning of his career, which has been to examine the particular style of citizenship that American philosophers and political thinkers have developed since Emerson (another frequent speaker and writer of short pieces), especially in the pragmatic and Protestant traditions. In engaging and arguing with that tradition, West has developed a model of the engaged intellectual tied to both the virtue and contest theories of citizenship: committed to offering social criticism, responsible for proposing concrete alternatives to the status quo, wedded to a spirit of experimentalism, and bound to articulate sources of hope—all features of his "nonacademic" endeavors. This chapter explores the significance of one particular aspect of West's efforts in this regard: his ideas regarding family. It is because there is much that is compelling about West's political ideas that they are worth taking seriously and criticizing.

6. Geoffrey Layman, *The Great Divide: Religious and Cultural Conflict in American Political Parties* (New York: Columbia University Press, 2001).

7. Edsall and Edsall argue that the political wing of the evangelical Christian movement in the southern United States had its specific origins in racial intolerance. I discuss this in the conclusion. (Thomas Byrne Edsall and Mary D. Edsall, *Chain Reaction: The Impact of Race, Rights, and Taxes on American Politics* [New York: W.W. Norton, 1992]).

8. West has written about Niebuhr extensively, especially in *The American Evasion of Philosophy* and in the essay "Pragmatism and the Sense of the Tragic" (*Keeping Faith: Philosophy and Race in America* [New York: Routledge, 1994], 107). Obama discussed his admiration of Niebuhr with the *New York Times*, calling him "one of my favorite philosophers" (David Brooks, "Obama, Gospel and Verse," April 26, 2007).

9. Recognizing—or capitalizing on—this connection, West published on the eve of the 2008 election a pithy and aphoristic summary of his ideas and the way they reflected on the Obama candidacy (and vice versa): *Hope on a Tightrope: Words and Wisdom* (Carlsbad, Calif.: Hay House, 2008).

10. Cornel West, *Prophetic Fragments: Illuminations of the Crisis in American Religion and Culture* (Grand Rapids, Mich.: Wm. B. Eerdmans, 1993), 25.

11. Cornel West, *Race Matters* (Boston: Beacon Press, 2001), 149.

12. Cornel West, "The Making of an American Radical Democrat of African Descent," in *The Cornel West Reader* (9). With these sorts of assessments, West is often unfair to Foucault. Foucault worked hard on political projects he believed in, including, most famously, prison reform. The fact that he did not believe any victory was final or unproblematic did not mean he thought we should avoid "any social project of transformation." Fred Dolan argues that Foucault's theory is not hostile to the politics of contest but rather offers a way to consider possibilities for political contest in more realms of life. "The Paradoxical Liberty of Bio-Power: Hannah Arendt and Michel Foucault on Modern Politics," *Philosophy & Social Criticism* 31, no. 3 (2005): 369–80.

13. West, "Nietzsche's Prefiguration," 189.

14. Honig, *Political Theory*, 72.

15. Ibid.

16. Referring in another case to Derrida, West summarized: "All he can do is try to unsettle the binary oppositions on which the dominant Western cultures rest, with very little possibility of mobilization and organization and so forth. . . . Then the feminists come along, and the blacks will come along and say look, we've got a movement. Serious movement here, not just a matter of talking about difference and heterogeneity, but difference and heterogeneity as a matter of concrete embodiment in a certain political direction" (*Beyond Eurocentrism*, 137–8). West's informal tone in this quotation is in part because it is taken from the transcript of a public lecture.

17. In this vein, West offers a critical overview of the tradition, picking out the

aspects of each thinker that he finds most useful and pointing out problems that prevented thinkers from fulfilling the potential their ideas possessed. Thus Emerson is praised as a prophet of self-creation but criticized for elevating personal integrity over political projects—"human personality disjoined from communal action" (*American Evasion of Philosophy,* 40). Peirce is commended for balancing individualism with a sense of the "higher duties" to the community imposed by the Christian notion of love. Dewey is appreciated for his activism but criticized as blind to the depth of the problems of the underclass. West thought Hook and Mills veered too far toward pessimism, while Niebuhr's religious and "tragic" sensibility might provoke a hopeful and heroic approach to seemingly insurmountable problems.

18. Rorty, "The Professor and the Prophet," 75.

19. Ibid., 77.

20. Ibid., 78.

21. Ibid., 77.

22. Young, "Cornel West on Gender and Family," 180–82. West's enthusiasm for combining the perspectives of other thinkers has also been noted by his harshest critics. For example, Leon Weiseltier suggests that West's work amounts to "a long saga of positioning" ("All or Nothing at All," *New Republic* [March 6, 1995]: 32).

23. Young, "Cornel West on Gender and Family," 179.

24. Ibid. Young extended this criticism to include the set of "economistic" policy proposals offered by West and Roberto Mangabeira Unger in *The Future of American Progressivism: An Initiative for Political and Economic Reform* (Boston: Beacon Press, 1999). Young is frustrated, for example, that despite "gestures acknowledging how racist, sexist and heterosexist structures intersect with economic class, [West and Unger] do not offer a description of the workings of privilege and disadvantage in America that integrates these different structural axes" ("Cornel West on Gender and Family," 186). Her criticism of West and Unger echoes very closely the terms that West used in *The American Evasion of Philosophy* (223) to critique Unger's *Knowledge and Politics* (New York: Free Press, 1975).

25. While West sometimes includes sexual orientation as another social divide and locus of discrimination or oppression in his other works, he and Hewlett do not discuss it in *The War against Parents*. Though they mention gay parents a few times, the authors defend the idea that the best parents for any child are the biological parents.

26. Had this suggestion been incorporated into the 2008 election, it likely would have cost Obama, for whom West campaigned, his victory. People with school-aged children slightly favored McCain (according to a CNN analysis of the exit polls).

27. Despite the absence of any desire to "offload their kids," parents did become fascinated by events that followed Nebraska's passage of a "safe-haven" law that

lifted any legal penalties if a parent chose to abandon a child at a church or hospital. While the law was intended to prevent young mothers from leaving newborns in dumpsters or trash cans, a number of parents took advantage of the law to turn over to the state older children, including teenagers. A *New York Times* article on the subject was one of the most read articles online that month. Erik Eckholm, "Older Children Abandoned under Law for Babies," *New York Times,* October 2, 2008, A21.

28. In that same book, West quotes Marx regarding the essence of man's species-life—that he "reproduces himself . . . actively and in a real sense, and he sees his own reflection in a world which he has constructed" (*The Ethical Dimensions of Marxist Thought,* 58). This desire to reproduce yourself and to see your own reflection would come to play a large role in West's exploration of the uses of parenthood for citizenship, as I discuss later.

29. Cornel West, "Introduction," in *The Cornel West Reader,* xvii.

30. Rorty, "The Professor and the Prophet," 73.

31. Sometimes West expresses the idea less abstractly—for example, speculating that "The most fertile seeds for democracy matters in the Islamic world can be found in the civic life of the Palestinians and Kurds—the most subjugated peoples in the region" (*Democracy Matters,* 142).

32. The question of what role the experience of suffering can play in the democratic politics of contest is the subject of Arendt's *On Revolution* (New York: Viking, 1963) and a larger theme in her political thought. Arendt argues that when the experience of suffering appears in the public realm, it tends to overwhelm all other claims and eventually sweep aside all the institutions of politics themselves. Discussing the French Revolution, she writes that "when [the poor] appeared on the scene of politics, necessity appeared with them, and the result was . . . freedom had to be surrendered to necessity" (50). West echoes this idea: "Oppressed people are preoccupied with survival rather than the struggle for freedom" (*Hope on a Tightrope,* 190).

33. West also doubts that Obama will make the black "underclass" a priority in his administration. "Any politician who makes it to the level of Barack Obama, . . . tends to be surrounded by spinmeisters and pundits who do not put the suffering of working and poor people at the center of their vision. I want Senator Obama to win, but I am going to criticize him intensely when he wins. I'm a deep democrat and he's a liberal. They're not the same thing. I very much support him, but it's a question of principle. The plight of everyday people is paramount" (*Hope on a Tightrope,* 144–45). As I discuss in the Conclusion, Obama does focus on the black underclass, primarily as parents.

34. All groups, of course, that include parents as well as nonparents.

35. The notion that "attention to affliction" is the most important political responsibility in democratic citizenship is explored by Simone Weil, another theo-

rist whose ideas about citizenship intertwine Christian and Marxist ideas, in her essay "Human Personality" (in *Selected Essays, 1934–1943* [Oxford University Press, 1962]). The application of this idea to the American political context is the subject of the strange but compelling film *Simone Weil: A Western* (Film archive of the Exploratorium Museum, San Francisco. Filmmakers unknown).

36. As the inclusion of Heschel as an example suggests, West does not think that one must be Christian to adopt this perspective. "I do not believe that . . . the Christian tradition has a monopoly on such insights, capacities and motivations" (*Keeping Faith*, 133–34). In fact, sympathy with victims rather than Christian faith itself is more central to West's identity and political outlook. "I would give up my allegiance to the prophetic Christian tradition . . . if I became convinced that another tradition provides a more acceptable or enabling moral vision" (133).

37. Honig, *Political Theory*, 62. The internal quotation is from Nietzsche's *Genealogy of Morals*, 22.

38. Honig, *Political Theory*, 62.

39. The problem of self-hatred in the black community is a topic West has continued to address up through his book reacting to Obama's candidacy (*Hope on a Tightrope*, 184–86).

40. In the essay "The Dilemma of the Black Intellectual," West offers a strikingly similar four-part schema in which self-contempt plays a prominent role (*Keeping Faith*, 67).

41. This description of Toomer bears a striking resemblance to Honig's descriptions of Nietzsche, and to a lesser extent Arendt, in describing them as theorists of *virtú*. For example, she says that both see "the self as a creature that is always agonistically engaged and implicated with established identities and subjectivities that never quite succeed in expressing it without remainder." She notes in each "the self's perpetual ill-fittedness" and that "each writes from a position of homelessness" (Honig, *Political Theory*, 9).

42. This can sometimes give West's writing on democratic citizenship a defensive air and call to mind the sort of righteous battle with evil one associates with virtue politics. In keeping with the notion of self-creation in the face of oppression, West often refers to the results of what we manage to create as our "democratic armor" or "cultural armor." However, in keeping with the balance between virtue and contest typical of West's ideas, in describing democratic armor, why we craft it, and what it is for, West incorporates the challenges of self-criticism. Crafting our democratic armor is a work on the self that delves into "the dark corners of one's own soul, the night alleys of one's society. . . . This pursuit shatters one's petty idols, false illusions, and seductive fetishes" (*Democracy Matters*, 208–9).

43. Nietzsche, *The Will to Power*, 543; *The Gay Science*, 328; *Ecce Homo*, 272.

44. Cornel West, "Pragmatism and the Sense of the Tragic," in *The Cornel West Reader*, 179.

45. The idea is central to Patterson's *Slavery and Social Death: A Comparative Study* (Cambridge, Mass.: Harvard University Press, 1982).

46. West frequently makes reference to the fragility of black families but also to their strength and resilience in tough circumstances. His explanation for their relative fragility bears a resemblance to the explanation offered by Daniel P. Moynihan in his 1965 report "The Negro Family: The Case for National Action" (Washington, D.C.: U.S. Department of Labor, Office of Policy Planning and Research). Black women often need to work long hours outside of the home. Due to discrimination in hiring and a relative lack of education, black men were often underemployed and driven to abandon their families because of feelings of emasculation. West explains that "out-of-work, poverty stricken men tend not to marry or [to] support their children.... Most men ... continue to see obtaining a 'real' job as a prerequisite for marriage and fatherhood" (*The War against Parents*, 77–79). Finally, social welfare policies encouraged women not to marry the fathers of their children. Temporary Assistance for Needy Families (TANF), for example, cuts the benefits of those women who live with a man who earns wages. West goes so far as to call TANF the "modern descendant" of slavery (181).

47. West has noted indirectly the connection between his own ideas about the black Christian church and Nietzsche's Dionyisan. He ends one section of the book *Hope on a Tightrope*: "Consciousness is just one brief moment within a larger organism. It is mind body and soul all tied together. Darwin is inescapable—even for Christians." Then he begins the next section: "Nietzsche says that the highest construct in his philosophic imagination is what he calls a 'gay Socrates' or a philosopher who dances" (40).

48. West's notion that "profound music leads us—beyond language" ("Introduction," in *The Cornell West Reader*, xvii) is prefigured in much of Nietzsche's writing about music—especially regarding Wagner in *The Birth of Tragedy*.

49. This was a project that seems to have warmed West up to the previous generation of black leaders, like Martin Luther King, of whom he had been critical in earlier books. While the book is not about parenting and focuses on political and intellectual leadership, children loom large in the project nonetheless. The book opens with a quotation from James Baldwin that begins, "For the sake of one's children, in order to minimize the bill *they* must pay, one must be careful not to take refuge in any delusion" (*Race Matters*, xxiii). In describing the problem of nihilism facing the black community, West places special emphasis on the consequences for children: "The collapse of meaning in life—the eclipse of hope and absence of love of self and others, the breakdown of family and neighborhood bonds—leads to the social deracination and cultural denudement of urban dwellers, especially children" (9).

50. Toni Morrison, *Beloved: A Novel* (New York: Knopf, 1987).

51. As alluded to earlier, Hewlett and West seem to sympathize with O.J. Simp-

son because his separation from his children after his divorce reenacted his own experience with an absent father. Hewlett and West seem to have special sympathy for Simpson because "he had to cope with the fact that his absentee father was a homosexual in a day when that was not cool" (*The War against Parents*, 167).

52. Hewlett and West point out that two-fifths of American children are growing up without their father in their primary residence (*The War against Parents*, 163).

53. Elsewhere, West provides more upbeat assessments of his parenting, including the way his participation in protests against Yale's investments in apartheid South Africa and his subsequent arrest "served as a fine example for my wonderful son, Clifton, ... an example he has followed as a progressive student body president of his predominantly black middle school in Atlanta" (*The Ethical Dimensions of Marxist Thought*, xxx). West has written movingly about his love for his children.

54. In his autobiography, West describes his long talks with his brother Clifton regarding their inability to create in their own lives "what Mom and Dad have, man, that's always been my ideal." But West has been married and divorced three times and had a daughter with a fourth woman. In a telling moment in the book, West describes his pleasure at buying a Cadillac like his father's. "Seeing how happy it made him, I always wanted a Cadillac of my own." He has driven it since 1988. West and Ritz, *Brother West*, 138, 153.

55. Hewlett was raised in Great Britain. She and West, however, are struck by how similar their childhood experiences were—another of their unexpected commonalities centered on family. "On the surface of things our lives began very differently—for what could be more different than black blue-collar America and white working-class Wales? But at a deeper level of reality, there were extraordinary similarities in how we were raised and the values we took from our parents" (*The War against Parents*, 3).

56. Young West had market cravings as well—especially music and "candy at Sam's store." But West did not rely on his parents to fund his habits. Instead, he and some friends "had an operation where we'd take little kids' money." West seems to think he deserved the "heavy-duty discipline" he received when caught in such schemes. He also points out that he would give the kids some candy (*The War against Parents*, 12–13).

57. West's father's pain did not last, and his parents are clearly happy with the way he turned out. They wrote a touching and charming preface to one of his books, in which they "unequivocally state that parenting this bright, high-spirited, loving and compassionate child was a challenge as well as a privilege. He has brought great joy to and pride to our lives. We are richer for having had such an experience" (*Beyond Eurocentrism*, viii).

58. Hewlett and West are quoting psychologist John Munder Ross.

59. Cited in Kelly Oliver, *Subjectivity without Subjects: From Abject Fathers to Desiring Mothers* (Lanham, Md.: Rowman and Littlefield, 1998), 6. At the Million Man March, attendees expressed respect for women but mostly in the context of shared parenthood. They recited a pledge that read, in part, "I pledge from this day forward I will never abuse my wife by striking her or disrespecting her, for she is the mother of my children and the producer of my future" (17).

60. Ibid., 13.

61. In looking at parenthood, West begins to give a different meaning to the black response to the experience of slavery, which is transformed from a resource for democratic capacities to a cautionary tale. "Slavery and its aftermath show us what can happen if we do not attend to the anguish of husbands and fathers" (*The War against Parents*, 182).

62. West discusses the meeting in his introduction to an excerpt from *The War against Parents* in *The Cornel West Reader*. He expresses pride that "after forty-five lectures in thirteen states the book received much attention—resulting in our being summoned to the White House." West mentions the problems "left critics" had with the book, especially the sections on the Promise Keepers and Nation of Islam, but maintains that "with the rise of the progressive Working Families parties in New York and other places, we are vindicated" (333).

63. The authors also praise celebrities who "have hung in there" in marriages that go through tough times and offer the example of Whitney Houston—who was repeatedly abused by her husband. In the years after the book was published, Houston remained in the marriage and became addicted to heroin. They scold Rosie O'Donnell, among others, for raising a child without a male partner (*The War against Parents*, 34).

64. Honig, *Political Theory*, 150.

65. West cites this passage in *Keeping Faith* (117) and repeats it in several public lectures that have gone on to be published. The passage is from Josiah Royce's *The Spirit of Modern Philosophy* (New York: Dover, 1983), 461–62. Royce himself cites Hegel regarding the experience in which "all that was most fixed in him has become shaken."

66. In this way, West's experience seems to parallel those described by Ehren-reich, which I discuss in the Conclusion, in which the young generation of the 1960s and 1970s, in embracing new ideas and rebelling against authority, led their parents' generation to begin to question themselves—to suspect they had grown soft and acquisitive in the relative comforts of postwar America. Barbara Ehren-reich, *Fear of Falling: The Inner Life of the Middle Class* (New York: Perennial Press, 1990).

67. This youthful hope and willingness to take on the work of politics seems to have taken West by surprise. Lacking an explanation for it, he is forced into contradictions. West had described how the younger generation had grown up

in conditions much more challenging than what he faced, having referred to the children of broken homes as skinless, burned, and bleeding. But West also says that Obama, the son of a single mother, "hasn't gone through the struggle and doesn't have the scars that we [older leaders] have. Thank God! That's why we went through it" (*Hope on a Tightrope*, 60).

68. West seems to have generalized to his generation the essence of a "bleak and bitter encounter" he once had at a community center. A young man seeking West's advice explained that he felt like "I belong on the streets, hustling, dealing, and hurting." He asked West, "Brother, what made you want to do all the hard work, what made you believe in some kind of different future?" West answered with stories about the love and discipline he got from his parents. The young man responded that his mother is "strung out and tuned out" and his father is gone. West reports he felt "totally helpless." He told the young man, "My god, I can't imagine—it's beyond my experience," and advised him "to stay strong and don't forget to pray." But West also tells the young man, "You've got things you can teach me—you've been somewhere I've never been. I've read tons of books on alienation, but I cannot grasp what you are living" (*The War against Parents*, 43).

69. The quotation begins the preface to the 1994 edition. It is from James Baldwin's *The Fire Next Time* (New York: Dial Press, 1963).

70. West, *Democracy Matters*, 81. The Baldwin quotation is from *The Fire Next Time*.

71. Ibid., 83.

Conclusion

1. Patrick Deneen explores the tendency of democratic thinkers to indulge in a hope for "ideal" democracy, and the antidemocratic consequences of this hope, in his *Democratic Faith* (Princeton, N.J.: Princeton University Press, 2005). He argues that there is often "an unperceived utopianism lining the antiutopian mantle of democracy, even a degree of overconfidence amid otherwise humble claims of democracy's rejection of overconfidence" (xvi). This overconfidence in the virtues of democracy, in turn, leads to a profound dissatisfaction with the actual capacities of citizens—a sort of "democratic cynicism" (8). As was the case with Rousseau's original use of parenthood for political purposes, claims of virtue lead to feelings of insecurity.

2. Macedo and Young, *Child, Family, and State*, 1.

3. White, *Sustaining Affirmation*, 8.

4. Connolly, *Neuropolitics*, 153.

5. The first two phrases are Connolly's characterizations of Nietzsche's ideas. The last is a quotation from Nietzsche that Connolly cites.

6. William E. Connolly, *Identity\Difference: Democratic Negotiations of Political*

Paradox (Ithaca, N.Y.: Cornell University Press, 1991), 164. Connolly is quoting from Nietzsche's *Twilight of the Idols*, 88.

7. Nietzsche's emphasis on multiple perspectives should not obscure his attraction to the idea of a singular approach to life into which those perspectives have been incorporated. "In the end, when the work is finished, it becomes evident how the constraint of a single taste governed and formed everything large and small. Whether this taste was good or bad is less important than one might suppose, if only it was a single taste!" (*The Gay Science*, 290). Alexander Nehamas offers a compelling account of this aspect of Nietzsche's thought in *Nietzsche: Life as Literature* (Cambridge, Mass.: Harvard University Press, 1985). Shapiro argues that family experience can be subjected to interpretations "that pluralize and open what cultural conservatives would like to close or restrict" (*For Moral Ambiguity*, 162). He compellingly defends the idea that "'family life,' however construed, is contingent as a condition of possibility and has an ambiguous relationship with civic life in general" (179). Shapiro defends this claim, however, by offering strong and singular interpretations of the meanings of particular family experiences as depicted in film, literature, and political theory. To the extent that Shapiro's interpretations of films like *Patriot Games* transform the way you think about the film, other interpretations seem less compelling.

8. Which is exactly what Arendt reminded Eichmann it is not: "For politics is not like the nursery; in politics obedience and support are the same" (*Eichmann in Jerusalem*, 279). After that "Grow up," Connolly quickly adds: "But if you won't, we will not try to compel you" (*Identity\Difference*, 195). Parents, of course, can also choose not to take on the task of compelling someone to grow up—Rousseau brought his children to the foundling home, Nietzsche never completed the project of procreation he explored so tenaciously, Rorty preferred (at least conceptually) to leave the job to teachers and professors, and West turns to his own parents for the task. But the evidence explored in the previous chapters is that this sort of resignation is not conducive to mature citizenship either.

9. This is also true of citizen Barack Obama, for example, who likes to remind people that Americans believe "raising kids with the right values" is "the most important moral challenge facing our nation." Even citizens who think about politics largely in nonfamilial terms often base their political claims on familial language. In *Avoiding Politics*, Nina Eliasoph describes the phenomenon of "mandatory public Momism" and "for the children" discourse among American activists. She notes that these activists often have complex notions of citizenship and public responsibility that they express in certain "safe" settings (246). But in public, they appeal to family-centered rhetoric. This is partly, Eliasoph finds, because they expect their ideas to resonate with other citizens when couched in these terms. But Eliasoph also sees this appeal to parental rhetoric as a retreat from the challenges of the politics of contest. Despite their political sophistication and awareness of

competing interests and claims, in public these activists resort to a rhetoric in which "there are no seriously opposing positions, no deep disagreements, no opposing interests.... Rather than questions about the future and children becoming political, politics becomes invisible, smothered in the sanctimoniousness with which we Americans surround children. Our concerns suddenly seem no longer to be about power, justice and democracy, but only about survival" (246).

10. Illness and death, because they are unavoidable and not subject to the pervasive "choice" that we experience elsewhere in our lives, provide unique access to the "given," according to de Zengotita. This connection between the experience of death and the experience of having children, the unique insight into our sense of ourselves that each can provide, is something Connolly would be wise to consider.

11. Richard Sennett, *The Corrosion of Character* (New York: Norton Press, 1998), 9.

12. William Connolly, *Pluralism* (Durham, N.C.: Duke University Press, 2005), 140–41.

13. Giorgio Agamben, *Homo Sacer: Sovereign Power and Bare Life* (Stanford, Calif.: Stanford University Press, 1998), 148.

14. These include the 1676 writ of habeas corpus, the Declaration of the Rights of Man, "the rapidity with which parliamentary democracies were able to turn into totalitarian states" and back again, de Sade's carefully structured orgies, Heidegger's concept of fallenness, the Hobbesian leviathan, and many others.

15. Nietzsche, *The Gay Science*, 292.

16. As noted in chapter 2, Nietzsche was intrigued by modern manifestations of this ancient power as well. Discussing the modern parent's sense of a right to impose his or her authority unconditionally over his or her child, Nietzsche noted, "Indeed in former times ... it seemed proper for fathers to possess power of life or death over the newborn and to use it as they saw fit" (*Beyond Good and Evil*, 117–18).

17. In fact, as Connolly points out, there was an anticipation of militancy working in the opposite way. "When the recount issue was still alive the electronic news media frequently reported that there would be a vitriolic response by Republicans if the official vote count went against George W. Bush" (*Pluralism*, 142).

18. On Jackson as "father," see Rogin, *Fathers and Children*, 192 passim.

19. Rogin, *Ronald Reagan*, 149.

20. Edsall and Edsall, *Chain Reaction*.

21. Ibid.

22. Ehrenreich, *Fear of Falling*, 15.

23. There are several manifestations of anxiety about permissiveness in contemporary rhetoric about security, terrorism, and radical Islam. One was the extraordinary media attention given to John Walker Lindh, "the American Taliban,"

the son of white, middle-class American parents discovered fighting on the side of the Taliban in 2001. More important is the persistent, if often unspoken, idea that one of the reasons for the "hatred of America" is the perception that our culture has become decadent, shallow, consumerist, and obscene and manages to export this decadence through its cultural products.

24. Michelle Rodino-Colocino, "War Mothering: The Fight for 'Security Moms,'" *Feminist Media Studies* 5, no. 3 (2005): 380–85.

25. Eric Boehlert, "The TV Ad That Put Bush Over the Top," *Salon,* November 5, 2004, http://www.salon.com/news/feature/2004/11/05/bush_ads. Political analysts found the ad to have been profoundly effective in the nine swing states where it was aired intensively.

26. As of the 2004 campaign.

27. Cited during interview with Sen. Robert Menendez (D-NJ), National Public Radio, *All Things Considered* (January 9, 2007).

28. Associated Press, "Bush: Obama Scoped Daughter's Bedrooms," November 11, 2008, http://www.msnbc.msn.com/id/27669864.

29. Katharine Q. Seelye, "Obama Selects Saddleback Founder for Invocation," *New York Times,* December 17, 2008.

30. Obama, *The Audacity of Hope,* 263.

31. Barack Obama, "What I Want for You—and Every Child in America," *Parade Magazine,* January 18, 2009.

32. Remarks of Senator Barack Obama, "Changing the Odds for Urban America," Washington, D.C., July 18, 2007, http://www.barackobama.com/2007/07/18/remarks_of_senator_barack_obam_19.php.

33. Paul Tough, *Whatever It Takes: Geoffrey Canada's Quest to Change Harlem and America* (New York: Houghton Mifflin Harcourt, 2008).

34. Ibid., 260.

35. Ibid., 4.

36. Tough suggests that baby college is "perhaps *the* essential part" of the Harlem Children's Zone (*Whatever It Takes,* 58).

37. Paul Tough, "Harlem Renaissance." Broadcast on *This American Life,* Chicago Public Radio, September 26, 2008. Quotation from an interview with Geoffrey Canada.

38. Ibid.

39. Obama has suggested he will ask Congress to dedicate "billions of dollars a year" to the initiative. Obama, "Changing the Odds."

40. Tough, *Whatever It Takes,* 52.

41. Tough describes how parents are encouraged to talk about "intense and personal issues: their feelings toward their own parents, the ambivalence they sometimes [feel] about their kids, and the guilt that ambivalence provoked in them" (Ibid., 200–201).

42. Ibid., 193.

43. Daniel Patrick Moynihan, "The Negro Family."

44. Obama: "Changing the Odds." In this "active recruiting" in Harlem, parents are cajoled, shamed, and tempted with gift certificates and other incentives (Tough, *Whatever It Takes*, 58–59).

45. Rousseau, *The Social Contract*, 64.

46. Rousseau, *Discourse on the Origin of Inequality*, 79.

Index

141, 152; and Indian law of Manu, 254–555; in *Julie*, 44, 64, 66; Kahn on, 12; in *King Lear*, 26; love for, 10, 185; and metaphysics, 148, 209; of the middle class, 219; moral codes of, 206, 207; morality imposed upon, 12; natural, care for as, 129; Nietzsche on, 103, 104, 110, 112, 249, 254–55; Obama on, 6; preservation of fathers through, 103; protection of, 118; and race/racism, 178, 218; and religion, 9; Rorty on, 118, 121, 129, 142–44, 146, 148, 151, 262; and Rousseau, 31, 34, 40, 43–44, 49, 50–54, 65, 67, 68, 110, 232, 240, 241; Sennett on, 210; socialization of, 143–44, 146, 151; and the state, 192–93, 256–66; suffering of, 173–74, 180; Taylor on, 10, 25; as transitional object, 131; transmission of values to, 6, 71, 72, 78–84, 113; violence against, 183, 217; and the wealthy, 135–36; West on, 174, 175, 178, 180, 185–89, 193–98, 269, 271; women as vessel for, 92; Young on, 24; Zarathustra on, 95. *See also* future as orientation for politics; imitation; inheritance; love; scrutiny

church, African American, 156, 161, 177–79, 186, 191, 197

civil rights movement, 158, 173, 188

class, 134–35, 138, 144, 219. *See also* inequality of wealth; middle class; poverty; wealthy, the

Clinton, Bill, 23, 192, 227

communication of values, 77, 79, 81, 85, 87–88, 93, 112, 160, 204

community: African American, 175, 184; Geoffrey Canada on, 223–24; and the individual, 42, 71–72, 250; moral, 128, 130, 258–59; Nietzsche

on, 90, 102, 163; political, 10, 13, 14; Rorty on, 139; Rousseau on, 42; Schopenhauer on, 89–90; West on, 156, 159, 165

Conant, James, 244, 246

conception, 48. *See also* pregnancy

consent, 22, 51, 239, 240, 241

Connolly, William, 11, 15, 20, 30, 61, 224, 233; on Agamben, 211, 214, 217, 220; on contest, 207; on death, 203–8, 273; on Nietzsche, 71, 205–6, 244–45

contest, 5, 15, 201–2, 224, 231; Arendt as theorist of, 234, 266; and citizenship, 2–3; in coexistence with virtue, 201; Connolly as theorist of, 207; Dolan on Foucault's theory of, 264; Honig on, 232, 233; Eliasoph on, 272; Nietzsche as theorist of, 13, 17, 21, 70–73, 88, 91–92, 94–95, 102, 112–14, 244, 254; Rorty as theorist of, 18, 116–19, 128, 139, 140, 147–48, 151, 152, 154, 257; West as theorist of, 156, 157, 159, 160–64, 170–71, 172, 182, 194, 195, 198, 263, 267

contingency, 3, 13; de Zengotita on, 208–11; Rorty on, 18–19, 117–18, 133, 141, 142, 154

contraception: Rousseau on, 33

Cranston, Maurice, 30, 53, 241

cruelty: Rorty on, 115–16, 144, 151–53, 262

culture: American, 3–5, 219–20; Nietzsche on, 75, 76, 77–79, 84, 89, 96, 101; West on, 169–70, 191, 193, 195, 197

Darnton, Robert, 31

Darwin, Charles, 214, 248, 268

death: Agamben on, 213–15; of a child, 4–5, 130; Connolly on, 205–7, 273;

82, 83, 87, 88; on *virtù*, 71; on virtue, 74; and Cosima Wagner, 69; and West, 162–63, 176–77, 178, 197; on will, 84–85; on women, 72, 91–92, 94, 96, 251; on Zarathustra, 90, 92, 94–95, 249

nihilism: West on, 155, 157, 160, 162, 163, 180–82, 183, 189, 195–96, 197

9/11, 220

1960s, the, 219

Obama, Barack: as father, 2, 4, 220–21; and gay marriage, 220–21; on his mother, 228; and poverty, 221–24, 266; and race, 158–59, 171; and religion, 158–59; and values, 4–5, 6, 228, 230; West on, 158–59, 171–72, 197

Okin, Susan Moller, 230

Oliver, Kelly, 190

ontology, weak, 202–4, 206–8, 232–33

oppression, 165, 170–71, 172

overman, 114, 117–18, 149

Pace, Peter, 220

Palin, Sarah, 5, 229

passion: Nietzsche on, 74; Rousseau on, 32, 56, 59, 64–66

past, the, 97, 124–25, 143, 153, 155, 186–88, 199

paternalism, 134, 215, 231

paternity: Rousseau on, 56, 62–63

patriarchy, 16, 48, 190

Patterson, Orlando, 178

philosophers: production of, 70, 79–81

Pitkin, Hanna, 230

pity, 90, 152–54

pluralism, 20, 206, 211, 233. *See also* ontology, weak

polis, 212, 216

postmodernism: Rorty on, 116, 124–25,

126–27, 127, 146–47, 150; West on, 162

poverty: and social programs, 221–24

pragmatism: prophetic, 159, 160, 173, Rorty on, 116, 119–20, 124, 125, 130, 147; West on, 156, 164, 165

pregnancy, 47–48, 53, 59–60, 72, 229

procreation, 5; as highest achievement of the individual, 83, 85, 90, 91, 96, 97, 113; as metaphor, 72–73, 76–77; and Nietzsche, 69, 72–73; prevention of, 102; as "the real bond," 82, 83

professional class. *See* middle class

progress: Nietzsche on, 75–76, 98; West on, 161, 199

Promise Keepers, 189–91

Protestantism, 9, 156; and the black church, 158, 161

public, relationship to private, 10, 18, 21, 22; Rorty on, 116, 117, 121, 127, 139–40, 141–42, 145; West on, 193

queer theory, 22–24

race, 2, 219; West on, 155, 158, 165, 171–72, 174, 175–76

Rawls, John, 230

religion: Nietzsche on, 74, 75, 96; West on, 156, 158, 161, 173, 177

reproductive futurism, 3, 23–24

responsibility, 3, 5 8–9, 11–12, 23, 27, 221, 256; and Nietzsche, 104, 109, 113–14; and Rorty, 136, 152; and West, 173, 185, 189–90, 192, 197, 199

ressentiment, 98, 103–4

Rogin, Michael, 217, 231

Rome, ancient, 212, 215

romanticism, 30, 122, 147, 159, 160–61, 162

Rorty, Richard, 14, 17, 115–54, 201, 203;

totalitarianism, 16, 283. *See also*
authoritarianism
Tough, Paul, 222
tragic sensibility, 158–59, 176–79
transcendence, 16, 21
transvaluation, 84, 102, 105, 109, 112, 113
Tronto, Joan, 21

unconscious, the, 71, 72, 82, 83, 85, 132
uniqueness, 77, 82, 83, 87, 88
unity: desire for, 163, 165; parenthood
as source of, 155, 163, 166–69, 172,
189
unnatural, the. *See* natural, the
utopia, 159, 161, 164, 189

values, 13; in American political rhetoric, 3–6; Nietzsche on, 71, 72, 78–84,
113; passing on of, 4, 6, 22; West on,
180–81
virtù. See contest
virtue, 13–16, 231; and citizenship, 2–3;
Nietzsche on, 73–74, 87, 102, 106;
Rorty on, 116–18, 128, 148, 151–53;
Rousseau on, 2–3, 6, 13, 21, 31–35,
38, 55–59, 66–67; West on, 169, 189,
194, 196

Wagner, Cosima, 69
Wagner, Richard, 69
Walzer, Michael, 26
Warren, Rick, 220–21
Weber, Max, 8–9, 210
weak ontology. *See* ontology, weak
wealthy, the, 135–38. *See also* inequality
of wealth
Weil, Simone, 266–67
West, Cornel, 14, 17–18, 19–20, 155–99,
201, 203; on African American
church, 156, 161, 177–79, 186, 191;
on African American community,

175, 184; on altruism, 182, 194; *The
American Evasion of Philosophy,* 164,
165, 170; on authoritarianism, 19,
156, 160–61, 162, 191; on Baldwin,
174, 197, 198–99, 268; on *Beloved,*
182–83; betrayal, 194; on children,
167–69, 173–75, 181, 183–89, 193–99,
269; on the civil rights movement,
158, 173; and contest, 156, 157, 159,
160–64, 170–71, 172, 182, 194, 195,
198, 263, 267; on Derrida, 258,
264; on divorce, 174, 185, 193, 197,
268–69; on exemplars, 197; on
Existentialism, 178; on failure as a
parent, 174, 180–81, 184–86, 189–92,
194, 196; on faith, 177; on fallibility,
156, 161, 172, 189; on family, 177–78,
180–81, 268; and family, his own,
185–86, 188, 269; on fathers, 174,
189–91, 197; on feminism, 168, 264;
foster care, criticism of, 193–94;
on Foucault, 162–63, 165; freedom,
184–86; and fundamentalism,
157–58; on the future as orientation
for politics, 155, 168, 176; on Marcus
Garvey, 171, 173; on gay parents,
265; on the generational divide,
197–98; and Sylvia Ann Hewlett,
155, 166–69, 185, on hope, 158, 159,
171, 177, 180, 182, 189, 195, 198; *Hope
on a Tightrope,* 172, 173, 178, 180,
197, 198; on humanism, 176, 179;
on humility, 173–74; on imitation,
9, 196–97; on Martin Luther King,
171, 172, 173, 174; love, 157, 182, 183,
196, 197; on Malcolm X, 162, 197;
on market values, 160, 180–82, 187,
193–94, 195; on marriage, 192–93;
on Marx, 156, 169; on the media,
160, 181, 184; metaphysics, 164–65;
on the middle class, 173; on the

BRIAN DUFF is assistant professor of political science at the University of New England.

www.ingramcontent.com/pod-product-compliance
Lightning Source LLC
Chambersburg PA
CBHW020840270326
41928CB00006B/492